T0345220

DRAGONS' TEETH
and THUNDERSTONES

DRAGONS' TEETH
AND
THUNDERSTONES

The Quest for the
Meaning of Fossils

KEN McNAMARA

REAKTION BOOKS LTD

To my children
Jamie, Kaitie and Tim
Fossil collectors extraordinaires

Published by
REAKTION BOOKS LTD
Unit 32, Waterside
44–48 Wharf Road
London N1 7UX, UK
www.reaktionbooks.co.uk

First published 2020
Copyright © Ken McNamara 2020

Printed and bound in Great Britain
by TJ International, Padstow, Cornwall

A catalogue record for this book is available from the British Library

ISBN 978 1 78914 290 7

CONTENTS

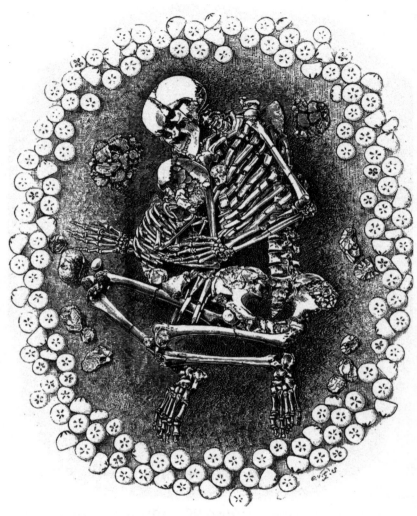

Engraving by Worthington G. Smith of a reconstruction of the skeletons of a woman (whom Smith named 'Maud') and child with just some of the hundreds of fossil sea urchins that he excavated from a Bronze Age grave in 1887. Smith used this as a frontispiece to his book *Man, the Primeval Savage* (1894).

ONE

A TIMELESS OBSESSION

Every human culture must find some way to explain the enigma of naturally-occurring plant and animal images in stone. In 'pre-scientific' cultures, explanations for fossils would likely entail the creation of myths. Fossils might easily inspire mythologies of design, creation, birth, death and spirit world.[1]

People have been collecting fossils for hundreds of thousands of years, drawn to them for a myriad of reasons. They are attractive objects to delight the mind and maybe adorn the body. Some believed that they could protect the body, in both life and death, and even to cure it of its ills. Other fossils, though, were just plain evil – spawn of the Devil, bringing ill-fortune and bad luck. Yet in many societies fossils were objects to be kept, revered and, in many cases, laid to rest with the deceased. But mostly people have just been obsessively curious about these enigmatic objects that so fired ancient imaginations.

Discovery

On 13 January 1690, a slight figure could be seen wandering through a vineyard at Sir Roger Dutton's estate at Sherborne in Gloucestershire. The young man, a 22-year-old physician named John Woodward, had been cooped up in Sir Roger's grand house for the previous few days, for a fearsome storm had been ravaging England. Two nights before, it had been reported that

> there was a most extraordinary storme of wind, accompanied with snow and sharp weather; it did great harme in many places, blowing down houses, trees, &c. killing many people. It began about 2 in the morning, and lasted till 5, being a kind of hurricane.[2]

Picking a route through the fallen branches and uprooted trees around the house, Woodward had made his way to the vineyard. The vines appeared for all the world to be dead, rooted into the bare, limy soils of this part of the Cotswolds. The torrential rain had washed much of the soil away, leaving a peppering of limestone fragments. It had also brought to the surface other, more unusual, things.

Woodward's eye was drawn to one of these objects. It looked like a little pebble. He picked it up. It was smooth. It was small. As the bitter winter wind snarled around him, Woodward toyed with the fanciful idea that it could be a frozen grape. Nothing would surprise him in this bleak, freezing place. It was the right shape and the right size. Yet it was made of stone. But the more he looked at it, the more it seemed to resemble a shell, not a grape. He was captivated by his find. He had never come across anything like this before. But he was also mystified. This must be what the

Anonymous portrait
of John Woodward
(1667–1728), *c.* 1720,
oil on canvas.

locals hereabouts called a 'pundib'. If it was a shell, it must once have lived in the ocean. How could it have arrived here, so far from the sea? And how had it been transformed into stone? Could this be evidence of the biblical Flood, part of the flotsam and jetsam left by the retreating waters and then turned to stone? Or was it just a sport of Nature, placed here by the hand of Providence to delude the unwary into thinking it was a shell? Woodward was not only completely mystified, but utterly captivated. And in this one moment his life was to change completely.

Writing in the catalogue of his collection some 35 years later, after a lifetime of unfettered curiosity spent collecting and acquiring many thousands of fossils from around the world, Woodward remembered how, after finding this, the very first, he, took notice of the like, lying loose in the Fields, on the plough'd Lands and on the Hills, even to the very top of the highest thereabouts. Nay, in many places of this Country, they lay exposed on the plough'd Lands so thick, that I have scarcely observed Pebles or Flints more frequent and numerous on the plough'd Land of those Countries that most abound with them. This was a Speculation new to me; and what I judg'd of so great moment, that I resolv'd to pursue it thorough [*sic*] the other remoter parts of the Kingdom; which I afterwards did, made Observations upon all sorts of Fossils, collected such as I thought remarkable, and sent them up to London.[3]

And this he did in style, accruing what was at the time the most extensive collection of not only fossils, but rocks and minerals. In early eighteenth-century London Woodward's collection was the talk of the town. Remarkably, it still exists today, largely intact, in its original cabinets in the Sedgwick Museum of the University of Cambridge. Perhaps most remarkable of all is that the little fossil found by Woodward in Ralph Dutton's vineyard still survives today and lies in a display case in the museum.

The first fossil collected by John Woodward, a terebratulid brachiopod, from Sherborne House, Gloucestershire, on 13 January 1690.

Woodward lived during exciting times. His was a world where science was emerging from the shadows of millennia of ignorance and superstition. In late seventeenth-century England, men like Robert Hooke, Isaac Newton and John Ray were beginning to explain the mysteries of the natural world in ways that had little to do with superstition or religion. When Woodward collected his 'pundib' in 1690, a number of the leading naturalists in England still believed that fossils like these were merely 'figured stones' formed by some 'plastic virtue latent in the Earth'. In a letter to the Royal Society in 1671, the naturalist Martin Lister wrote: 'I am apt to think, there is no such matter, as Petryfying of Shells . . . but that these Cockle-like stones ever were, as they are at present, *Lapides sui generis*, and never any part of an Animal.'[4]

What he meant by *Lapides sui generis* was that they were 'formed stones' or 'figured stones' that merely resembled formerly living creatures, but which had in fact been created by formative powers latent within the Earth. Their resemblance to any living creature was, he believed, purely coincidental. In England one of the few lone dissenters was the polymath Robert Hooke, who, in 1665, argued succinctly in his book *Micrographia* that shells and other so-called 'figured stones' found in rocks were undoubtedly the remains of organisms that had once been alive (see Chapter Ten).[5]

In Italy this view had been particularly promoted by the Sicilian artist and naturalist Agostino Scilla in his book *La vana speculazione disingannata dal senso* (1670).[6] The idea, though, was slow to catch on in England. Apart from Hooke, two other men did embrace this view. One was Sir Thomas Browne, writing in his *Pseudodoxia epidemica*, first published in 1646. The other was John Woodward, who thought that fossils were striking evidence to support the biblical account of the Flood. As the waters receded they had, to Woodward's eyes, left

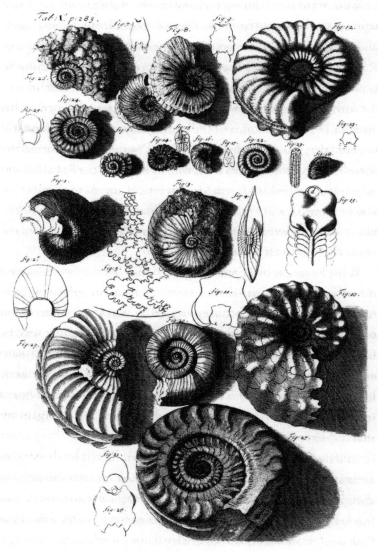

Engraving of Robert Hooke's drawings of ammonites, published by Richard Waller after Hooke's death in *The Posthumous Works of Robert Hooke* (1705).

Frontispiece to Agostino Scilla's *La vana speculazione disingannata dal senso*, published in 1670. It shows Sense vainly trying to convince 'vain speculation' that the fossils on the ground were once living organisms, like the sea urchin he is holding in his hand.

behind evidence of this watery domain in the fossilized remains of animals and plants that had once inhabited the Earth.

In Woodward's time, superstitions about fossils were rife. Writing in 1728, he recorded how some fossils were known as *brontia*; others *ombria*. Both were believed to have landed on Earth during thunderstorms.[7] However, he prosaically pointed out that they were, in fact, fossil sea urchins. 'These Kinds of Stones the Country People here in England call sometimes *Fairy Stones*, but commonly *Thunder Stones*, in which Fancy they agree with the People of Germany, and likewise with Pliny.'[8] In other words, the idea that fossils were of supernatural origin was widespread across Europe and had been for a very long time: at least 2,000 years. Woodward, though, was dismissive of such superstitions.

But such ideas prevailed among country people in England and, indeed, were to remain so in some places in the English countryside until well into the twentieth century. These were beliefs that had arisen deep in the shadowy past and had been handed down, generation to generation, over countless millennia. They were certainly established in Oxfordshire at the end of the eighteenth century. In 1798 James Parkinson, surgeon, palaeontologist (or, as he liked to be known, oryctologist), political activist and author of an article on 'shaking palsy' (later to be called 'Parkinson's disease'), decided to take a trip. It was time, he thought, to pursue 'scientific research, and an enthusiastic admiration of the beauties of nature'. So, he 'quitted London . . . with my daughter, accompanied by our old friend Wilton, whose lively manners . . . render him an excellent companion'. Parkinson's aim on his research trip was to visit 'the most interesting parts of this island'. Even before the end of their first day's journey, when they were 'within about ten or twelve miles of Oxford . . . Wilton, looking out of the window of the chaise

THE ALEHOUSE SERMON.   *See Page* 10.

A physician, presumed to be James Parkinson himself, visiting an ale house; frontispiece engraving from Parkinson's *The Villager's Friend and Physician* (1804).

exclaimed, "Well, I never saw roads mended with such materials as these before!"' What most arrested the travellers' gazes was 'a labouring man breaking to pieces, with a large hammer, a stone nearly circular, half as large as the fore-wheel of our chaise, and bearing the exact form of a serpent closely coiled up.' They asked the workman what it was. '"This stone, sir" says he, "is a snake stone."'[9]

Parkinson and his travelling companions were inspired to pursue this further. Where better to gather information on these strange stones than at the local hostelry? Having alighted from their chaise, they sauntered along until they came to a small 'hedge ale-house'. Delighted by the profusion of roses and honeysuckle in full bloom around the door, they 'had very little hesitation in determining to stop, and partake of such refreshments as our cottage would yield'. While they were waiting Wilton was attracted by a range of curious objects arranged neatly on the mantelpiece. Neither he, nor Parkinson nor his daughter, had any idea what these curious stone objects were. While they were examining the specimens the 'landlady made her appearance; and from her we learnt that this was her collection of curiosities made in the neighbouring parts of the country'. Picking up one of the stones, she began to tell the travellers about them.

'This,' said she, 'is a petrified snake, with which this part of the country abounds. These were fairies, and once the inhabitants of these parts, who for their crimes were changed, first into snakes, and then into stones.' She then showed them a conical stone. 'Here is one of the *fairies night-caps*, now almost become stone.' Picking up other pieces she explained that 'this and this are pieces of the bones of giants who came to live here when the race of fairies was destroyed'. As well as the bones she also showed them other objects that she called thunderbolts, 'stating that these were the very thunderbolts with which these people were, in their turn, also destroyed'.

As fanciful as the Oxfordshire landlady's beliefs may seem to us today, these were the legacy of a fascination with fossils that has an extraordinarily long history, stretching back many thousands of years. While people like Woodward in the early eighteenth century, and Parkinson in the early nineteenth century, were beginning to forge new ideas about the origins of fossils, those before them, who for thousands of years had found, collected, used and treasured these remarkable stones, had, in all likelihood, been interested in them for very different reasons. Some might just have thought them fascinating and attractive objects, worthy of collecting and keeping, much as we do today. Others could have believed that they were much more: the possessors of magical powers, with the ability to heal the body, or perhaps the spirit, affording the owner strength or protection, in this life or even in the next.

Ancient Collectors

For those living across Europe, Africa and Asia before the last great Ice Age had begun to melt away, some 15,000–12,000 years ago, stones were all. People were nomadic, travelling great distances each year to follow their food sources, the herds of animals that migrated with the seasons. The right stones had to be found that could become the tools to kill animals for food and provide hides or fleeces to stave off the bitter cold. They were also needed to dig up plants to eat when hunting animals failed, or to cut branches to make wooden tools or shelters. These stones were even, perhaps, used to kill other people. In warmer periods, around 125,000, 250,000 and 400,000 years ago, between the freezing pulses, people would have hunted herds of deer, bison and sometimes larger prey, such as elephants. Their fashioned stone tools – axes, arrow heads and scrapers made often from hard flints with broken edges as keen as scalpels – kept them alive. Sometimes the stones they turned into these tools had fossils embedded within them. Sometimes they were even fossils themselves.

Then, when the Earth was plunged into prolonged cold periods and glaciers slid like giant slugs slowly across the land, the tools were also used to hunt great woolly mammoths – for their meat, skins and bones, and tusks to carve into ornaments, charms, musical instruments, boomerangs and even to construct shelters. The frozen landscape was scoured for hard chert and flints, which made the best and sharpest tools. And these rocks were ones that would often contain fossils. Did these nomadic peoples ignore them? Probably not, for, as I will show, some of the tools were manufactured with great care to show off the fossils that studded their surface. Other fossils were collected and turned into personal ornaments – necklaces, bracelets or even sewn into clothing – symbols of wealth, and of status.

Today fossil collectors scour the ground looking for stones with embedded fossils. As a palaeontologist, I have been doing it for more years than I care to remember. These ancient peoples, living many thousands of years ago, did just the same as me. While today those of us bitten by the fossil-collecting bug may be specifically searching for a fossil, did our ancient ancestors similarly hunt them out, or did they just pick them up by chance? While they were looking for rocks to fashion into stone tools, their fancy would occasionally, in all likelihood, be drawn to a stone that was more interesting than the rest: maybe it was a spiral; or perhaps had curved lines coursing across it, or, most special, a star shape branded onto its surface. These were sometimes collected, kept, maybe worked or discarded with our ancestors' earthly remains. And a few, thousands of years later, were found again, second-hand fossils to intrigue another generation.

Who were these people, living hundreds of thousands of years ago, the very first fossil collectors? Can we delve into their minds to try and understand what drove them to collect? If they shared our fancy for collecting fossils were they so very different from us? Well, in some ways they were. For, as I will show, it was not only early members of our own species that developed the knack for finding fossils. *Homo sapiens* was not the only fossil-collecting species of *Homo*. The archaeological record provides intriguing evidence that Neanderthals (*Homo neanderthalensis*) were also adept at fossil hunting and used the fossils they discovered for different purposes. Perhaps even more remarkable is that – based on evidence from fossils found embedded within flints that were made into tools nearly half a million years ago – *Homo heidelbergensis*, the ancestor of our species who lived even before the Neanderthals, also collected fossils. And maybe most intriguing of all are fossils found in association with remains of an even earlier species of *Homo*. This raises the intriguing possibility that one thing that maybe links all the various species of *Homo* to have lived in Europe for the last 1 million years is their rather strange penchant for collecting fossils.

Fate Changers

In the many places and times in which people have left us tantalizing clues as to what they thought about fossils, they have done so in a variety of ways. Sometimes the clue is in the way the fossil was modified. Or it may be the way in which a stone was crafted into a tool on which a fossil proudly sat. Often they were placed in their houses, their shrines or temples, and very often in their graves. In essence what this means is that any fossil found in an archaeological context is a 'pre-loved' fossil that may well have been collected before, and passed through someone else's hands. To some, it may have been a fleeting acquaintance. To others, the fossil may have been of some practical use. But in many cases the fossils have emerged from sites, such as burial chambers or graves, that could attribute a reverence or even a spiritual dimension to why the fossil was collected. These were treasured possessions. The fossils may have been readily recognizable shells or teeth. They might have been huge bones preserved in stone that would have inspired legends of giants or monsters.[10] Or they might have been more cryptic spirals or fan-shaped structures; or stars in rocks suggesting gifts from the heavens.

Before we started giving names to fossils, like 'brachiopod', 'ammonite', 'dinosaur' and so on, and before we started popping them in boxes with labels – arranging them in drawers and sliding them into cabinets in our museums – after digging them up from their stony graves, people had been collecting and storing fossils in a myriad of ways and bestowing them with a rich catalogue of names for an extraordinarily long time. As James Parkinson discovered, following his meeting with the 'hedge ale-house' landlady, people's imaginations have conjured up a wealth of names for these 'formed stones' – fossils that they found in their everyday life in the countryside. In the vacuum of a rational explanation prior to the seventeenth century for what these fossils could represent, the human imagination invented a welter of stories to try and explain their origins. Some were incorporated into pre-existing mythologies. Others engendered their own, unique legends.

Many are the names bestowed on fossils, such as 'shepherd's crowns', 'St Cuthbert's beads', 'thunderstones'. Passed down through the generations, they have been reported by writers for the last thousand years or so. But to delve further back in time before written records, to the shadowy world of thousands, tens of thousands, even hundreds of thousands of years ago, we have to chase the fossils themselves. To break, as it were, the archaeological record. This way there is a chance of investigating why people might have developed the urge to collect fossils, even though we may not know what they called them.

If you crack open a rock with a hammer, and you are lucky enough for a fossil to pop out, seeing the light of day for the first time in maybe hundreds of millions of years, then there is no doubt that it had never been collected before. But to get a handle on what our forebears thought about fossils we need to search for second-hand objects: ones previously collected then discarded, or lost, or maybe placed somewhere safe by our ancestors thousands of years ago.

So how to recognize a second-hand fossil? While you might generally prefer to avoid damaged second-hand goods, in the case of fossils, damage, caused intentionally or otherwise, can be a useful indicator of prior ownership. For ancient people searching for a chunk of flint to fashion into a tool, the presence of a fossil was sometimes a bonus – indicated by the flint having been carefully knapped to preserve the fossil's shape. Or a fossil might show signs of having been altered in some way – a bit taken off to make it into a scraper; or a hole drilled through, with which to thread twine to create a fetching necklace.

The locations where fossils were discarded can provide potent insights into the significance they might have had to their original collectors. Fossils may be found with other archaeological objects, or

Neolithic hand axe crafted around the fossil sea urchin, *Micraster*; from Camp-à-Cayaux, Belgium; found by Roland Meuris.

in specific locations within and around dwellings or other buildings. Most useful are fossils placed in graves, either with interred bodies or with cremated remains. It could, of course, be argued that the fossils might have just fallen into the graves inadvertently. However, their frequent occurrence as grave goods, and the discovery of fossils placed carefully around deceased bodies or even, in one instance, held tightly in a hand, provide compelling evidence for the importance of fossils to past societies. Fossils discovered by archaeologists in the 'wrong' place are excellent indicators of the movements and behaviours of these ancient peoples. So, if a fossil preserved in flint and derived from Cretaceous chalk deposits is found in a tomb constructed in granite country, it suggests the hand of ancient people must have been at work, transporting or trading the fossils, sometimes over great distances.

The archaeological record of fossil collecting is quite extensive, but relatively poorly studied. As I have indicated, fossil collecting may have been practised by more than just our own species of *Homo*. Given that many fossils appear to have been collected for no apparent functional reason, it raises the question of what inspired people to collect them in the first place. Certainly, there is ample evidence of fossils being used as medicines in 'modern' (medieval) pharmacopoeia.[11] This practical use of fossils probably originated many thousands of years ago. Some, we know, that were collected 10,000 years ago, were used in early attempts at weaving.[12] But many people seem to have collected fossils simply because they liked the look of them, much as many people do today. It was their aesthetic attributes that were paramount.

When viewed over the long span of human existence (and I use the term 'human' in the broadest sense to include all species of the genus *Homo*), then patterns emerge of what fossils meant to ancient peoples. The perceptive palaeoanthropologist Kenneth Oakley argued that there has been an overarching pattern in humans' relationship with fossils.[13] The first people to take notice of them, in what is known as the Early Palaeolithic, hundreds of thousands of years ago, were probably attracted by some aspect of their symmetry – bilateral, pentameral, radial, spiral – all organized shapes that stick out in a sea of otherwise irregular rocks. Their curiosity was piqued. The objects were pleasing to the eye. This was the first smouldering sense of aesthetic sensibility.

The fossils may then, Oakley thinks, have become objects that could bring the possessor luck in some form or other. A little nearer to the present day (that is, 5,000–10,000 years ago), when people stopped wandering the land as hunter-gatherers and settled down to become sedentary farmers, fossils seem to have stimulated their imaginations even further. They bestowed them with a much deeper meaning, becoming great symbolic objects: magical or even spiritual. They were fate changers. Eventually, as other faiths and beliefs emerged, fossils faded back, once again, into the realm of objects, to ward off evil or to impart 'good luck'. Then, finally, they transformed into whispers of ancient cultural memories: objects to be collected and placed maybe on a window ledge or by a front door, because, well, that's what you do.

Mythology, folklore, archaeology – all tools to be used to explore the motives of fossil collectors across the ages, and across the world. Some fossils were subsumed into established mythologies, many for thousands of years, their origins lying deep in the myths of time. Other fossils have become the stuff of legends and passed into local folklore. What archaeology reveals, in addition to the written and oral record of myths and legends, is paramount to our understanding of how ancient societies viewed and used fossils. Some fossils, though, were not for collecting. These were tracks and trails preserved in rock that marked the passage of heroes and villains of myth and legend. What we now see as fossilized behaviour of dinosaurs, mammals, reptiles and humans was seen by prehistoric people as the spoor of myth makers and the enduring legacy of legends.[14]

From the people of the European Middle Ages to those living in the Near East at the time of the Romans, 2,000 years ago; from the Vikings in northern Europe to Bronze Age (4,000 to 2,800 years ago) and Neolithic (7,000 to 4,000 years ago) communities across Europe, Asia and Africa: all have collected fossils. So too Mesolithic hunters and gatherers living 11,000 to 7,000 years ago in northern Europe and 13,000 to 10,000 years ago in the Mediterranean region. This was a time when the Earth was emerging from the grip of the last great freezing, to the first Neolithic farmers. These were enthusiastic fossil collectors. But we can go even further back, into the deep archaeological time of the Palaeolithic, to a world of nomadic hunter-gatherers. These, the first fossil hunters, lived hundreds of thousands of years ago. These were people not quite like us. They were different enough to be classified as other species of the genus *Homo*. But still they collected fossils.

However, after hundreds of thousands of years of collecting fossils that inspired or were subsumed into a cornucopia of myths and legends, the quest for the meaning of fossils took another, altogether strikingly different, turn. Other ways of seeing fossils emerged and the old ideas, with their myriad of superstitions, crumbled into dust. Scholars came to realize that these strange, attractive and often mesmerizing figured stones were the remains of animals and plants that had once lived an unfathomable time ago: creatures frozen in rock for hundreds of millions of years. In some ways this was something even more astounding than all the myths and legends that had evolved as humans themselves had evolved. This book, though, does not tell the story of this, the 'true' nature of fossils. Rather, it is a tale of peoples' timeless obsession with these stony gifts from the gods.

And where better to start than with a dragon.

TWO

IN THE MYTHS OF TIME

For pre-Enlightenment communities the easiest way for them to come to terms with the nature of what we now call fossils was to subsume them within their most fundamental mythologies. So in China the fossilized remains of mammals and other vertebrates slid into mythologies centred on the dragon. And in Europe fossil sea urchins and belemnites conveniently became bit players in powerful Norse mythologies. In these instances the fossils were objects to be revered, as they brought with them powers bestowed by the dragon or by the gods.

Concerning Dragons

It was a simple hessian bag, more suited to carrying yams than its current bulky contents. It was heavy. Time for Thomas Kingsmill to lighten his load. He opened the mouth of the bag and slid in his hand. Slowly he drew out a large tooth, as though extracting it from the maw of some exotic creature, and handed it to the somewhat bemused Robert Swinhoe. Like a magician, Kingsmill then pulled another out of the bag, and another, and another. Soon 21 teeth of all shapes and sizes had erupted onto the table, much to Swinhoe's delight. The place was Shanghai, China. The date, May 1868.

'What are they?', asked Swinhoe.

'*Lung chi*, my friend. Dragons' teeth.'

Swinhoe, a 33-year-old consul for the British Foreign Service in China, was fascinated. On his way from Hong Kong to Peking (now Beijing), he had stopped off at Shanghai, in part to visit his friend, the engineer, architect, geologist and long-term Shanghai resident Thomas Kingsmill, but mainly to scour the markets for birds. For as well as being a diplomat of some standing, Swinhoe was an ornithologist. All of his spare time on his many trips through the depths of China was spent collecting birds. These he would either send back to other naturalists in England, such as John Gould, or he would describe and publish descriptions of his trophies himself. In his short life (he died of syphilis aged just forty), he described an astonishing 93 species of birds and seventeen species of mammals from China.[1]

When Kingsmill placed teeth that were clearly mammalian, and not dragon, in his hands, Swinhoe was obviously intrigued. Some were like no other mammal teeth he had ever seen. And big. Very big. He could understand why they had been called dragons' teeth. Some looked very familiar, for all the world like rhino teeth. Kingsmill had not collected this set of teeth himself, but had bought them from some of the many shops in Shanghai that specialized in selling animal remains for traditional Chinese medicinal purposes. But these were not from living animals. They were fossils.

Kingsmill realized that he had to explain to Swinhoe some of the myths about dragons' teeth. The local Chinese, Kingsmill told Swinhoe, believed that, in olden times the world consisted of monsters who were incessantly fighting and killing one another, until man came on the scene and initiated a more peaceful state by clearing the country and cultivating it. The monsters were large and powerful brutes; and in their teeth and bones existed their strength, hence the remains of these ground to powder and taken internally must give strength to the weak invalid.[2]

Many myths have survived in China concerning dragons. The concept of these animals has been ingrained deep in the Chinese psyche for thousands of years, because of the dragon's association with the imperial rulers, and most importantly with rain – and with thunderstorms in particular.

One of the attributes accorded to dragons was that they protected the emperor. Whenever Emperor Kao Ti (founder of the Han dynasty), who was rather fond of his wine, became too drunk for his own good, he was guarded by a dragon.[3] The emperor and the dragon were almost interchangeable beings, the former being known as 'the real dragon'.[4] He sat upon the dragon's throne, which was embellished with paintings and carvings of dragons, as were the emperor's robes.

Dragons were important because they ruled the sea, the rivers and the rain. During the summer wet season, the dragons live in the clouds. When they quarrel there comes thunder and rain. The philosophical essays of Wang Ch'ung (AD 27–c. 100), who wrote on astronomical and meteorological matters, contain a vivid description of the part believed to have been played by dragons in influencing the weather:

When the summer is at its height, the sun reigns supreme, but the clouds and rain oppose it. The sun is fire, clouds and rain being water. At the collision with water, fire explodes and gives a sound, which is the thunder. Upon hearing the sound of thunder, the dragon rises, when it rises, the clouds appear, and when they are there, the dragon mounts them. The clouds and rain are affected by the dragon, and the dragon also rides on the clouds to Heaven. Heaven stretches to the farthest distance, and the thunder is very high. Upon the clouds dispersing, the dragon alights again. Men seeing it riding on the clouds believe it to ascend to Heaven, and beholding Heaven sending forth thunder and lighting, they imagine that Heaven fetches the dragon.[5]

Yet, if the dragon is thirsty he will suck water up from the sea, creating waterspouts. In autumn, as the rains abate, the dragons leave the sky and descend to the depths of the oceans and lakes. It is at this time and when they reascend to the heavens in spring that they create violent equinoctial disturbances in the atmosphere.[6] Because these huge animals were all-powerful, as Kingsmill had explained to Swinhoe, they were imbued with great strength. So, any part that

Rubbing of a Chinese stone engraving of a dragon, age unknown.

could be harvested from a dead dragon and then processed for human consumption was thought to impart this power to the recipient.

References to dragons appear very early in China's written and artistic history, with the earliest known depiction of the dragon symbol on pottery found at a Neolithic site in Shanxi Province, a product of the Yangshao culture (5000–3000 BC). Dragons (and especially their teeth) also figure prominently in an early myth that explains the repopulation of the Earth following a great flood. The late Scottish sinologist Dr John Chinnery recounted the myth of Fu Xi, and the way that dragons' teeth helped repopulate the world.[7] On a day of storms, Thunder, in the guise of a dragon, came down to Earth. Unfortunately for him, he was captured by a peasant. Caging the thunderous dragon who had destroyed his crops, the peasant left the beast in the care of his children, a boy and a girl. He assured them of their safety, so long as they didn't give the dragon any water to drink. Unfortunately, after her father had left, the girl gave the dragon a few drops. Immediately, he broke free of his cage. Rather than eating the children, the dragon gave each of them one of his teeth. 'Bury them,' he instructed them, 'and harvest the plant that grows.'

When their father returned and found the dragon had escaped, he realized that it would unleash a great flood upon the Earth. So, what else to do but build a boat. Meanwhile, in a single day the teeth miraculously grew into a vine that bore a gourd. Slicing its top off the children saw rows of sharp dragons' teeth within, like the one they had planted. Pulling them out, the gourd was transformed, rather conveniently, into a boat, just as the storm broke. As the seas rose higher and higher, the peasant and his children in their little boat rose up to the ninth heaven, the land of the thunderous dragons and the gods. The Water Spirit Goy Goy was angered by the peasant's presumption to knock on the door to gain entry and made the flood recede so quickly that the boat was hurled to Earth and the father was killed.

His children, though, survived. Calling themselves Brother and Sister Fu Xi, after the gourd that had saved them, they married. Sister Fu Xi (sometimes known as Nu Wa) became pregnant and, somewhat surprisingly, gave birth to not a child, but a 'meatball'. Once it was born, the children chopped it into pieces and wrapped them in paper. A gust of wind then came and blew them away, scattering the fragments of the 'meatball' down to Earth, where they became humans. So the Earth was repopulated after all had been destroyed in the great flood. And all thanks to a dragon's tooth.

The question is, what became of Kingsmill's dragons' teeth? Rather like the Fu Xi brother and sister, they took a voyage on the high seas, accompanying Swinhoe back to England in September 1869. Knowing that the great anatomist Richard Owen at the British Museum would be interested, as he had described a single fossil mammal tooth from China some eleven years earlier, Swinhoe presented them to him. The subsequent study and description of the teeth in the *Quarterly Journal of the Geological Society of London* by Owen just a few months later was a landmark in vertebrate palaeontological studies.[8] It not only showed the world that in the not too distant past China was populated by modern types of animals, like rhinos and hyenas, that have today vanished from the region, but revealed that the people of the area shared their land with a number of huge, strange, now extinct animals. So, in addition to the eight rhino teeth, three hyena and seven tapir teeth, Owen also identified two teeth of a genus of the sister group to elephants, *Stegodon*, plus a single tooth from the huge extinct ungulate *Chalicotherium*. It was

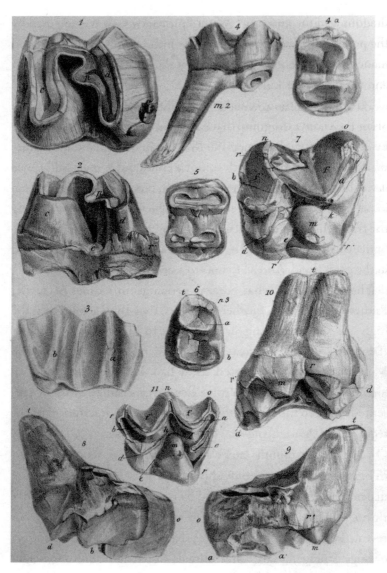

Engravings of 'dragons' teeth' among the 'Chinese fossil mammals' illustrated in an article by Richard Owen in the *Quarterly Journal of the Geological Society of London* (1870). Figs 1–3, *Rhinoceros sinensis*; 4–6, *Tapirus sinensis*; 7–10, *Chalicotherium sinense*; 11, *Anoplotherium commune*.

not a dragon, perhaps, but of dragon-like proportions, weighing 1.5 tonnes and standing more than 2.5 metres (8 ft) at the shoulder, though it was probably a much more benign animal. Ironically, all of these teeth that Kingsmill showed to Swinhoe that were originally collected for their supposed mythical powers, having been thought to have been shed by dragons, mark the beginning of modern vertebrate palaeontology in China.

Where there are teeth, there will be bones. Given that vertebrates have more bones than teeth, dragons' bones feature even more prominently in traditional Chinese medicine. The earliest reference to *lung ku* (dragon bones) appears in an account of the history of Han-shu written by Pan Ku (AD 32–92).[9] He recorded how a 'dragon's bone' was discovered at a digging site for a canal. The canal became known as *Lung-shou ch'ü*, or Dragon Head Canal.

When such bones were first used medicinally is not known, but this cultural heritage probably stretches back thousands of years. Their use is recorded in the *Han Medical Tablets* of Wu Wei, which were probably written in the first century AD.[10] Intriguingly the *lung ku* in powdered form were used in a preparation to help cure 'sword wounds with protruding intestine'. Powdered *lung ku* was added to fermented beans and the patient was made to drink the concoction two or three times a day. This was said to encourage the intestines to return into the abdomen. Another potion to aid in curing dysentery involved adding the powder to honey. *Lung ku* appears quite regularly in other medical works from this time.

The source of many of the bones seems to have been from cave deposits (as were Kingsmill's teeth). Some authors thought that the bones came from dragons that had died in these caves. Others thought that they came from living dragons who regularly shed them.[11] Li

Shizhen (1518–1593), a renowned naturalist and physician, in his *Classified Compendium of Materia Medica* (*Pen-ts'ao kang-mu*) discusses these counter-arguments in detail, coming to the conclusion that since there are indications that dragons were killed and sometimes eaten, then they were probably derived from dead individuals.

The colour of the bones had a big impact on how efficacious they were thought to be in curing various ailments. Lei Hiao (AD 420–77) wrote that black bones (often the remains of extinct elephants or rhinos) were the least effective (and so fetched a cheaper price). White and yellow dragon bones or teeth (which could be the remains of horse fossils) were of much greater medicinal value. But most prized of all were multicoloured bones, some with up to five colours. These were by far the best. Different colours harmonized with different internal organs. So the greater the number of colours, the more effective the *lung ku* would be in treating the disease. The use of dragon bones was not confined to China. Chinese communities overseas also wanted to be serviced. The extent of the trade in these fossils is shown by the records for the amount of material exported in 1884–5, amounting to some 20,000 kilograms (44,000 lb) of bones and teeth.[12]

In the same way that Owen's description of Kingsmill's teeth kick-started vertebrate palaeontology in China, so the quest for dragon bones inadvertently led to the first discoveries of ancient humans in China. And in a similar manner to Swinhoe's role in facilitating the study of dragons' teeth, so another naturalist and doctor, Karl Haberer, played a similar role with the mammal bones, as well as with the discovery of the first fossilized human remains in China.

In 1903 Max Schlosser of the University of Munich published the most extensive description to date of fossilized mammals from

China, based on material that he obtained from Haberer. He had arrived in China in 1899, hoping to explore the country for natural history specimens. As a European he couldn't have chosen a worse time, for later that year saw the beginning of the Boxer Rebellion, the reaction against foreign, especially Western, influence in the country. As a result he was confined to touring apothecary shops in the so-called Treaty Ports, in particular Shanghai, Ningpo, Ichang and Peking.[13] Haberer's view was that he was freeing important scientific material from the clutches of ruthless businessmen:

> I found the greatest sources of these fossils in Shanghai – not in the apothecary shops . . . which although very luxuriously put together, only yielded a few mostly broken pieces and charged very expensive prices for them, but in the nondescript ends of large drug traders, as I only really found in Shanghai. These are found in great numbers (around 50) in the truly Chinese districts, in narrow Chinese-style thatched-roofed alleyways, quite far apart from European trade.
>
> The material itself is sewn up in straw mats into round bales, which are bound with ropes. White and black lung chi are specially packaged and carefully divided. In order to investigate them, the bales were poured into a shallow basket and searched carefully, because the material is mixed with a quantity of small stones, bone fragments and bits of earth. In particular the lung chi are mixed up with plenty of recent teeth of horses, buffalo and so forth, so that picking out the most valuable fossil material must be left to the experts. This mixing of the lung chi with recent teeth is clearly intended to deceive the public, because only heavily mineralized fossils have medicinal value in the eyes of the Chinese.

As a result, my thorough searching through the chaos of stones, bones, fossils and recent skeletal material was met with some resistance from the Chinese traders, and I usually had to pay a very high price, or else the business fell through entirely, and my laboriously sorted fossils were taken back.[14]

This extensive collection that Haberer made yielded more than eighty mammalian species. Like Owen, he found the remains of hyenas and rhinoceroses, but also the fossilized relics of extinct camels, giraffes, pigs, hippopotamuses, antelopes and elephants. The most common fossil, though, was the extinct three-toed horse, *Hipparion richtofeni*, which had 670 teeth.[15] But among this great menagerie of mammals one in particular intrigued Schlosser, as it was quite human-like in its form. His conclusion was that it came from either a human or an unknown anthropoid ape.

Little further research was carried out on this fossil fauna until the Swedish geologist Johan Andersson and colleagues, working for the newly established China Geological Survey, decided in 1917 to try and find out where these dragon bones, so common in traditional drug stores, actually came from.[16] The task was no easy one. Often the fossils had passed through a number of intermediaries before finding their way into shops. Not surprisingly, many of the dealers were reluctant to reveal their sources. So as well as traipsing around countless shops, Andersson and his colleagues contacted missionaries and foreign residents in China, asking them for their help in searching for 'dragon bone mines'.[17]

This strategy proved successful, and Andersson and his colleagues were soon heading off on their dragon quest into deepest central Hunan Province. Once there, aided by Swedish missionaries, they were soon excavating the red loess clay and uncovering not just dragons' teeth but complete jaws and teeth of rhinos and hyenas. Other sites were visited in nearby Hubei Province and a large collection was made. Andersson soon realized that he needed help in describing the material, as he was almost drowning in the abundance of dragons' bones and teeth. He called on his colleague, Carl Wiman, a professor of palaeontology at the University of Uppsala, to help with identifying the material and collecting more.

Wiman travelled to China with a young palaeontologist, Otto Zdansky, and arrived in 1921. Initially they concentrated on a locality known to Andersson as Chou Kou Tien (now Zhoukoudian), about 60 kilometres (37 mi.) southwest of Peking. Here, cavities in the limestone, representing ancient caves, were now infilled by sediments along with large quantities of bones and teeth. Joined by the American palaeontologist Walter Granger, the men were excavating material from a locality called Chicken Bone Hill (so-named because it contained lots of fossil bird bones), when a local inhabitant told them: 'Not far from here there is a place where you can collect much larger and better dragons' bones.'[18] The site yielded a large number of mammalian bones, though none were human. Andersson noticed, however, that a number of quartz fragments with sharpened edges occurred in the deposit, evidence perhaps of ancient tools. Frustratingly, there was no sign of any human bones or teeth. It was not until 1926 that Andersson received a report from Zdansky, by then back in Uppsala studying the material they had collected, explaining that he had recognized a molar and a premolar tooth, both of which looked human-like. The find was reported in *Nature* later that year, but received a rather lukewarm reception. More material was needed.

Unsurprisingly the hunt was on to find more specimens. One of Wiman's colleagues, Birger Bohlin, undertook further excavations in April 1927 on behalf of the China Geological Survey. Any human material discovered was to be described by the Canadian palaeo-anthropologist Davidson Black, who worked at the Peking Union Medical College. By October of that year Bohlin found a human-like tooth. Black was convinced that it was an ancestor of *Homo sapiens* and formally named it *Sinanthropus pekinensis*, or 'Peking Man' as it became known. These days it is regarded as *Homo erectus*. As excavations continued, more material was unearthed, including an almost complete cranium. By 1941 the Geological Survey had more than forty specimens, confirming an early human presence in China. With the threat of invasion by Japan, the decision was taken to transport the material to the United States for safekeeping. The fossils were entrusted to the U.S. Marine detachment in Peking prior to transportation to the United States. Sadly, the specimens disappeared en route.

Many conspiracy theories have arisen concerning the ultimate fate of the fossils. Did the invading Japanese military take them back to Japan? Were they just dumped in the sea by unsuspecting Japanese soldiers? Are they buried somewhere in China? Or, could they, somewhat ironically, have found their way back to an apothecary shop to be sold as dragon bones?

Some Talk of Thunderstones

The relationship between fossils, thunder and rain was not confined to dragons' bones and teeth in China. In 1911 the archaeologist Christian Blinkenberg found that it existed throughout Denmark. Blinkenberg's book *The Thunderweapon in Religion and Folklore: A Study in Comparative Archaeology* had been published that year in England, two years after its original publication in Denmark, where

Blinkenberg was based. He had long been interested in the historical relationships between concepts of the 'thunderweapon' that
had existed in and around Greece at various times. For example,
in the Mycenean age (the last part of the Bronze Age, 1600–1100
BC), the thunderweapon was a bronze double-axe. But by early historical times it was the *keraunos*, or the thunderweapon of Zeus.
More recently the name was sometimes given by people to ancient
stone axes that they discovered in the ground. In Scandinavia it had
an altogether different meaning that lay at the very heart of Norse
mythology – one inexorably linked to the god of thunder, Thor.

Blinkenberg was well aware that particular stones often found in
the Danish countryside were known as 'thunderstones'. However,
few studies had ever been systematically carried out to try and understand the background to why a range of different naturally occurring
objects were called 'thunderstones' and probably had been for millennia. He was also interested in finding out what powers people
associated with these objects. Blinkenberg considered the different
options of achieving his objective: he could wander around villages
and farms, interviewing people or he could pursue research in a very
modern way – he could use the media. The latter, he decided, was
the way to go. He placed advertisements in newspapers regularly for
three years, from 1908 to 1911, asking anyone with any knowledge of
the folk traditions attached to any naturally occurring objects that
they called thunderstones to write to him.

Blinkenberg must have been delighted by the response he received.
Clearly, folklore was alive and well throughout Denmark at the time,
for he received more than seventy replies, containing a wealth of fascinating information. The letters flowed in from all over the country.
What rapidly became apparent was that, as Blinkenberg had suspected, a number of quite different things were called thunderstones

Thunderstones (belemnites), Devil's toenails (bivalves) and snakestone (ammonite).

– some natural, others artificially created. Less expected was that there were distinct regional differences in what people called thunderstones. About half of the replies came from people living in North Jutland, and on the islands of Sealand, Funen and Langeland. Overwhelmingly to people in these areas, ancient flint axes, dating back to Neolithic times more than 5,000 years ago, were known as thunderstones. But some people living in the southern islands of Falster, Lolland and Bornholm had a very different idea of what thunderstones were. To them, thunderstones were things that looked for all the world like bullets. But these were very strange bullets. They were made of calcium carbonate – if you pop them in a jar of vinegar, they dissolve. And that's because these 'bullets' were fossil belemnites.

Belemnites are among the most distinctive of fossils, mainly because of their strange bullet shape. These fossils are the remains of an internal structure in an extinct group of cephalopods (the group of molluscs that today encompasses animals like cuttlefish, squid and octopus). This hard bullet-shaped structure, known as the guard, attached to an internal chambered tube that helped the squid-like animal adjust its buoyancy in the sea. What the 'bullet' did was to provide a stabilizing structure, such that when the animal zipped through the water using jet-propulsion (water sucked in through a tube and shot out the other end), it could swim in a straight line, rather than flashing through the water like an out-of-control firework. Belemnites are amazingly common as fossils, sometimes occurring in such dense accumulations of many millions of individuals that they are called 'belemnite battlefields'. In all likelihood such aggregations probably represent death assemblages that formed after mass spawning events.

But to most people living in southern Jutland, thunderstones were something quite different. Fossils, yes, but not fossils that masqueraded as bullets. These were fossils that looked more like rocky buns or tiny loaves of bread. But no hot crosses lay on these buns. Rather, they all sported a rather fine five-pointed star splayed across their rounded surface, looking as though an exhausted starfish had collapsed on the stone. These were fossil sea urchins (echinoids).

I suspect that when the term 'sea urchin' impinges upon your consciousness what springs to mind is an animal that resembles a rather crowded pin cushion – sporting a fearsome array of long, poisonous spines – that lurks in shallow rock pools. This type is known as a 'regular' sea urchin. We will meet their fossils in an archaeological context later. But there is another, far more reclusive type of urchin that today, and for the last hundred million years or so, has evolved the ability to burrow into marine sediments, whether sand, silt or mud. Instead of flourishing a modest quantity of big spines, like their 'regular' counterparts, these animals increased the number of their spines enormously, but greatly reduced them in size, so that they look for all the world like little hedgehogs. Indeed, Thomas Browne, writing in his *Pseudodoxia epidemica*, called these fossils 'Sea-hedg-hogs'. Many of these so-called 'irregular' urchins spend their entire lives in the sand or mud. When they die, they are buried in the same sand or mud. They are about as pre-prepared for fossilization as you are ever going to get. It is a bit like spending your whole life in your grave. So this is why so many of them have been fossilized, and why people,

Fossil irregular sea urchin *Echinocorys scutatus* collected by Alan Smith from a field in Linkenholt, Hampshire. Sometimes known as a 'thunderstone' or 'shepherd's crown'.

wandering along, looking at the ground for food or rocks, or whatever, have been finding them for a staggeringly long period of time. While we can collect one of these fossils today and smugly know that they are the fossilized remains of once living sea urchins, this intellectual luxury has only been available to us for the last three hundred years. For the preceding 500,000 years or so of human existence it is very likely that this association was never made. For this is how long people have been collecting these particular fossils.

Thunderstones were also, in classical times, called *brontia* and *ombria*. And they had come from the heavens. They were the Roman equivalents of thunderstones. This view had been expounded by Pliny (AD 23–79) in his *Natural History*, the go-to source for many explanations of the natural world until the Renaissance. Pliny wrote:

Ombria, which some call Notia, is said to fall from heaven in stormes, showers of rain, and lightning, after the manner of other stones, called thereupon Ceraunia and Brontia: and the like effects are attributed to it . . .[19]

Georgius Agricola (1494–1555) in his influential book *De natura fossilium* (On Natural Fossils), published in 1546, reported that 'the ignorant believe that these [*brontia*] fall when it thunders. If it is raining when they fall they were called *ombria*. In Germany *brontia* were known as *Donnerkeile,* and *ombria Regensteine.*'[20] Even as late as 1677 Robert Plot (1640–1696) was ambivalent about the origin of thunderstones. In his book *The Natural History of Oxfordshire* he discusses stones that:

(by the vulgar at least) are thought to be sent to us from *inferior Heaven,* to be generated in the *clouds,* and discharged thence in the time of *thunder* and *violent showers*: for which reason, and no other that we know of, the ancient *Naturalists* coined the suitable names, and called such as they were pleased to think fell in the *thunder Brontiae*; and those that fell in *showers*, by the name *Ombriae*: which though amongst other authors has been the only reason why these have had place next the *stellated stones*, yet methinks it is due to most of them, by a much better pretence, having something upon them that rather resembles a *star* of five points, than anything coming from the *clouds* or the fish *Echinus*; to the shell whereof deprived of its prickles, *Ulysses Adrovandus*, and some others, have compared them, and therefore called them *Echinites*. However, I think fit rather to retain the old names, though but ill applied to the nature of the things than put myself to the trouble of inventing new ones.[21]

The thunderstone myth has its roots deep in Norse mythology, especially that of the god Thor. Renowned as a rollicking red-bearded weather, or sky, god, Thor's strength was legendary. In one hand he carried his hammer Mjöllnir; from the other he hurled thunderbolts to Earth. His hammer carried great powers, principal among which was the ability to bring creatures back to life. One Norse saga tells the tale of Thor's exploits one night when he stayed as a guest at a farm. Wishing to contribute to dinner, he killed his trusty goats. Now this was a rather problematic action because these two steeds (Gaptooth and Toothgnasher by name) drew his chariot across the heavens, creating thunder as they went. Indeed, this was a rather brazen act, because food certainly was not in short supply. But Thor just wanted to impress his host with Mjöllnir's power. After a fine meal of roasted goat he collected all the bones of these culinary casualties together

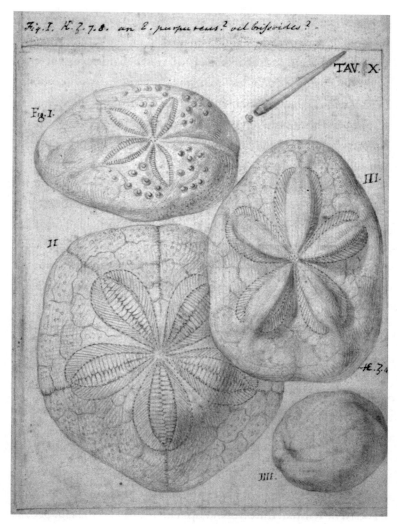

Original pencil drawing by Agostino Scilla for Plate 10 of his *La vana speculazione disingannata dal senso* (1670), showing irregular sea urchins: spatangoids (figs 1 and 4) and clypeasteroids (figs 2 and 3).

and lay them on the goatskins. With a prestidigitator's flourish of his hammer over the remains, Thor brought the animals back to life. But the best-laid plans, and all that. He had stressed in no uncertain terms to his host that the goats' legs were not, under any circumstances, to be broken to extract the marrow. Unfortunately, one of his host's sons disobeyed Thor's order. In consequence, one of the goats was made lame, ever after limping across the heavens. Thor, unsurprisingly, was not amused.

Despite Thor's reputation as a belligerent god, forever tossing his thunderstones from the sky, the people loved him and thought him the best of the gods. This is partly because, with the help of Mjöllnir, he protected the people from all sorts of unpleasant creatures. He happily slew serpents and giants alike. Most important from the peasants' perspective was his ability to control the weather. Yes, Thor made thunder and lightning, which can be pretty terrifying and, at times, destructive to man, home and beast, but he was also the Norse fertility god, responsible for the fertility of the fields, animals and people. Thor ensured the fruitfulness of the crops and the continuity of the seasons. He brought the rain that made the fields fertile and the crops bountiful. Useful attributes indeed. He guarded travellers and warded off disasters. He even protected the dead in their graves.[22]

Of all the gods, it was Thor who fought most determinedly to protect the world against evil. Thor was the peasants' god. He was a god to be trusted, the one who upheld justice and the law. So, any strange object found in a field following a storm, whether it be an old stone axe, a fossil belemnite or sea urchin, must be imbued with luck if it was dropped by Thor. Where else could it have come from? As Thor is the great protector, so must any of his objects be. Stick it in your pocket; hang it round your neck; place it by a door or on a window ledge – wherever you put it the thunderstone will protect you from evil and misfortune. How could it do otherwise? It is a present from the mighty Thor.[23]

Of all the different types of fossils that people have plucked from the crusty skin of the Earth for hundreds of thousands of years, one type of thunderstone, fossil sea urchins, seem to have been by far and away the most popular, if, as I will show in the succeeding chapters, the archaeological record is to be believed. Perhaps this is partly the reason why they have garnered the greatest number of names, in addition to 'thunderstone'. Nothing demonstrates this more than what Blinkenberg discovered in the heart of Jutland. The catalogue of names for these thunderstones was breathtaking: *sebedai, Sebadeje, spadæje, spadejesten, sebedæjsten, pariko, paradisko, paddeko, palliköer, marmorsko, marrimusko, smördie, smörsten, smör-lykke.* Blinkenberg was unable to provide any sort of explanation for what these names meant.

However, a more recent study by Viggo Sørensen from the University of Aarhus has shed light on their meaning. *Spadejesten, sebedæjsten* and *spadæje,* which were used in central and eastern Jutland, essentially mean 'Zebedee-stone'. Even in this name, thunder can be heard rumbling in the distance. The folklore concept of such fossils as charms falls neatly into the realm of pagan (that is, pre-Christian) beliefs, as with many of the 'old religion' ideas that were consumed by Christianity as it spread its power two millennia ago. It extended beyond Easter and Christmas even to thunderstones. Zebediah was the name of the father of the apostles James and John, and they were sometimes known as the 'sons of thunder'. So, 'Zebedee-stone' becomes 'thunderstone'.[24]

The terms *paradisko, paddeko, palliköer* and *pariko* were used only in North Jutland, and mean, literally, 'paradise cow'. This is clearly far removed from thunder, though 'paradise' might refer to the idea that the animals fell from the heavens during thunderstorms. The names *smördie*, *smörsten* and *smörlykke* relate to the power attributed to thunderstones of preventing butter or milk from spoiling.[25]

Many of the fossils that these Danes were calling thunderstones derived from Cretaceous chalks, or from more recent glacial deposits that incorporate flinty fossils eroded from the chalks, and were tough enough to have withstood the ravages of the ice. The chalk deposits that occur in Denmark, Germany, the Netherlands, northern France and southeast England are rich in fossil sea urchins. Sometimes the original urchin shell, known as a 'test', has been replaced by calcium carbonate in the form of the mineral calcite. Fine chalk fills these fossil 'eggs', which were long thought to have a particular medicinal value. But often, during cooler periods of deposition during the Cretaceous, there was abundant dissolved silica in the oceans. This often precipitated as the familiar layers or nodules of flint. But often, the silica worked its way inside the fossil urchin before hardening. Over time the outer shell dissolved, but an internal siliceous mould made of a type of chert called flint remained. And it is such fossils that not only are extremely resilient to the ravages of weathering processes, but frequently erupt in ploughed fields, like flinty potatoes.

As I will show in later chapters, people have been finding and keeping these fossils for hundreds of thousands of years. So when Danish Vikings in the years between AD 800 and 900 decided they wanted to explore lands to the west, and set off across the North Sea to Britain, could the thunderstone tradition have been one of the many that they took with them? While perceived wisdom has it that waves of Danish people populated parts of southern and eastern England over that century, a recent major study, called the People of the British Isles (POBI), has argued that, on the basis of DNA analysis of thousands of people living today, there is 'no clear genetic evidence of the Danish Viking occupation and control of a large part of England'.[26]

However, not all archaeologists agree. A strong counter-argument has been proposed of a significant immigration from Denmark to England during this period, with upward of 35,000 people making the journey across the water.[27] The evidence used relies on archaeological and linguistic studies. Moreover, by looking at the range of 'folk' names given to a particular natural object it might be possible to provide some further insight.

Support for a pervasive migration of Danish Viking ideas related to Norse mythology comes from some of the folk-names used in England for both fossil urchins and belemnites. In the 1860s the folklorist Edward Lovett recorded seeing fossil urchins placed neatly on windowsills of cottages in Wiltshire and Gloucestershire, mirroring the behaviour in Denmark.[28] Lovett was told that these fossils protected the dwellings from thunderbolts, as they did in Denmark. In the 1920s and '30s, fossil urchins in some parts of Dorset, Northamptonshire, Sussex and Hampshire were also known as thunderbolts.[29] In some parts of Sussex they were also called thunderstones. Just like in Denmark, the fossils were sometimes carried around in pockets, or placed on windowsills or mantelpieces, and for exactly the same reason: to protect the person or house from lightning.

There is archaeological evidence supporting a long association between fossil sea urchins and stone hand axes in the thunderstone myth. In Southborough, Kent, in 1910, a small funerary pot was found, along with a larger cremation urn. It was thought to have been placed there in the Iron Age.[30] The pot contained a fossil sea urchin and a broken Neolithic stone axe-head – again showing the association between these two objects, both called thunderstones in Denmark. Their burial, as part of a cremation, suggests a deeper spiritual association to these objects; they were not merely items to protect an individual from lightning. This therefore points to a long heritage for the thunderstone myth. People were also not averse to independently burying flint axes and fossil urchins. In recent times in Denmark it has been known for Neolithic axes, when unearthed, to be reburied when planting seed for a crop in order to ensure a bountiful harvest.

So, while the use of the term 'thunderstone' in southern and eastern England supports the idea of a migration of folk beliefs across the North Sea, as in Denmark, fossil sea urchins were known not only by this name. But in England the panoply of recorded folk-names for these fossils is even more extensive than in Denmark, suggesting that there were other myths associated with the fossils.

Thunderstones – the fossil sea urchin *Micraster* from the Chalk and an incomplete Neolithic axe head; from an Iron Age cremation burial, Southborough, Kent.

Not only is the diversity of names much greater than in Denmark, but so too is the disparity – in other words the linguistic range of the names. These can be grouped according to various themes, mainly related to either shepherds or fairies, but bishops also make an appearance, as 'bishops' knee' and 'bishops' mitre'.[31] The name most commonly given to fossil urchins in southern England was 'shepherds' crown', but other variations on this theme include 'shepherds' hats', 'shepherds' hearts' and 'sheep hearts'.

Exploring the derivation of these names takes us far back into the distant times of the Bronze and Neolithic ages, where inferences can be made from the archaeological associations of these fossils: in what context they are found – in association with the remains of the living or the dead? The much greater disparity of these names attributed to fossil sea urchins in England compared with Denmark suggests independent acquisition of folk, or probably spiritual, beliefs attached to these fossils in much earlier societies, and a very long history of interest in these fossils.

Both the Chinese concept of fossil vertebrates as dragons' bones or teeth, and the European folklore associating fossil belemnites and sea urchins with Thor, show how these particular fossils became incorporated into mythology as people tried to explain the world in which they were living. What links them both is their association with thunder, lightning and the bringer of the precious rain, be it a dragon or Thor. Other fossils, however, have engendered their own stories, by either instigating their own legends or sliding into pre-existing ones.

THREE

THE STUFF OF LEGENDS

What of fossils other than mammals, sea urchins and belemnites
commonly found by people as they tilled the ground or searched
for rocks to fashion into useful tools? Among other fossils they
often came across and were attracted to were brachiopods (lamp
shells), ammonites and crinoids (sea lilies). Rather than being
swallowed by existing mythologies, they carved their own
legends. These are legends that were borne of the fossils and
which existed in relatively recent times (that is, within the last
thousand years or so) and so made their way into early, medieval
writings and oral traditions. This is not to say that the legends
arose in these times. In all likelihood they were saturated with
prehistoric memories stretching back thousands of years. We
know this because these fossils often appear in archaeological
contexts, such as in burials: a nest of brachiopods in a Bronze
Age burial mound; an ammonite set into the construction of
a Neolithic long barrow; and tiny pieces of sea lilies placed in
Bronze Age graves. These were legends in the making.

Brattingsborg Pennies

'In Shi-Yen Shan,' wrote Li Tao-Yuan in China near the end of the fifth century AD, 'there are a sort of stone oysters (*shih kan*) which look like swallows. Hence the name of the mountain [the Stone Swallow Mountain]. There are two varieties of these stone shapes, one large and one small, as if they were parents and offspring. During thunderstorms these "stone-swallows" fly about as if they were real swallows.'[1]

These stone-swallows (*shih yen*) fascinated early Chinese writers, for both their beauty and their value, which is why they were collected as gifts for the emperor. These bird-like stones with permanent outstretched wings were what today we call brachiopods.

For more than half a billion years this group of animals with a pair of hard shells has inhabited the oceans. Similar in external appearance to bivalves (clams), brachiopods are fundamentally different, to such an extent that they are classified in another group, the lophophorates, rather than molluscs, within which bivalves belong. What characterizes brachiopods is a spiralling ribbon-like structure called a lophophore that nestles within the tightly clamped, curved brachiopod shells. Tiny hairs on its surface trap microscopic particles of food, which are carried into the shell by currents in the water.

In pre-scientific times some brachiopods attracted more interest than others and so generated more folk names and legends. This was probably a question of recognizability. A round, pebble-like blob may not attract the casual collector as much as a beautiful shell decorating the face of a rock looking like an elegant swallow or butterfly. That is, unless you are John Woodward, wandering through a windswept vineyard and spotting a pebble-like 'pundib'.

This type of brachiopod, known as a terebratulid, is very common in Jurassic and Cretaceous rocks in many parts of the world. It has attracted no special folk legend, just its rather peculiar name, and that was probably only used in parts of the Cotswolds. One of its claims to fame is to have prompted the common name of brachiopods today, 'lamp shells', because of the terebratulid's similarity to a Roman lamp. So, clearly not a name of much antiquity.

The Chinese stone swallows, the *shih yen*, are another type of brachiopod. They are what we now classify as spiriferid brachiopods, common in far older Palaeozoic rocks, 450 to 250 million years old. They also bear a resemblance to butterflies, both in shape and size, hence their folk name in Devon, 'Delabole butterflies', named after the quarry where they commonly turn up. Few brachiopods are very large; they are never more than the size of a clenched fist. Some brachiopods, called rhynchonellids, that have shells covered by radiating ridges and furrows, also seem to have piqued the interest of ancient people, quite commonly turning up in Late Palaeolithic archaeological sites of the Magdalenian culture (*c.* 12,000–17,000 years ago) in the Mediterranean region.[2] More recently, in the Swabian Alps in southern Germany, these brachiopod fossils have been called *täubli*, meaning 'little doves'.[3]

The spiriferid brachiopod *Punctocyrtella australis*, from the Permian of Western Australia. This type of brachiopod is known in China as a 'stone swallow'.

One type of brachiopod, though, is very small; the shells are flat and near circular in outline, about the size of a little fingernail. These somewhat strange brachiopods are called craniids. Although seemingly insignificant, these brachiopods have engendered a number of legends. And this is probably because when you look at one of these shells it seems to be staring back at you. On one side of the shell is what appears for all the world to be a face.

All brachiopods have the ability to open and close their paired shells. They do this by using two pairs of muscles. These are cunningly arranged so that when one pair contracts, the shell opens; when the other pair contracts, it closes. In many brachiopods the attachment of the muscles on the inside of the shell surface leaves a distinctive scar. In the case of the craniids, the scars resemble a face (which no doubt was what inspired Anders Jahan Retzius in 1781 to call the genus *Crania*). One pair resembles staring eyes; the other, set closer together, a nose.

Unlike most other brachiopods that attach to their aquatic substrate by a fleshy stalk called a pedicle, the craniids are either free-living or, more usually, cemented to a hard surface, such as another, larger shell. As the craniids are usually almost flat and circular, and with an apparently embossed face, they have long been thought to resemble little coins, particularly in southern Sweden where they are found in 70-million-year-old rocks.

The first reference to them is in Swedish medieval texts, in which they are described as *brattingsborgpenningar* (Brattingsborg pennies). On the southern Swedish island of Ivö, in Ivösjön Lake, Scania, is Brattingsborg castle. A number of separate legends exist to explain the origin of the fossil craniid brachiopods. Two involve a rather unpleasant character called Atte Ifvarsson, sometime king. Renowned as a distinctly evil character who lived in the castle, he

The craniacean brachiopod *Isocrania costata* from 70-million-year-old Cretaceous chalks in Maastricht, the Netherlands. This type of brachiopod is known in Sweden as a 'Brattingsborg penny'.

was infamous for greedily extracting taxes from the villagers, even from the sick and old. But thanks to divine intervention his castle was destroyed and swallowed by the lake. All the money he had taken turned into small calcareous discs. And each disc carried a grinning face.

Another tale is one of incest. Ifvarsson and his wife decided that their son and daughter should get married to each other, as there was no one else, in their opinion, who was good enough for them. However, the gods clearly disapproved of this strategy, as during the wedding dinner a landslide smashed into the castle and pushed it into the lake. Ifvarsson was the only one to survive. Rushing to the stables, he leapt on a horse and galloped off to faraway lands, where he and his trusty steed eventually perished. It is said that in memory of the tragedy you can still find white 'coins' embossed with what look like faces in the sand beaches of Ivö island – commemorations of the unfortunate fate of the deceased newly-weds.[4]

In yet another legend emanating from the same island, the thirteenth-century archbishop Anders Sunesen, dying of leprosy, was said to have seen out his days sequestered in a castle. One day he was told that soldiers had stolen a large amount of money from the castle after spending the night in the cellars, boozing and gambling. The archbishop promptly cursed the stolen money, so that when the soldiers awoke hungover the next morning they realized that the last laugh was on them. All the money had been turned into little, white, flattened stones. And on each, a death's head was laughing at them.[5]

Snakestones

On Christmas Day 1896, s.s. *Cornwall* steamed quietly out of London on its maiden voyage to Australia. Deep within its hold it carried a most unusual Christmas present: eight boxes that contained what was described at the time as 'one of the most complete [and] compact collections of British fossils stratigraphically arranged which has ever been made.'[6]

Unfortunately, upon its arrival in Western Australia disaster struck. The barge to which the boxes containing about 8,000 fossils were then consigned sprung a leak on its short trip between the port of Fremantle and the jetty in central Perth, where they were to be unloaded. As a result, much of the collection sat in bilge water for 36 hours. To make matters worse, when Bernard Woodward, the first curator and director of the Western Australian Museum, unpacked the soggy boxes he discovered that many of the fossils had, owing to inadequate packing, come adrift from the small, wooden tablets to which they had been glued on their journey out from England. Sad to say, all the information about each fossil had been written on these tablets.[7]

The assemblage of fossils had formed the personal collection of James Tennant (1808–1881), a major dealer in geological specimens in London and a professor of geology at King's College London. A well-known figure among England's geologists and geology enthusiasts, Tennant collected few specimens himself. Rather, he either exchanged with other collectors, purchased collections or employed people to collect for him. One of these was Edward Simpson. Tennant had employed him in 1852 and he worked for Tennant for two years. Simpson's main task was to collect fossils, often from ships' ballast and stone-yards, in order to form sets of geological specimens, which were Tennant's stock in trade. For many years Simpson, an experienced collector, had roamed northern England collecting and selling fossils, and also antiquarian objects, such as flint axes and arrowheads.[8] Tennant had first met him in 1847 or 1848, when Simpson was the one to approach Tennant offering him fossil specimens, many from Yorkshire.

What Tennant did not know at the time, until Simpson returned to London some ten years after he left Tennant's employment, was that Simpson had spent much of his adult life as a forger. He had forged fossils and a whole range of antiquarian objects, from flint-axe heads and arrows to pottery, all crafted with great skill. As a result, he had picked up a range of sobriquets (in addition to a few pseudonyms) as he wandered the country, including 'Flint Jack', 'Fossil Billy', 'Bones', 'Shirtless' and 'Snake Billy'.

Tennant's personal fossil collection, which 'Flint Jack' helped put together, contains all the standard types of fossils from throughout England and Wales: bivalves, gastropods, sea urchins and lots of ammonites, among others. Like bivalves and gastropods, ammonites are molluscs. They are one type of (generally) coiled cephalopods (the group that contains squid, octopus and the nautilus) called ammonoids. Among the ammonites in James Tennant's collection is one specimen that stands out from the others: one that has clearly

A 'snakestone' – an early Jurassic ammonite *Dactylioceras commune* from Whitby, Yorkshire; the snake's head was artificially carved in the 19th century.

been tampered with, a meddling of the fossil of which Tennant must have been well aware.

The ammonite in question is a beautiful specimen of *Dactylioceras commune*, from the early Jurassic 'Lias' deposits at Whitby. This was a place well known to Flint Jack, who was born nearby and who collected and sold many fossils from the fossiliferous deposits in the area. What marks this ammonite out as something rather special is that this tightly coiled, stony shell bears a very fine snake's head. This is not a natural feature, but a delicate carving. In all likelihood it is Flint Jack's handiwork. However, Simpson was not alone in tampering with fossil ammonites in this way to create snakestones.

Carving snake's heads on ammonites was a relatively common 'industry' in nineteenth-century England. Travellers were tempted to Whitby, and would part with their cash for a fossil legend.

The snakestone legend was particularly prevalent in England and associated with the towns of Whitby in Yorkshire and Keynsham in Somerset, where ammonites commonly occur. Similar legends also existed in southwest Germany. The earliest reference to snake-stones in England is said to be in William Camden's *Britannia; or, A Chorographical Description of Great Britain and Ireland, Together with the Adjacent Islands*, published in 1586:

> Here are found certain stones resembling the wreths [*sic*] and folds of a serpent, the strange frolics of nature, which (as one says) she forms for diversions after a toilsome application to serious business. For one would believe them to have been serpents, crusted over with a bark of stone. Some ascribe them to the power of Hilda's prayers, as if she had transform'd them.[9]

Camden further reported that he had 'seen a stone brought from thence, winded around like a serpent, the head whereof, tho' but imperfect, jutted out in the circumference, and the end of the tail was in the centre.'

Hilda (or Hild), whom Camden holds responsible for incarcerating snakes into stone, lived from AD 614 to 680. Revered by the locals, she was regarded as having had both the gift of foresight and the power to petrify all the snakes in the vicinity of her Abbey at Whitby. When found in rocks, as Camden had observed, they were also *sans* heads. This decapitation in some quarters was ascribed to St Cuthbert (*c.* 634–687), who will appear later in the chapter in association with fossil crinoids (sea lilies). As much as Victorian tourists to Whitby wanted to take home evidence of Hilda's handiwork, some entrepreneurial souls, like Flint Jack, decided the snakestones deserved to be reunited with their heads. Thoughtfully, they would carve one on the end of the serpentinous, stony bodies. And so the snakestone legend slithered comfortably into local folklore.

But deeper in time ammonites were viewed quite differently. They were objects of magic. Writing in his *Natural History*, Pliny the Elder observed that: '*Hammonis cornu* is reckoned among the most sacred gems in Aetheopia; it is of golden colour like a ram's horn in shape, and ensures prophetic dreams, it is said.'[10] *Hammonis cornu*, or the 'horn of Ammon', reflected the similarity of fossil ammonites to rams' horns, sacred to the ancient Egyptian god Amun. The third-century Roman writer Solinus, probably echoing Pliny, also wrote on golden ammonites: 'Beeing layde under a mannes head when he sleepeth, it is said to represent unto him heavenly dreams.'[11]

While Ethiopia is not noted for the occurrence of ammonites, golden or otherwise, in other places, such as southern England, they are quite common. Here, either the shell or the inside of the shell have been replaced by pyrite (iron sulphide), giving a golden, metallic lustre to the fossil. Unfortunately, on exposure to the air the pyrite will often, quite rapidly, disintegrate into a sulphurous pile of powder.

It is not only in Europe and Africa that ammonites have engendered legends. High in the Himalayas in Nepal, in some of the rocks continuously being worn by the fast-flowing streams and rivers, are found ammonites. Many thousands of metres above sea level, these hard, black, 150-million-year-old limestones and mudstones that outcrop along the banks of the Gandaki River in Nepal were sediments in a warm, shallow ocean called the Tethys. With the arrival of the Indian subcontinent, ploughing into the Asian continent about 65 million years ago following its separation from Western

Australia about 65 million years earlier, the Himalayas were created. As the Indian subcontinent continued to barge like a rugby front-row forward into the immovable Asian continent, the crust was rucked up, folded, lifted and reborn as the vast Himalayan mountain range. Along with the sediments, now hardened into rock, the enclosed fossils were carried aloft, including tightly coiled ammonites. These are known to the locals as *Salagrama*.

The *Salagrama* are regarded as the embodiment of Vishnu, one of the principal deities of Hinduism. The fossil is closely linked with the holy basil plant, which, annually, is 'married' to the *Salagrama*. The anthropologist Sir James Frazer, author of *The Golden Bough*, originally published in 1890, recorded how the marriage of the basil plant to the ammonite *Salagrama* must be performed before the tasting of fruit from a newly developed orchard is allowed. During the celebration, the basil plant is carried by a woman, the *Salagrama* by a man.[12] To one Rajah who supported and funded the celebrations, money was no object. It is said that on one occasion more than 100,000 people were present. The procession was suitably impressive, led by eight elephants, 1,200 camels and 4,000 horses. The most elegantly decorated elephant had the honour of carrying the fossil ammonite.

Turn of the Screw

Whether you are walking across the sharp, adumbral rocks of the Pennines, the mustard-coloured limestones of the Cotswolds or siltstones the colour of tea in the Kennedy Range in Western Australia, there is every chance you will find, nestled in the rocks, little discs. Looking like Lilliputian CDs, they are sometimes stacked together to form columns. More often they occur alone, either in the rocks or weathered out and waiting to be picked up. When naturalists in the seventeenth century were coming to grips with the true nature of these fossils, they called these columns *entrochi*; isolated discs were *trochi*. These terms were originally introduced by the German mineralogist Georgius Agricola in 1546. *Trochi* means 'wheel'.

About the size of a fingernail, these discs often have a hole in the middle, accentuating their CD-like nature. The first naturalist to wrestle with the nature of these enigmatic objects was the late seventeenth-century naturalist Martin Lister. Unsurprisingly, given their stem-like form, he conjectured that they were the petrified remains of plants. Given that he also recognized in the same rocks the frequent occurrence of 'certain rude stones, of the bigness of Walnuts', which he thought formed part of the plant, it was not an unreasonable explanation given what we know about the form of these organisms today.[13]

A Silurian crinoid from the Wenlock Limestone, Shropshire, showing the column comprising a series of ossicles, and the tulip flower-like calyx.

The hard calcareous discs, called ossicles, form part of the supportive column of a group of animals called crinoids. They really are one of the strangest of animals. Many cannot move. In life they are tethered to a rock, or a shell; or they are rooted, plant-like, into the sand. Their long, stem-like column of discs ascends to a bulbous 'head' (Lister's 'walnut'). From this emerge five (or multiples thereof) arms for catching microscopic food particles. Still in existence today, despite having evolved about 450 million years ago, they look, as Lister thought, more like plants than animals. Some closely resemble tulips, though their common name today is 'sea lily'.

Not all crinoids have columns made up of circular discs. Some are like little five-pointed stars. And this gives away the nature of their biological affinity – for they are echinoderms. This is the group that today includes starfish and sea urchins. Conrad Gesner, in his 1565 book *De rerum fossilium, lapidum et gemmarum maxime, figuris et similitudinibus liber* (A Book on Fossil Objects, Chiefly Stones and Gems, their Shapes and Appearances) thought that they owed their shape to stellar influences and called them *Asterias separatus* (separate stars). As such, they were believed to have great restorative powers.

Writing in 1652 in his *The Lapidary; or, The History of Precious Stones*, one Thomas Nicols observed that 'Asterias or Starre-stone is worth two crowns, since it has power to give victory over enemies, is good against Appoplexies [*sic*], and by the very touch of the body to hinder the generation of worms.'[14] Certainly, an efficacious and wide-ranging cure-all.

Folk explanations for crinoid discs in medieval Germany were many and various. In Lower Saxony they were known as *Sonnenräder* (sun wheels). However, in Thuringia and Hessia they were *Bonifatinspfennige* (St Boniface's pennies – so named because the saint who baptized the German tribes was said to have cursed pagan money and turned it into stone). In other parts of Germany they were called *Hexengeld* (witches' money).[15]

To medieval writers in England these little discs were clearly beads. Lister noted that they were known as St Cuthbert's beads, probably getting the information from naturalist John Ray, who noted that when visiting Northumberland in 1671 he rode to 'the Holy Island . . . where we gathered, on the sea shore under the town, those stones which they call St Cuthbert's beads which are nothing else but a sort of entrochi'.[16]

Cuthbert had something of a cult status. Bishop of Lindisfarne on Holy Island for just one year (AD 685–6), he was renowned for his sanctity and austere life.[17] Viking raiders, up to two hundred years later, having destroyed the monastery of the island, took his body with them when they left. Maybe it was because of this that, writing in 1783, Francis Grose noted, 'according to the vulgar belief, he [St Cuthbert] often comes thither in the night, and sitting upon a certain rock uses

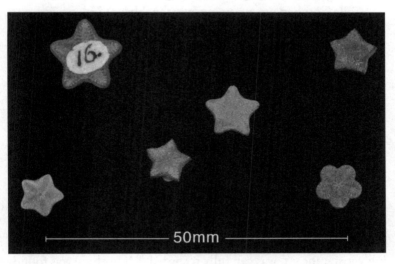

Individual ossicles of isocrinid crinoids known colloquially as 'star-stones', from John Woodward's collection.

another as an anvil, on which he forges his beads.'[18] Sir Walter Scott, in his epic poem *Marmion* (1808), immortalized the legend:

> But fain Saint Hilda's nuns would learn
> If, on a rock, by Lindisfarne,
> St Cuthbert sits, and toils to frame
> The sea-born beads that bear his name:
> Such tales had Whitby's fishers told,
> And said they might his shape behold,
> And hear his anvil sound;
> A deadened clang – a huge dim form,
> Seen but, and heard, when gathering storm
> And night were closing round.
> But this, as tale of idle fame,
> The nuns of Lindisfarne disclaim.

While Cuthbert was presiding over the abbey at Lindisfarne, 640 kilometres (400 mi.) to the south a woman was being buried on Kingston Down in Kent. We do not know how old she was when she died, but when her grave was exhumed by Reverend Bryan Faussett on 26 July 1771, it was clear from the grave goods buried with her that she was a woman of some standing in seventh-century Saxon society. Her grave (numbered 142 by Faussett) is one of more than three hundred that he excavated between 1767 and 1773.[19] Along with James Douglas, Faussett was one of the pioneer 'barrow diggers' of the eighteenth century, excavating burial mounds on the high chalk downland of southern England. Both men did this with meticulous care. Every item found with each body, however seemingly insignificant, was carefully recorded.[20] If nothing was found, Faussett simply wrote: 'Nothing'.

The most spectacular find in all the graves Faussett excavated was one of the greatest Anglo-Saxon treasures unearthed in England – the magnificent Kingston Brooch, of garnets and turquoise in an intricate gold-filigree setting. The woman buried in grave 142 was not so sumptuously adorned. However, she was still buried with an impressive array of jewellery, including earrings made of a cluster of a dozen amethysts, a gold neck-piece inset with garnets, silver bands and crosses. At her feet lay a wooden box. It had once measured about 35 centimetres (14 in.) square, but was very decayed when Faussett delved into her grave. What it had contained was an eclectic mix of items that must have meant a great deal to her during her life. There was a large ivory comb, a brass bracelet, a pierced sheep bone hanging on a silver bracelet, a cowrie shell, knives, shears – but, most unusual of all, the grave held what Faussett described as 'a piece of fossil substance, called by naturalists a screw'.[21]

Forty-two years before Faussett wrote his manuscript describing his finds, John Woodward's catalogue of his collection, now housed in the Sedgwick Museum in Cambridge, was published.[22] This was the go-to book at the time for those interested in fossils. Among the thousands of specimens in Woodward's collection are what he called 'screw-stones' or just 'screws'. Mainly from Derbyshire, the dozen or so specimens represent the internal moulds of what we now recognize as crinoid stems. Each of the discs that comprises the column of the stem is often, to varying degrees, hollow. After the animal dies, fine sediment can infiltrate this space. If the sediment cements together, and the actual calcitic stem dissolves away, what remains is a mould of the inside of the crinoid stem. These are generally screw-like in form, hence the common name, screwstone.

For the woman in grave 142 to have been buried with a piece of fossil crinoid suggests that it must have meant a lot to her during her life. As we sink further back in time, and peer into the excavated graves of those who lived thousands of years before the Kingston woman, we will see that placing crinoids (and indeed many other kinds of fossils) in graves, either with bodies or their cremated remains, was a regular pastime. People clearly have enjoyed collecting fossils for a very long time. And some wanted to take them with them into the afterlife. Other Saxon graves have been found with pieces of actual crinoid stems, not just the internal moulds.[23] Older graves have yielded much larger fossil hoards. A Bronze Age barrow at Tynings in the Mendip Hills was recycled in the Iron Age, around the middle of the first millennium BC. Within it were found two hundred isolated crinoid stem ossicles contained in an urn. Examination of them gave no indication that they were ever used as beads.[24] Sliding further back in time, and into Bronze Age cremation burials in the Mendips, more crinoid beads were found buried with cremated bodies.[25] Such occurrences are quite common in Bronze Age graves throughout Wessex. Often they are isolated ossicles, probably used in bracelets or necklaces. A single crinoid ossicle was found in a necklace that otherwise was composed of 150 perforated pieces of black shale.

Even earlier – 5,000 years ago, during the Neolithic – in southern England are some graves that had been seeded with crinoids. Stem fragments lay in a Neolithic burial in Aurignac (Haute-Garonne) in France, and in graves of the same age in Algeria.[26] Yet even older examples have been found in the Mendips: a short piece of cyclindrical stem from a layer about 12,000 years old in Gough's Cave, near Cheddar. Digging deeper we begin to pass into the realm of the hunters and gatherers of Mesolithic times who roamed northern Europe, moving north or south depending on the waxing and waning of the great layers of ice. Some of these people had an attraction for the crinoid stems with a five-pointed star outline, the Jurassic genus

Pentacrinites. Some have been found with decorative shells in a layer of Magdalenian age (12,000–14,000 years old) in the Dordogne region of France.[27] Even the mammoth hunters who roamed much of northern Europe during the Late Palaeolithic, 20,000–30,000 years ago, had a penchant for fossil crinoids. Pieces have been found not in graves but in the hut sites used by the hunters, particularly at Dolní Věstonice in the Czech Republic, where both cyclindrical and star-shaped crinoids appear to have been used as beads.

The fact that these fossils were being collected and used for decorative purposes as long ago as nearly 30,000 years is startling. Yet it pales into insignificance when compared with two tiny fossil crinoid ossicles found in an archaeological site in the Jordan Valley. For it is possible that these fossils were picked up and used more than 700,000 years ago by a species of *Homo* that looked very different from us, but which also was rather fond of collecting, and perhaps wearing, fossils.

The Venerable Bead

In the northern part of the Dead Sea rift valley in Israel, along the steep sides of the Jordan River, are sediments recording what that part of the world was like between 700,000 and 800,000 years ago. More than that, they contain the story of the ancestors of modern humans who lived there, inhabiting a world very different from ours. They left behind evidence that rather than being intellectually challenged, hirsute cave people, who we today classify as *Homo erectus*, they led a complex, structured social life and were adept at manipulating and utilizing their environment. A detailed study of one horizon at the site, known as Gesher Benot Ya'aqov, and dated at 780,000 years before the present, revealed the hearths of the fires around which they sat and the remains of the fish, nuts and game that they ate.[28] There is also evidence of a complex manufacturing industry of stone tools that they fashioned there: hand axes, chopping tools, scrapers and hammers. They crafted their tools from three rock types: basalt, flint and limestone. All the raw material had been sourced from elsewhere and brought to the site.

Among the thousands of manufactured stone artefacts found by the team of archaeologists led by Naama Goren-Inbar of the Hebrew University of Jerusalem, which has long worked at the site, were two small fossils. Easily missed in this riot of stone tools, they are small, disc-shaped and centrally perforated crinoid ossicles, each a smidgen under 4 millimetres (0.16 in.) in diameter. Both showed signs of wear when found. The question is, were these fossils naturally occurring at the site or had they been brought in by the same people who had collected the large quantities of limestone, flint and basalt? Like other human species who had utilized such material for tools, these people knew a thing or two about rocks. They knew the best ones to collect to fashion into handy artefacts. Did they perhaps, while rock hunting, spot these two small, perforated discs and decide they were worth keeping?

The closest natural occurrence to Gesher Benot Ya'aqov of Jurassic and Cretaceous rocks that contain such crinoid fossils is about 25 kilometres (16 mi.) away. A careful analysis by Goren-Inbar and her colleagues showed that geomorphologically it was unlikely that they could have been transported by natural agencies, such as streams, into the site.[29] The inevitable conclusion, therefore, is that somebody brought them in. If so, why did they do it? As I have pointed out earlier, it is known that other, younger Palaeolithic societies collected crinoid ossicles and probably used them as ornamental beads. It has been suggested that the presence of the central perforation in the disc made the crinoid ossicles ready-made to be used as beads in personal ornaments.[30] The two crinoid 'beads' from Gesher Benot Ya'aqov both show signs of wear. Whether this was caused by natural erosion or by the beads rubbing against adjacent ones when threaded together is not clear.

Verifying whether or not these crinoid beads ever graced some part of the anatomy of an individual of *Homo erectus* from the Jordan River Valley will require the discovery of more specimens. In the meantime we are left with just the tantalizing possibility that these distant ancestors of our species may not have been quite so primitive as we have been led to believe. The signs, perhaps, of an aesthetic sensibility towards this venerable bead.

FOUR

FASHIONING THE STONE

Two flints. Each alike in many respects: the size and shape of a thumbless hand. One carefully crafted 400,000 years ago, the other up to 100,000 years later. Both are objects of beauty and may have seemed so to those who made them. But they are also creations of great use: knapped to create razor-sharp edges to slice through flesh, roots, even bone. These two are extra special, however, different from the thousands upon thousands of similar tools crafted for aeons. For each carries, embedded prominently on its surface, a striking fossil.

Cutting Edge Curiosity

December 1673 was a bitterly cold month in London. Not a time to be rummaging through gravel as cold as ice. But on 11 December that was exactly what John Conyers was doing, in a gravel pit opposite the well called Black Mary's Hole, in Battlebridge (now King's Cross, London). Conyers, an apothecary and antiquarian, was looking for artefacts to add to his burgeoning collection. And on this freezing cold day he struck gold. Well, bones and a strange piece of flint, to be more precise.

For nearly 25 years Conyers had plied his trade from his shop in Shoe Lane, off Fleet Street. Here he concocted his own compound medicines and dispensed prescriptions for physicians, though he never indulged in medical practice himself.[1] Conyers was, by all accounts, an all-round good man. He was one of a select few apothecaries and physicians who remained in London in 1665 and 1666 during the last great plague, when most of their colleagues were fleeing London like proverbial flea-bitten rats from a floundering ship.

What Conyers enjoyed most was not grinding up his lucrative medicaments, but searching London for 'Antiquities . . . both Egyptian, Jewish, Grecian, Roman, British, Saxon, Danish . . . their Dieties or Idols . . . Amulets, Tallismans, ancient Urns, Medals, Coyns, Shields, Weapons.'[2] With the huge amount of rebuilding that took place in central London following the Great Fire in 1666, many of the shadows and memories of earlier settlements were exposed, providing rich pickings for Conyers and like-minded antiquarians. So, while Christopher Wren and Robert Hooke were undertaking the monumental task of rebuilding central London, John Conyers, on that cold December morning, was digging through what he thought were the remains of a lost river in the gravel pit. However, what he found, no doubt to his great surprise and delight, was rather unexpected: not only some huge bones, but what Conyers perceptively identified as the teeth of an elephant. What on earth, he must have thought, were the remains of an elephant doing in London in 1673?

Conyers reasoned that the remains were from animals that had come over to Britain during the time of the Roman invasion. We now know that they were, in all likelihood, the remains of the extinct straight-tusked elephant (*Palaeoloxodon antiquus*). This elephant had roamed through much of Europe, including Britain, between about 780,000 and 50,000 years ago. Conyers and other seventeenth-century naturalists and antiquarians had no awareness that animals as exotic as elephants could once have trod the cool, damp meadows of England.

Conyers, though, found more than just elephant remains:

> Then upon ye discovery of ye bones & Teeth . . . in ye side of ye River over agt. Black Marys in great pits that were made for Gravel . . . wch have lain as long as Claudius Caesars time . . . the Beasts as I suppose having been then slain at Landing . . . by one of ye Teeth was found a Brittish [*sic*] weapon made of flint dextrously shaped . . . to be seen at my home in Shoe Lane.[3]

This 'dextrously shaped' piece of flint looks for all the world like a large frozen teardrop, and it probably felt as such that cold day. Conyers seems to have been the first to realize that such a shaped flint, one among thousands of river gravel pebbles and cobbles, was not the product of physical erosion, but had been fashioned with skill and precision as a 'weapon' by someone living a very long time before.

The perceptive realization by Conyers that ancient man had crafted this teardrop-shaped flint opened antiquarians' eyes to the understanding of the existence of a type of stone tool that was the hallmark of Early Palaeolithic people. Known as Acheulean hand axes, following the discovery of many of these distinctive hand axes at St Acheul in France in the late nineteenth century, these tools mark one of the most significant advances in human cognitive evolution. This was the attainment of an awareness and appreciation of symmetry and the ability to manipulate irregular-shaped objects from the environment and fashion them into both useful, and aesthetically pleasing, bilaterally symmetrical objects. This was, perhaps, the awakening of the human preoccupation with art. It also meant that these ancient peoples could kill other animals more effectively.

For well over a million years the Acheulean hand axe was essentially the sole type of tool manufactured by two of our ancestors – *Homo erectus* and *Homo heidelbergensis*. Often called the 'Swiss army knife' of the Palaeolithic, these flint tools served a multitude of uses. They would have been used for cutting, chopping, slicing and scraping, both animals and plants; for hunting, butchering and skinning game, both large and small; for cutting down small trees; and for digging. In Europe they first appeared nearly 750,000 thousand years ago, coincidentally (or not) around about the time of the appearance of the straight-tusked elephant.

Fashioning one of these tools took skill, planning and foresight. It has been argued that for the necessary skill to be passed on from one generation to another, complex communication skills, a form of speech perhaps, must have evolved in the early *Homo* species. Choosing the right rock was paramount. Of course, it had to be hard and capable of producing a sharp edge when knapped. Flint was ideal, but so too were igneous rocks like basalt and hard limestone. Using a hammerstone, flakes were knapped off each side with care and precision. First a flake from one side then from the other. Then back to the first side, and so on, knapping from side to side. The flakes themselves, as sharp as slivers of glass, were also used in appliances for slicing and cutting. For the more teardrop-shaped axes a greater amount of rock was knapped off one end, to create a distal point. Final treatment was with a soft hammerstone such as a hard bone implement.

Sites like Swanscombe in Kent, where thousands have been found, was one of many that appear to have been manufacturing sites for these tools on an industrial scale. And while looking for the right piece of stone to knap, every so often it would seem that the eye of the searcher was drawn to something embedded in the stone that took their fancy – such as a fossil.

The further we go back in human history the more likely it is that people were generally more familiar with fossils than they are today. This is for the simple reason that much of their time would have been spent hunting for rocks to transmute into tools, a necessity for survival in a dangerous world. The extent of this proto-palaeontological knowledge would have depended a lot on the location across which these archaic humans roamed. Before the advent of metallic tools, the material used to craft artefacts to hunt, kill, eviscerate and create food and clothing were, primarily, rocks, and to a lesser extent bone and wood. For most purposes rocks were the best, especially flint. And with flint come fossils. A variety of chert (silica) that occurs as layers within chalk deposits across southern and eastern England, and parts of northern mainland Europe, flint was the hunter's rock of choice. A no-brainer, really. Flint is extremely hard and has the capacity for making a razor-sharp edge that cuts through bone and flesh with ease. As well as peppering the land under which chalk deposits now lie, it has, over tens of millions of years of relentless weathering, accumulated in river gravels and even in glacial deposits, far from the original chalk deposits.

Flint owes its existence, somewhat surprisingly, to animals. In particular, sponges. Not the sort that mattress layers of cream and jam, but back-scrubbing sponges that sit like pallid shrubs on the sea floor. They are the strangest of animals, with a heritage stretching back about 600 million years; animals that, in the evolutionary stakes, got a head start on their metazoan rivals. Their lives are essentially spent sucking in water and spitting it out, extracting any planktic morsel that might be caught up in their sieve-like internal structure. There have been times in the geological past when the land's rivers have been rich in dissolved silica and spewed it into the oceans. Other times have seen extensive upwelling of silica-rich subterranean volcanic magma. This was all manna from heaven for most sponges, as their bodies are supported by a mesh of tiny needles made entirely of silica.

It is then perhaps a little remarkable that a flint Acheulean hand axe that once nestled in an archaic human's palm nearly half a million years ago would have started life as part of a forest of sponges that lived on the floor of a Cretaceous ocean, some 70 million years ago. Transforming a marine animal into a flinty weapon of mammalian destruction required a particular set of circumstances. The tiny needle-like skeleton of sponges is a particular type of hydrated silica known as Opal-A. Over time the needles would have dissolved and worked their way into the chalky mud on the sea floor in a gel-like form. As the gel penetrated deeper into the mud, oxygen levels progressively decreased until the environment became anaerobic (this boundary between oxygenated and non-oxygenated conditions is known as the redox boundary). And in this anaerobic microbial world the gel-like opal hardened into tough, solid flint, replacing the chalk as it did so.

Many organic remains in the chalky sediments fossilized as flint. Often the surface of a nodule of flint will bear the impression of a bivalve, a starfish, a brachiopod or a sea urchin. Think shell pressed into a piece of plasticine. That's the impression they make. Sea urchins, hollow after decay of their viscera, seem often to be preserved whole. In reality they are the mould of the inside of the urchin's shell into which the silica gel oozed before hardening. The shell then dissolved away, leaving a round or heart-shaped fossil, but always impressed with a five-pointed star.

Fossils preserved in flint are really quite common. Anyone spending much of their waking hours collecting flints to craft into tools will, understandably, see many fossils. And sometimes our ancestors decided that the stone tool they would make would be much better if it was embossed with a striking fossil.

Tucked away in a small box, in a drawer, in a cabinet in a former tram depot in Bootle, Merseyside, is a very unusual piece of flint. Where once trams trekked in and out of the building, trolleys now trundle, bringing archaeological treasures to and from this Liverpool Museum storage facility. The flint (of perfect size to nestle snugly in your hand) is, to all intents and purposes, 'just' an Acheulean hand axe. Collected far to the south in Swanscombe, Kent, it is one of some 60,000 flint implements about 400,000 years old that have been excavated from here since 1880. But it differs from all others in two respects. First, it was only largely knapped on one side. This is most unusual, given that the methodology for making these tools was to knap flakes alternatively from either side. And, second, it carries quite blatantly on its surface a striking five-pointed star.[4] This was

Early Palaeolithic
Acheulean flint hand axe with
the fossil sea urchin *Conulus*,
from Swanscombe, Kent.

not a feature engraved with meticulous care by its original owner long ago. It is a natural five-pointed star that once graced the underside of a sea urchin that slowly ploughed its way through chalky mud about 70 million years ago before becoming entombed in flint. This particular type of urchin we today call *Conulus*.

The only real way to figure out if this artefact was made from a particular flint because it contained the fossil is to try and get inside the mind of its creator, who lived some 400,000 years ago. Clearly a somewhat challenging task. However, we have their handiwork to guide us in their thought-making processes; they have left clues as to what they were thinking in the way they made it.

A piece of rather gnarled flint is found, picked up and hefted to decide whether it would make a useful tool. (It is hard to imagine that the finder would not have noticed the fossil.) The tool has been broken off a larger block of flint. This is clear from the fresh, black, vitreous surface on one side, in stark contrast to much of the other side, which bears the fossil. This is brown and deeply weathered. The 'dark' side, away from the fossil, has been further carefully knapped so that the artefact looks like a relatively standard Acheulean hand axe. Perhaps it was just fortuitous that the other side has the fossil on it. Or maybe not.

There is another scenario. The flint is picked up because the eye is drawn to the prominent five-pointed star on its surface. What was it? Did this archaic human species have the cognitive capacity to even think about what it might be? What could they have seen in that pattern? A stick-like representation of the human form? Or perhaps, like so many people today who clothe and bejewel themselves with five-pointed stars, they just thought it would be rather cool to have a hand axe with such a nice pattern on it. Either way, it is likely that they crafted it because of the fossil, not despite it. This *Homo heidelbergensis*, it would seem, was a very early fossil collector with fashion sense.

The tool has been knapped all along one side, to the left of the fossil sea urchin. Only a small part of the right-hand side, near the top, has been worked. The final blow on the left side may well have caused the knapper to stop, for with that one blow a sliver of the fossil flew off. Can they have reasoned that to continue would have resulted in more of the fossil being lost? Is this why they didn't knap the right-hand side? Should they have had the power of speech at this stage in human evolution, would it be unreasonable to suggest that their response to this final misguided blow was an early, archaic human's version of 'Oh, fuck!'? Maybe, yet somehow I suspect that this person knew very well what they were doing with each blow, maybe even with the final one. This is for the simple reason that I, too, have had the pleasure of holding this remarkable object in my hand. It is hard to imagine such a tool fitting any more perfectly into the palm of your hand than this one. The heel of the tool fits perfectly along the unknapped, weathered surface. And, by good fortune (or maybe good design), the top of the bent thumb sits perfectly in the thin, scalloped scar on the fossil sea urchin. Is this what the knapper actually wanted? To be in tactile contact with the fossil when they were using the tool? Held like this, it becomes a simple extension of the hand: a perfect tool for cutting, slicing or hacking. This person, it would seem, prized their fossil. Maybe they thought it would bring them luck. Perhaps more than that: magical power. But this all presupposes that our ancient ancestors had the necessary cognitive abilities to reason, to plan for the future and to be aware of the concept of fate.

As one swallow generally fails to make a summer, so one fossil on thousands of flint artefacts would hardly make a convincing argument for the proto-palaeontological proclivities of early humans. But this particular flint axe is far from unique. In another museum, the Museum of Archaeology and Anthropology in the University of Cambridge, is another Acheulean hand axe – a 'proper' one. This axe does not lurk in a cabinet deep in the museum collections, but has pride of place in a showcase in the museum's newly refurbished displays. One of a small number of similar hand axes found in West Tofts, Norfolk, in 1911, its age is uncertain. It was made during an interglacial period, probably either about 250,000 years or 320,000 years ago. Either way, it is very old. Its creator was probably one of our ancestral species, *Homo heidelbergensis*. The consensus among those who have studied this tool is that it was carefully crafted to highlight the fossil bivalve that sits in a prominent plinth on one surface.[5] More than that, it sits exactly in the centre of the face, knapped carefully all around it. The bivalve, probably a species of *Spondylus*, is, like the sea urchin, a striking fossil. Many fine ridges radiate in an elegant fan on its convex surface. Little surprise, then, that it attracted someone who, even hundreds of thousands of years ago, must have been imbued with an aesthetic sense, to so carefully construct such a tool.

The creation of these hand axes incorporating the fossil urchin and bivalve signify that early human species were curious about these objects and attracted to them by their shape and by their symmetry. Although it is impossible to know whether the artisans who crafted these tools thought the fossils imposed any sort of power to their artefacts, sometimes the fossil itself became the tool.

If it was so important to possess a flint implement bearing a fossil, then what could be better than if the tool itself was the fossil – and the fossil the tool. No extraneous rock. Just the fossil. Would this not indicate that the fossil, in the eye of the holder, was something out of the ordinary? Maybe something others wanted, or even feared.

Early Palaeolithic Acheulean flint hand axe crafted around a bivalve, *Spondylus*, from West Tofts, Norfolk.

Among some Acheulean artefacts recovered from river gravels at Saint-Just-des-Marais in France was a fossil sea urchin. This one was obviously a pre-loved fossil, as it has been worked. A species of Late Cretaceous heart urchin called *Micraster*, the fossil had been carefully knapped around its entire periphery.[6] It had been transformed by the hand of one of our ancient ancestors, probably *Homo heidelbergensis*, into what seems at first glance to be the perfect tool, with razor-sharp edges all around: ideal, you would think, for a range of tasks, such as cutting, slicing and scraping. And if their imagination did bestow on these fossils some sort of intrinsic power, this must surely have been the finest. Its star-rayed pattern of five ambulacra rakes across its smooth, rounded surface. The fossil would rest firmly against the user's palm. Yet was this object really a weapon of utility? When firmly clenched in the fist, the sharpened edge would have cut into the hand. In whatever way it was handled it is hard to imagine the fossil being a very functional tool. Yet whoever made it was clearly prepared to while away their time, carefully knapping and transforming the fossil into the idea of a tool. So, maybe not so much an item of obvious utility, but an expression of the aesthetic imagination of its creator.

Fast forward a 'mere' 40,000 years or so ago, the beginning of the Upper Palaeolithic, and a very similar-looking object was being created. However, this was not by an individual of *Homo heidelbergensis*, but one of another archaic human species, *Homo neanderthalensis* – Neanderthals. The Grotte de la Roche-au-Loup is a cave in central France between Paris and Lyon. The tool industry found in the cave belongs to a type known as Châtelperronian, and is thought to have been manufactured in this region by Neanderthals between 40,000 and 45,000 years ago. The tools that they made differ markedly from the earlier Acheulean types in that their creators forsook a bilaterally symmetrical form for one that is distinctly asymmetric – a sharp blade on one side, and a smooth, even surface on the other. In this way the user avoided slicing off their own thumb when using the tool.

The cave is sunk deep in Jurassic limestone country. Yet it contained tools made of flint derived from Late Cretaceous chalk deposits. These attest to transport of the raw material over at least 30 kilometres (19 mi.) from the site of the nearest Cretaceous outcrop. One of the flint implements is a fossil reminiscent of the fossil sea urchin from Saint-Just-des-Marais. It too is a complete specimen of *Micraster*. Yet it differed in one distinctive way – it was only worked on part of the periphery. About half had been knapped, removing two of the five star-rayed ambulacra, meaning it is very Châtelperronian in its style of manufacture.[7]

The similarity between the two worked fossil sea urchins – crafted by two different archaic human species living hundreds of thousands of years apart – raises the question of whether their interest in fossils was a shared passion that was passed down through the generations, as echoes of past curiosities. If so, was the technique of transforming the fossil into a tool somehow transferred from one species to another? Could they really have communicated with each other about such esoteric pursuits? Or was it just an independently shared curiosity, a simple desire to possess a fossil that arose in the early evolution of the human psyche?

There is a good deal of evidence to show that Neanderthals collected many types of fossils: bivalve shells, corals, brachiopods, trilobites, as well as sea urchins. And they searched widely for them, carrying them, in many cases, far from where they first were found. Rather than being the savage brutes of popular myth, Neanderthals were a more sensitive group of late-age Palaeolithic people: caring for more vulnerable members of the group, burying their dead, adorning themselves with ornaments, such as fossil and shell beads, and even creating basic forms of artistic expression.[8] The bones of their hands and arms were anatomically much the same as ours.[9] They relied on not just force, but precision. Hence their ability to manipulate objects like fossils to turn them into ornaments and to craft elegant flint tools. And this must have been combined with suitably developed cognitive abilities akin to those of *Homo sapiens.*

Homo heidelbergensis, from which both our species and the Neanderthals are thought to have evolved, also had this penchant for fossil collecting – of bivalves, crinoids, sea urchins and even sponges. The first three they fashioned into their Acheulean technology tools. Near the mouth of the River Charente in France, large numbers of Palaeolithic worked flints have been recovered by archaeologists.[10] As well as sea urchins, other fossils have found their way into elegant hand axes fashioned with care by this early human species, including brachiopods, oysters and crinoid stems.

So what of our species, *Homo sapiens*? Have we been as imaginative as our early ancestors? Well, as you would expect, we have. Again, there are close parallels between flint tools made relatively recently (that is, just a few thousand years ago) and those made hundreds of thousands of years ago. Humans have long been drawn to the shape and elegance of the fossil, selecting them while searching for just the right piece of rock to knap and craft. By the time people cast off their hunter-gatherer ways a little over 10,000 years ago, heralding what we now call the Neolithic, they started leaving other evidence of their proclivity for collecting fossils. Gathering fossils not simply to embed on tools, or use as tools, these people began to leave them in their houses, in their temples and shrines, even in their graves. But old habits die hard, and some still fancied possessing a tool adorned with a fossil.

At Spiennes in Belgium, by a hill called Camp-à-Cayaux, Roland Meuris, expert collector of archaeological artefacts, has found an astonishing number of flint axes, scrapers and picks, many containing fossils around which the flints have been fashioned. Often the fossils take pride of place on the tools. Of the more than a hundred artefacts found by Meuris with fossils in them, about three-quarters are sea urchins. The other quarter contain bivalves, brachiopods and belemnites.[11] Surprisingly, these Neolithic flint workers emulated their Neanderthal archaic relatives in, at times, transforming isolated sea urchins into tools, by knapping part of the periphery. When it came to how to use a fossil sea urchin as a tool, the brain seems to have been hardwired the same way in all three species of humans who collected these fossils.

As people in the Mediterranean region began to settle down and domesticate animals and plants 10,000–11,000 years ago, they were finding fossils that were not preserved in flint. One of these, an altogether different type of sea urchin, they began to modify in a most intriguing and novel way. Soon they realized that they could use these fossils to help make their clothes.

Neolithic flint hand axe with ornament of the fossil sea urchin *Micraster*; from Camp-à-Cayaux, Belgium.

Spinning a Yarn

Many areas of the Levant, especially in present-day Jordan, are covered by pale, fossiliferous Cretaceous limestones. The warm seas in which these limy sediments were deposited about 70 million years ago were particularly rich in echinoderms – starfish, brittle stars and sea urchins. From the nature of their shells, sea urchins, unlike starfish and brittle stars, do not readily break up after death. Hence the entire hard parts of the animal are more likely to be preserved and become fossilized. As I have argued earlier, the five-pointed star pattern engraved naturally on the fossil's surface was particularly attractive to prehistoric fossil collectors. As the global climate began to ameliorate 10,000–12,000 years ago, people made the transition from a predominantly hunter-gatherer existence to a sedentary social system. Animals were domesticated, and plants for food were sown and harvested on the land the people inhabited. Permanent settlements were created and the dead were buried close to the living. These Neolithic people living in the eastern Mediterranean region had time for things other than just hunting for their next meal. But still they needed rocks for tools and found the time to collect fossils, especially fossil sea urchins. Many fossils preserved in these Levant limestones are small and pebble-like, and always bear the five-pointed star. As the limestone erodes on hillsides or in wadis, the fossils naturally weather out and can just be picked up from the ground.

Neolithic examples have been described from some of the earliest-known permanently inhabited sites in present-day Jordan: Beidha and 'Ain Ghazal. Five specimens are known from the former site, but have yet to be studied, and four from the latter.[12] But the richest early Neolithic site by far is at Basta, where 99 examples have been excavated.[13] Whereas the other Neolithic and also many Iron Age sites have fossil sea urchins of a similar type (species of *Mecaster*, *Heterodiadema* and *Coenholectypus*), those at this rich site at Basta are dominated by an urchin called *Nucleolites*, which is not found in any other archaeological site in the region. Of these 99 fossils, 84 are *Nucleolites*, suggesting that the species may have been targeted by the area's early fossil collectors. None show signs of alteration, but were found in rooms in settlements, along with cultural debris. The shepherds and flint-mining specialists working near Basta may have been collectors of these specimens. There is no clear indication as to why they collected these fossils, but even today, bedus of the nearby Petra area still collect them to sell to tourists. In the past as well as today, fossils are found in bedu households or as personal property, and they have held some symbolic significance. Probably like us, individuals from early Neolithic Basta found the shape and symmetry of the fossils appealing, and it impelled their instinct to collect.

Some of the fossil sea urchins found in other archaeological sites in Jordan, from the Neolithic to the Iron Age, show obvious signs of having been collected in the past because they have an artificial hole running through them – and (nearly always) right through the centre.[14] So, it is clear that such fossils have been 'pre-loved' because of their extensive modification. The profiles of the holes are always the same – hour-glass shaped and drilled from both ends with great precision to pass exactly through the centre of the stony doughnut. But were these holes drilled just so the fossil could be slid on to a thread to be worn as a personal decoration? Maybe. But they almost certainly had another quite different function.

Attach a thread to a short shaft, or spindle; drop the centrally perforated fossil urchin over it; give it a twist to set it spinning and

Regular sea urchin *Rachiosoma major* with hole centrally drilled in the Neolithic; specimen probably used as spindle whorl; from 'Ain Ghazal, Jordan.

it transforms into a spindle whorl, stabilizing and prolonging the turning, working its own special magic. And when the early inhabitants of the Levant learnt to domesticate sheep and goats, realizing that the animals' hair fibres when twisted together could be used to make cloth, the spindle whorl became a crucial tool in the manufacturing process. Many were made from clay, or carved from limestone. But it soon became clear that, if you could find them, a great source of spindle whorls were fossil sea urchins – these little round stones branded with a five-pointed star. They were the perfect shape, size and weight. All they needed was to have the hole drilled through them.

The distribution of these drilled fossils in Jordan from the Neolithic to the Iron Age demonstrates a usage over a period of about 8,000 years. In other regions, fossil urchins were collected and perforated for even longer, for about 40,000 years. While some of the early examples may have been used as personal decoration, many were used as spindle whorls. In a survey of their occurrence in Palaeolithic to Roman-age archaeological sites in France, 184 examples were recorded, mostly from southwestern and northern parts of the country, especially Charente and Charente-Maritime.[15] Just a single specimen has been found in England, discovered in the 1840s from an Anglo-Saxon grave in Fairford, Gloucestershire.[16] So, while many of the Neolithic to Anglo-Saxon perforated sea urchins may well have been used as spindle whorls, a variety of fossils from earlier in the Palaeolithic also often had holes drilled through them. But this was for an altogether different reason: fashion.

Wearing the Stone

For our distant ancestors (gatherers as well as hunters) with a penchant for fossil collecting, one way to keep the fossils safe was to carry them around embedded in tool-kits. But there was another way: to wear them. For at least 70,000 years our species has been making necklaces and other types of personal ornaments using a cornucopia of material – teeth, bones, carved rock, shells and plant matter. Neanderthals were also adorning themselves with such items for even longer. The shells used as personal ornaments by these people, widely through space and time, were not confined to modern marine, freshwater or land shells. These people were also using fossils. We know this from the many examples that have been uncovered from archaeological deposits of perforated or grooved fossils. Probably attracted first by the aesthetic qualities of the fossils, these ancient people wore them as another way of safeguarding these curious objects and easily transporting them.

Wearing objects such as fossils was obviously not just for aesthetic reasons. Anthropologists have argued that wearing any type of naturally occurring object, whether it be a shell, tooth or bone, is part of a shared communication system.[17] Some have argued that the appearance of items such as personal ornaments marks a significant change in human cognitive evolution – the evolution of 'modern behaviour', including language. Wearing these figured stones is thought to have been important in terms of recognition by other members of the same or other social groups – a potent form of visual communication to clarify a person's perceived status, much as visible material goods are evident proof of wealth or status today.[18] 'Hey look! My fossil is bigger and better than yours.'

It didn't matter what the weather was like. You just had to put up with it, or die. Clothing was paramount. No time to worry about what it looked like. It just had to keep you warm. Very warm. But this didn't mean that you had to forego a sense of fashion. It wasn't just what you wore. It was how you wore it. It all came down to bling.

Around 30,000 years ago, vast ice sheets began a 10,000-year inexorable crawl south from the Arctic Sea and northern Europe, deep into central Europe. What was not covered by ice was unbelievably cold – windy permafrost plains so dry the air was infused by lung-clogging dust. Trees, sensibly, only inhabited the warmer lands of the south. People had to adapt or move somewhere else. Many chose to stay. These were some of the earliest so-called 'modern humans', the people who had developed a lifestyle that, while hard, was not just one of survival – hunting animals to kill, or searching for tubers to dig up and cook. They also found time for art.

In this progressively harshening landscape the people managed to eke out an existence. So too the animals – wolves, foxes, rabbits, hare, deer, horses and mammoths: food for ever hungry humans, and the source of clothing and hides to construct their ephemeral shelters. Some such shelters were impressive structures, made from bones of the mammoths the hunters killed. Huge ribs and limb bones were stuck in the ground, raised vertically, and covered by hides or circles of massive mammoth jaws. Bones were also burnt as fuel. But some bones and tusks were put to more creative uses – to carve figurines of mammoths, bears, lions, horses, owls and humans, usually females. Other parts of animals, especially the teeth of foxes, were pierced, threaded and hung as necklaces, bracelets or head bands or sewn into clothing. So why not do the same with fossils?

The material culture of the people living through the period leading up to the last glacial maximum – the period when the Earth was at its coldest for at least 130,000 years – and after, was one of change. As archaeologists, like other scholars, like to classify things, the periods when tools and other cultural artefacts transformed from one distinctive type into another, have spawned a variety of names. The early modern humans, *Homo sapiens*, living from about 43,000 to 33,000 years ago, before the cold reached its greatest intensity, developed a rich cultural identity called the Aurignacian. As well as their own distinctive type of flint implements, these people also used bone and antlers as tools; produced some of the earliest cave art, such as that at Lascaux and Chauvet in France; and carved figurines from ivory, of people and animals (such as mammoths, horses, lions). They even made flutes, carefully fashioned from the delicate wing bones of vultures and swans – music and art evolving side by side.

As the cold intensified around 30,000 years ago the material culture passed into what is called the Gravettian, as the glaciation reached its peak, until about 20,000 years ago when the glaciers slowed their advance and began to withdraw north. This period of climate amelioration is called the Epigravettian. The Gravettian people were specialized mammoth hunters and made a wide range of tools, including blunt-backed knives, often crafted from mammoth tusk. They also conjured up boomerangs.

In 1985 in a small cave in southern Poland in the Obłazowa Rock, archaeologists made an unusual discovery.[19] In what appears to have been a pit excavated in older, Aurignacian strata, were the remains of an eclectic set of items from the early Gravettian culture (also known as the Pavlovian), between 20,000 and 30,000 years old. Set within a ring of granite and sandstone blocks was a worked, curved mammoth tusk interpreted as a boomerang; a decorated wedge made from the distal end of a deer's antler; a pierced Arctic fox tooth; an ivory bead; a pair of human finger bones; more than thirty flint tools – and a pierced fossil *Conus* shell. The gastropod fossil shell, boomerang and wedge show signs of having been coated with ochre. The cave may have been a religious or ceremonial site, perhaps representing a symbolic grave. Subsequently two more pierced fossil *Conus* shells were found.[20] The leader of the excavation, Paweł Valde-Nowak, suggested that because the perforation of the shell was not just a simple hole, but an elongate slit, the shell could have been used either as a pendant or maybe as a bullroarer.[21] These are objects used in recent times by Australian Aboriginals; when attached to a cord and swung around, the shell makes a whistling sound that can carry over vast distances.

There was a long tradition during the Upper Palaeolithic in central and western Europe of collecting fossil gastropods to be used as personal ornaments. Many have neat holes in them. Some may have been deliberately made to turn the fossil into a wearable item. Others may have been made in the gastropod by other carnivorous gastropods while it was living and before it was fossilized, creating for the fashion-conscious a most useful hole through which a cord could be strung. The Gravettian mammoth hunters seem to have particularly liked to wear gastropods. Other fossils they largely eschewed, except for the occasional fossil that also spirals like a gastropod, but on a plane and not helically – such as an ammonite. Two beautiful ammonites pierced through their centres have been found in an early Gravettian deposit at Kostenki on the Don River in Russia.[22]

In the famous Gravettian site of Dolní Věstonice in Moravia in the Czech Republic, fossil Cenozoic gastropods, some with holes, along with fossil bivalve shells, have been recovered. These shells are thought to have been used as small ochre dishes. Some of the richest fossil collections have been found in Epigravettian deposits, 14,000–15,000 years old, in the Dnieper Basin in Ukraine. Here occur hundreds of fossil gastropods of a wide range of different types. Many have holes pierced through them, either by hungry gastropods when the fossil was living, or much later by humans.[23] The importance of these fossils to these late Palaeolithic people is shown by the fact that they had to source them from far away – at least 200 kilometres (124 mi.). Clearly personal ornaments were worth travelling a long way to obtain, or they had a high trade value.

It is the summer of 1886. In July, the French army surgeon and amateur archaeologist Adrien-Jacques-François Ficatier is using his leave to explore some caves just south of Arcy-sur-Cure in Bourgogne. The limestone cliffs here that hug the river's edge are riddled with caves. He finds a small entrance to one quite high above the river. Slowly shedding light from his lantern into the darkness of the cave, he sees fragments of bones and pieces of flint littering the ground. There is bound to be much more, he thinks, if he digs deeper. And so he does. And so there is. There are bones of horses and reindeer; debris – worked flints, spears and needles – left behind by ancient occupiers of the cave; and intriguing personal items, pierced presumably to be worn as personal ornaments. There is a wolf's tooth and some marine shells, including scallop shells; a beetle carved from a piece of lignite derived from a pine tree; and, preserved in a dark grey piece of shale, a weathered, but nevertheless distinctive, trilobite. What better name for the cave, thought Ficatier, than the Grotte du Trilobite.[24]

While the lower layers of the deposits in Ficatier's cave have sub-sequently been shown to be about 35,000 years old, the upper layers that he excavated have been dated to around 15,000 years. This period of occupation of the cave corresponds closely to what has been

Entrance to the cave site at Arcy-sur-Cure, Renne, France.

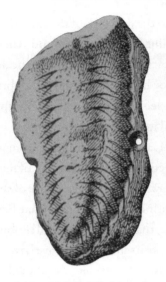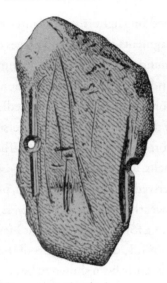

Worn trilobite with hole drilled through one end for use as a pendant (and
now in the Musée de l'Avallonnais, Avallon); from Upper Palaeolithic deposits,
about 15,000 years before present, Grotte du Trilobite, Arcy-sur-Cure, France.
The illustration is by its discoverer, Adrien-Jacques-François Ficatier, and reproduced
from an 1891 paper by him.

called the last glacial maximum. These caves would probably have
been important dwelling sites for people living through such harsh,
freezing times.

The trilobite pendant that Ficatier found is the only one of its
type unearthed in such old archaeological deposits. Trilobites were
the dominant marine arthropods for nearly 300 million years, becoming extinct about 250 million years ago during the great end-Permian
mass extinction event. These segmented animals, looking rather like
modern-day woodlice or slaters, consist of a fused head plate, often
sporting a pair of prominent eyes; a multi-segmented body and a
fused segmented tail. The fossil from Grotte du Trilobite lacks a
head, but is otherwise complete. While the cave in which this
second-hand fossil was found is in Jurassic limestone country, the

trilobite originated from much older, Ordovician deposits that formed about 450 million years ago. The closest natural occurrence of strata of this age in which this type of trilobite occurs is in the Armorican Massif, some 700 kilometres (435 mi.) to the west of the Grotte du Trilobite. This fossil must have meant so much to somebody, or maybe a number of somebodies, that they pierced it and wore it as a prominent, personal ornament, carrying it with them over a vast distance.

Unlike the Gravettians, the earlier Aurignacians collected a wider range of fossil types to use as personal ornaments. These include belemnites, sea urchins and their spines, and Devonian age fossil corals. All these fossils had been pierced (by humans) in order to be worn. While gastropods were also used by the Aurignacians, these were more often than not shells of living species, not fossils. Of four second-hand belemnites found at Kostenki, two have been heavily altered. They have been engraved and cut in such a way as to enhance their beautiful, translucent amber-coloured lustre.[25]

What caused this change between the Aurignacian and Gravettian periods in the preferred type of fossil to use for personal ornamentation? Wearing fossils or other types of beads was about more than being fashionable. It was a cogent statement of who the wearers were in their communities. Archaeologists Marian Vanhaeren and Francesco d'Errico have promoted the view that the Aurignacians' personal ornaments, such as beads, were a powerful indicator of ethno-linguistic identity and diversity. That is, they made it easier to identify your friends – and your enemies. 'Symbolic behaviours,' they have written,

such as artistic activities, mortuary practices, and decorations on utilitarian and non-utilitarian objects, which need to be transmitted from generation to generation through language, are probably among the more informative elements for tracking down ethno-linguistic entities.[26]

While their study assessed regional differences, it is possible that temporal changes in types of fossils collected reflected, at least in part, changes in the cultural identities of these groups through time.

The Aurignacians, who represent the early spread of modern *Homo sapiens* across Europe, co-existed, at least for a time, with Neanderthals. These latter people have had bad press. In popular culture they are the epitome of all that is ugly, all that is stupid. The reality is likely to be far from this conception. Like us they collected fossils (a most worthy occupation, some of us would argue). Moreover, they made stone tools that carried fossils. And like us they were not averse to bling. Far from it. One fossil gastropod discovered in a layer in Fumane Cave, northern Italy, shows signs of having been not only artificially perforated, but deliberately coated with dark red haematite.[27] The layer has been dated at between 47,600 and 45,000 years old and pre-dates the arrival of modern humans (the Aurignacians) in Europe. Stone tools

Artificially drilled fossils from Kostenki, Russia, from Upper Palaeolithic (Spitsynean: 42,000–36,000 years before present), presumably worn as personal adornments. Top row, three pairs of elongate Mesozoic belemnites and a small pair of Devonian corals; bottom row all Devonian corals.

found associated with the fossil are of Mousterian type, typical of manufacture by Neanderthals. The fossil is considered to have been suspended by a sinewy thread, on the basis of wear marks on the shell, and worn as a decorative pendant. The fossil was sourced far from the cave in which it was found. The closest geological deposit that contains this Miocene- to Pliocene-age fossil species, *Aspa marginata*, is about 110 kilometres (68 mi.) away in the Po Valley.

Other fossils have been found that are associated with Châtelperronian and Mousterian technologies typical of manufacture by Neanderthals which show other examples of their use as personal ornaments. A fossil brachiopod from the Grotte du Renne in France has had a groove cut in it to enable a cord to be tied around it. Two pierced belemnites have also been found there and apparently used for personal decoration. There is plenty of other evidence for Neanderthals' interest in fossils. In the caves at Arcy-sur-Cure in France, fossils clearly brought in to the caves are associated with Neanderthal tools of the Mousterian type. In the Grotte de l'Hyène, a slightly gnarled piece of spiralling fossilized gastropod and a small, globular coral were found. And in another cave a terebratulid brachiopod was brought from at least 30 kilometres (18 mi.) away. Very little raw material for tools also found in the same deposits was transported from very far away. Neanderthals, like everyone else, treasured their fossils.[28]

In 2018, the world-view of Neanderthals as sluggish brutes was cast aside with the publication of the discovery at Cueva de los Aviones in southeast Spain of marine bivalve shells in a context indicating that they were used in a symbolic fashion. The shells, about 115,000 years old, had been artificially pierced and coated with ochre and used, most likely, as personal ornamentation.[29] And the discovery of Neanderthal cave art in the Iberian Peninsula dated at about 65,000 years old pre-dates any comparable artwork by modern humans.[30] The question then arises, at what point does the manipulation of natural objects, such as fossils, by piercing them and wearing them, or incorporating them into everyday tools, become indicative of a propensity for artistic, as well as symbolic expression? Whether it was *Homo heidelbergensis*, *Homo neanderthalensis* or *Homo sapiens*, it is the creative mind here at work, transforming everyday, humdrum objects into something much more. Something of meaning to lighten the soul and delight the mind.

FIVE

DELIGHTING THE MIND

To see beauty in a grain of sand, or a gazelle in a water-worn pebble or broken bone. In many societies people spent much of their time searching for rocks suitable for turning into utilitarian objects, and were drawn to attractive or unusually shaped stones that couldn't be used for any practical purpose. Sometimes it could be the way the rock had naturally weathered, perhaps creating a subtle circular shape looking for all the world like an eye staring back to the finder. If that coincided with other features of the rock reminiscent of a leg or a snout, then it was collected and probably treasured. Even better if the stone was a perfect spiral or carried a five-pointed star.

Vitruvian Woman

'Ain Ghazal they called it – Spring of the Gazelle. Ten thousand years ago this place in present-day Jordan was fertile woodland, of tamarisks, oaks and poplars. Many animals gravitated here. So too did humans. People had foregone their hunter-gatherer ways and some chose this perfect spot to settle. It must have seemed an idyllic place

– fresh supplies of meat and hides from wild animals, such as deer, horses, wild pigs and hares, and fields of edible wild plants. Soon they began to domesticate their own animals – sheep, goats, pigs – and grow their own selected grains. From its first settlement about 9,250 years ago it grew to become one of the largest early Neolithic towns, with upward of 2,500 people.[1] But therein lay the seeds of its own destruction. The wild game was hunted out; the goats overgrazed the abundant vegetation, ably assisted by the sheep, pigs and cattle. And soon this wooded, bountiful paradise had become a rocky wasteland, unable to support the swollen population and barely able to support a few goats. Now it is just part of an outer suburb of the capital, Amman, through which roars a major highway.

Yet in the 2,000 years during which the site was settled, people were able to spend time not just hunting and farming, but being creative – and in quite novel ways. The early period of settlement was a time before anyone had learnt to fire clay to pottery. The only pots and bowls were made from sun-dried clay. After becoming adept at crafting these vessels, they turned their attention to making less utilitarian objects feeding not just the body, but the soul. Archaeological excavations, principally by Gary Rollefson and his colleagues in the 1980s, have turned up many stone and bone tools, broken pieces of pots and other useful everyday items made from clay. Significantly, they also unearthed the results of these people's creative minds – a wealth of figurines. While many were crafted from clay, others were carved from chalk rock and limestone that outcrops in the area. The figurines are mainly of the animals the people spent much of their time with – chiefly cattle. These were not simple representations of your average cow, rather they emphasized the animals' horn-laden heads; so, too, many of the human figurines were depicted in suggestive ways. While some depicted the entire body in proportion, others

The archaeological site of 'Ain Ghazal in Jordan that has yielded fossil sea urchins modified by the site's original inhabitants. Located on the outskirts of the city of Amman, it was excavated in the early 1980s. Here a step trench has exposed a stone wall and plaster floor at the bottom. All of the stratigraphy from the red clay to just above the excavator's head is known as Middle Pre-pottery Neolithic B and dates between 9,250 and 8,200 years before present.

Excavations led by Gary Rollefson in the early 1980s at 'Ain Ghazal on the outskirts of Amman, Jordan. Here fossil sea urchins, modified by the inhabitants some time between 9,250 and 8,200 years ago, have been found.

had a swollen abdomen and pendulous breasts, interpreted as fertility figurines. Other images were of dismembered heads or torsos.

However, the most stunning pieces, neither crafted from clay nor carved from rock but carefully made out of reeds and white plaster, were fifteen statues and the same number of busts. At about 1 metre (40 in.) in height, these amazing figures stare out from piercing eyes of bitumen harvested from the shores of the nearby Dead Sea. As humans are not white, so the manufacturers of these plaster figures applied a pink wash, possibly made by mixing some animal blood with the plaster, to make them more lifelike. To this pioneering Neolithic society the celebration of life and its renewal was central to the very fabric of the community's existence, and it was encapsulated in these different types of figures and figurines. This concept of life and replenishment may also have been embodied in one of the four remarkable fossil sea urchins, found during the archaeological excavations at 'Ain Ghazal.

Four fossil sea urchins: all modified by people who lingered for a long time over them. Each is the size of a small button and shaped like a tiny hot-cross bun, but with five rather than four arms to the cross splayed across the fossil's surface. Three of them have holes drilled through the centre – classic spindle whorls. But the fourth is very different. It is a striking and quite beautiful specimen. The five ambulacra on its convex surface that form a prominent five-pointed star are deep red scars that radiate across the salmon pink surface of the fossil. Somebody, more than 9,000 years ago, exposed this deep red colour by picking very carefully at the white crystalline calcite that originally formed the five ambulacra.

The fossil was also modified in another, more significant, way. Coursing through the 15-millimetre-wide (0.6 in.) urchin from one side to the other is a hole, but quite unlike those in the spindle whorl

Early Neolithic plaster figure from 'Ain Ghazal, Jordan.

fossils. It starts off on the flatter surface (keep thinking domed hot-cross bun), where the fivefold pattern is only weakly developed. Here the hole is 5 millimetres wide. As it moves through the fossil it narrows to about half that width. Unlike holed urchins used as spindle whorls that are drilled equally from both sides, producing the hour-glass-shaped profile, this urchin was only drilled from one side.[2]

The trouble with this hole is that while it was started at dead centre, where the original animal's mouth had been located, it wasn't drilled perpendicular to the outer surface, like urchins drilled for use as spindle whorls. This was drilled way off-centre. It would have made a useless spindle whorl. Maybe the driller just got it wrong. Or perhaps they knew exactly what they were doing. The hole emerges on the domed surface of the fossil exactly between a pair of ambulacra – two of the rays that make up the five-rayed star pattern – close to where they meet. It seems to be so carefully located that it looks as though the driller intended the hole to emerge exactly at that point.

What if somebody, when looking at this or another fossil urchin, made a great cognitive leap and saw in the pattern on the fossil sea urchin not just a pretty five-pointed star but something else entirely? A figure. A figure of a human. A human stick-figure imprisoned on the surface of the little stone bun. The significance of the hole then becomes quite clear, because it is placed exactly at the junction of the fossil sea urchin's 'pair of legs'. Another 'Ain Ghazal fertility figurine, but one transformed from a natural object into a unique work of art.

So, maybe in the five-rayed star on the fossil urchin the artists of 'Ain Ghazal were seeing their own reflection on these little pebbles – head held high, arms outstretched and legs akimbo. The manner in which this pattern lies on this circular object bears an uncanny

Regular sea urchin *Coenholectypus larteti* with hole drilled off-centre between the posterior pair of ambulacra, possibly representing a fertility symbol; from the Neolithic of 'Ain Ghazal, Jordan.

resemblance to Leonardo da Vinci's *Vitruvian Man*. If you want an illustration that the hole on the fossil is representative of female genitals, then all you have to do is to superimpose the two images, and the genitals match up perfectly. Vitruvian Man meets Vitruvian Woman, incised on a fossil.

Like in other societies, intercourse and pregnancy played a significant role in Near Eastern mythology. Child-bearing was a metaphor for the mysteries of the origins of the universe, the planets and stars. Nammu, the primaeval Mesopotamian deity, gave birth to An-Ki (the gods of sky and Earth, respectively). This inseparable pair gave birth to water, wind, the Sun and Moon, and the stars. The renewal of vegetation each year was Ki's doing by consorting with An. Likewise, in Sumerian/Babylonian times the deity Inanna/Ishtar caused the plants to germinate in spring by intercourse with the god Dumuzid.[3] The Neolithic female statuettes at 'Ain Ghazal are regarded as fertility symbols that embody a mythical figure who helps crops to grow each year. So too, perhaps, the Vitruvian Woman.

Leaving No Stone Unturned

The transition in *Homo sapiens* from a nomadic hunter-gatherer to a sedentary lifestyle did not happen overnight. It is not as if someone suddenly thought, 'Oh, bugger it. I've had enough of this wandering lark. Can't we just stop in one place for more than just five minutes?' Rather, the transition, between about 12,300 and 15,000 years ago, saw people adopt a semi-sedentary way of life. Known as the Natufian culture and centred in the Levant, it was characterized by the building of semi-permanent settlements, or base-camps, primarily composed of round and oval-shaped huts. Although still chiefly hunter-gatherers, the Natufians remained settled for long enough to make what some might consider to be one of the great breakthroughs in human cultural evolution – the ability to brew beer.

The earliest evidence for brewing, perhaps for ritual feasts, has recently been found at a Natufian site in present-day Israel.[4] The Natufians were also the first to bake bread.[5] When not imbibing their new concoction, hunting the local fauna (especially gazelles) and harvesting seed from pistachios, lentils and wild barley to bake their bread, they were avidly collecting natural objects – tortoise shells (sometimes placing them in their graves), semi-precious stones and strangely shaped rocks, which they sometimes either engraved or transformed into erotic sculptures,[6] and fossils.

Wadi Hammeh 27 is the oldest-known Natufian base-camp in the Levant, dated at about 14,500 to 14,000 years old. Detailed excavations by Phillip Edwards and his colleagues from La Trobe University in Melbourne, Australia, have revealed a rich material culture of flint, limestone and basalt artefacts, along with nearly eighty portable art objects.[7] Many of these show evidence of

A weathered fossil regular sea urchin, possibly *Leioechinus* sp., from the Natufian site of Wadi Hammeh 27 in Jordan. The pattern of the plate structure seems to have inspired artificial engravings of the same pattern on other carvings from the same site.

engraving with abstract geometric patterns. The inhabitants of this ancient site also collected fossils: a lucinid bivalve, a baculitid ammonite (an ammonite not coiled into a spiral, but a straight shaft), different types of high-spired gastropods and, of course, the ubiquitous sea urchin. This urchin is a 'regular' type called *Leioechinus*. In its fossil form it is shaped like a balloon, but in life it would have been covered by pox-like tubercles that supported an array of protective spines. Before being picked up by a Natufian collector, the fossil had been very abraded by natural weathering. The tubercles and surface features had faded away, revealing the chunky, underlying plates of the internal structure that make up the animal's protective shell, looking like row upon row of rectangular bathroom tiles.[8]

This pattern seems to have fascinated the Natufian artists. Two of the pieces of artwork from Wadi Hammeh 27 are zoomorphic – that is, objects sculpted to look like animals. One is a flat piece of limestone, carved into a body with a pair of legs, possibly meant to represent an agamid lizard.[9] The other is a piece of bone carved to look like the head of an animal, maybe a gazelle.[10] In both pieces their surfaces have been engraved with a rectangular pattern, finely incised longitudinal and transverse grooves creating a pattern virtually identical with that on the fossil sea urchin.

Fossil sea urchins may also have inspired another piece of more functional artwork. Many miniature bowls less than 5 centimetres (2 in.) in diameter, carved from basalt or limestone, have been found at Wadi Hammeh 27. Another fossil sea urchin found at el-Wad Cave, Nahal Me'arot, Mount Carmel, Israel, has, on its lower surface, been ground to produce a sunken bowl, its overall shape becoming just like that of the manufactured bowls.[11] In the pristine fossil the area artificially ground away was naturally a little sunken. Perhaps this provided the inspiration for the manufactured bowls – again the natural world inspiring the human mind.

So, are we really any different today from a Natufian who picked up a pebble resembling an animal's head with a penetrating eye at Wadi Hammeh 27? While a rock, like a weathered cobble of calcite, may at times have suggested something animate to its finder, embellishment was sometimes needed to fulfil its true artistic potential. Arguably the most renowned of such Natufian pieces is the sculptured rock in the British Museum's collections interpreted as depicting a copulating couple. Just a few deft carvings on a water-worn calcite cobble and it was transformed from a hinted-at couple embracing into a blatant erotic sculpture. While the metamorphosis from cobble to work of art arose from the sculptor's imagination crystallizing a pleasurable memory, many Natufian artworks created from natural objects like stone or bone were carefully engraved with abstract geometric

Underside of Cretaceous fossil regular sea urchin *Heterodiadema lybica* artificially worked to produce a miniature bowl; from the Natufian el-Wad Cave, Nahal Me'arot, Mount Carmel, Israel.

patterns. Did this non-representational expression derive freshly imagined from the artist's mind, or could it have been inspired more rationally by natural objects, such as fossils?

Before leaving this ancient Natufian site, there is one more piece that provides tantalizing evidence for nature inspiring art, albeit on a small scale. Finding a fossil sea urchin, especially one abraded to show the rectangular plating structure, is no easy task. Serendipity plays a significant part. So, if you cannot find one of your own, then why not just make one? This is precisely what one Natufian did. A piece of limestone, roughly fossil-urchin-shaped, had a deep groove carved into it to represent one of the five ambulacra. Either side are two rows of carefully engraved plates – a longitudinal incision and scores of transverse ones. An instant 'fossil' sea urchin was born.

This mimicking of a fossil was not unique. Perforated fossil sea urchins were apparently so popular that at a number of different times and places some people thought, 'Well, if I can't find a fossil to turn into a spindle whorl, I'll make my own.' In Cyprus a little more than 4,000 years ago somebody chose to make a pottery spindle whorl that looks just like a perforated fossil sea urchin.[12] An even older Neolithic clay spindle whorl was unearthed in Ober-Jonsdorf, Reichenbach, Germany.[13] It too had been fashioned to look exactly like a fossil urchin. Some 3,000 years later in Woodhouse in Northumberland, a spindle whorl was crafted with five 'ambulacra' and intervening tubercles – again an object that was made for a functional reason but artistically inspired by fossil sea urchins. This one was not made from clay, but from lead, no doubt to give the spindle an extra spinning boost.

In the great scheme of artistic achievements, these examples may all seem relatively inconsequential. Yet they are, I believe, in many ways a fingerpost to explain some of the great examples of Neolithic art – the abstract Megalithic art of northern Europe. Art that may well have been inspired by fossils.

Fossils Inspiring Art

They chose to build it – this place for the dead – on a small, rocky hillside close to the river. The slabs of limestone were the perfect shape and size – flat and the length of a man's thigh. Three circles of stone they built – an outer one about seven paces in diameter, the innermost just four paces wide. A short passage led into small inner chambers. And here, 5,000 years ago or so, they came to bury the cremated remains of their dead and to ease their passage into the afterlife.

Situated just over 3 kilometres (1.8 mi.) east of Tralee in County Kerry in Ireland, the remains of this passage were discovered in 1996 when county archaeologist Michael Connolly led an excavation at this site at Ballycarty. The burial mound the archaeologists discovered was one of a number of structures revealed following notice of the construction of a motorway nearby.[14] On this limestone hill they found evidence of ditches, ramparts, enclosures and stone cairns, along with a number of small mounds. One of the mounds was under the most threat from the motorway construction, so it was chosen for excavation.

The discovery that this mound was a passage tomb came as a great surprise to the archaeologists. Such structures had previously only been known in eastern Ireland, and included the spectacular passage tombs at Brú na Bóinne, notably Newgrange, Knowth and Dowth. But this tomb here in Ballycarty is far away in the southwest of the country, making it the most westerly known of this type of structure in Europe.

Little did the Neolithic inhabitants realize when they decided to build their rather modest passage tomb at Ballycarty that 345 to 330 million years earlier the hillside of broken rocks on which they stood had once been a mudmound in a warm Carboniferous sea. Such structures are known as Waulsortian mudmounds, accumulations of very fine carbonate mud derived from precipitated calcium carbonate and finely comminuted mud derived from the bioerosion of carbonate-bearing organisms, such as corals, bryozoans and other invertebrates, built up into mounds of mud many tens of metres high.

The invertebrate inhabitants of these mounds included crinoids, brachiopods and gastropods. Swimming over them were cephalopods

Aerial view from the west of a Carboniferous limestone reef at Ballycarty, County Kerry, Ireland, showing location of Neolithic passage tomb.

Close-up of a passage tomb at Ballycarty, County Kerry, Ireland, that contained a cache of fossils.

– coiled ammonoids called goniatites, and many types of nautiloids. After they died all of these invertebrates contributed their shells or other skeletal structures to the mudmounds. These rapidly cemented on the sea floor to become limestone. The consequence, hundreds of millions of years later, was a limestone peppered with the fossilized remains of these invertebrates, especially the brachiopods, gastropods and nautiloids. What was to become a tomb for the remains of Neolithic humans had long before been a tomb for the myriad invertebrates that lived on and above the mudmound.

As they collected the slabs to make the passage tombs, these Neolithic people could hardly have failed to notice this mineralized menagerie of the past inhabitants of the Carboniferous seas. What they made of this great assortment of strange objects is anybody's guess. Fossiliferous limestones of this age occur commonly across Ireland and the Neolithic settlers of this region would have been familiar with such fossils. When Michael Connolly and his team carefully excavated the passage tomb they discovered an interesting collection of grave goods interred with the cremated human remains. There was a stone pendant carved from the local limestone; a bead made from a deer antler; bones of dogs, cattle, sheep, pigs and even birds – mainly corncrakes and song thrushes. And with this eclectic mix was an equally high diversity of fossils – thirty in all.

From the Waulsortian mudmound on which they were building their passage tomb, these Neolithic palaeontologists collected six species of brachiopods.[15] The shells varied greatly in shape, from the grape-like terebratulid to two species of large, convex productids and three species of spiriferids – the brachiopods called stone swallows by the Chinese. It is not hard to see the attraction of these particular fossils, shaped as they are like an open fan, with fine radiating ribs. These ancient people also collected other, quite different fossils. They found many types of shelled cephalopods, ancient

Carboniferous fossil spiriferid brachiopod *Spirifer coplowensis* from the Neolithic passage tomb at Ballycarty, County Kerry, Ireland, showing pronounced radiating rib ornament reminiscent of pattern on stone engraving at Brú na Bóinne.

ancestors of the present-day squid and octopus. Some nautiloids have shells shaped like ice cream cones. Others are gently curved or coiled into a tight spiral. Gastropods were popular too. These ones spiral like a spring, unlike the helically spired gastropods favoured by the Gravettians for their body ornaments. Apart from the gastropods, most of the eighteen different fossil species are represented by single specimens.[16] This includes just one piece of crinoid stem, despite this type of fossil being very common in these limestones. The Neolithic fossil collectors, it would seem, were being very selective in what they placed in the tomb. But not when it came to the spiral-shelled gastropods. These make up one-third of all the fossils in the tomb. Overall the fossil grave goods are dominated by forms with a spiral, serpentinous shell – gastropods, goniatites, nautiloids – and, to a lesser extent, fan-shaped brachiopods.

Carboniferous fossil gastropod *Euomphalus pentangulatus* from the Neolithic passage tomb at Ballycarty, County Kerry, Ireland. One of many spiral-shaped fossils found inside the tomb.

All of these fossils, brought to the surface of their mudmounds by the combined efforts of tectonism and erosion more than 330 million years after they lived, had been plucked from the Earth's surface by the human inhabitants of this area about 5,000 years ago, only to be placed back in the mound from which they had escaped, to accompany the remains of dead humans into their afterlife. These marine invertebrates experienced a rather ironic cycle of death, rebirth as a fossil, then reburial by another's hand. Just no escape. The obvious question is why did these humans do this? Why place so many fossils with their dead? They appear to have been quite selective in their choice of fossil. Apart from one gastropod which seems to have been freshly broken from a piece of rock, the others had weathered quite naturally out of the limestone and so were ripe for plucking from the ground. Placing the fossils as grave goods in the tomb might suggest that they had great spiritual significance to these gravediggers. Then again, maybe they were viewed merely as attractive curios. How to resolve this dilemma?

Of all the Neolithic, Bronze and Iron Age burial sites in Europe that contain fossils, the little passage tomb at Ballycarty contains by far the greatest diversity of types. Certainly the Neolithic palaeontologists had plenty to choose from in these limestones. Fossils have been found in burial sites elsewhere in Ireland though. However, in each case they are known from just single specimens – a fossil coral of unknown age from a discrete grave in County Mayo,[17] and from an excavation in the Neolithic passage tomb at Newgrange, a fossil rugose coral, whose end had been cut off, exposing the delicate flower-like internal septal structure within.[18] Why so few fossils in these massive passage tombs, given their common occurrence in the Brú na Bóinne area? Perhaps it was because they came up with a better idea.

In 1699 Edward Lhwyd, then Keeper of the collections of the Ashmolean Museum in Oxford, was touring Ireland. Lhwyd's visit to Newgrange was particularly timely, as it was shortly after land-owner Charles Campbell decided to remove stones from a mound on his land overgrown with vegetation to reuse in a new home he was building. Lhwyd stopped Campbell from ransacking the structure any further once he realized its great significance. Writing to Tancred Robinson, Fellow of the College of Physicians and of the Royal Society, on 15 December 1699, Lhwyd observed:

We continued not about three Days at Dublin, when we steer'd our Course towards the Giants Causway [*sic*]. The most remarkable Curiosity we saw by the way, was a stately Mount at a Place called New Grange near Drogheda; having a number of huge Stones pitch'd on end around about it, and a single one on the Top. The Gentleman of the Village (one Charles Campbel [*sic*]) observing that under the green Turf this Mount was wholly composed of Stones, and having occasion for some, employed his Servants to carry off a considerable Parcel of them; till they came at last to a very broad flat Stone, rudely Carved, and placed edgewise at the Bottom of the Mount. This they discover'd to be the Door of a Cave, which had a long Entry leading to it. At the first entering we were forced to creep; but still as we went on, the Pillars on each side of us were higher and higher; and coming into the Cave, we found it about 20 Foot high. In this Cave, on each hand of us was a Cell or Apartment, and an other went on streight [*sic*] forward opposite to the Entry . . . The great Pillars round this Cave, supporting the Mount, were not all hewn or wrought . . . But . . . some . . . had such Barbarous Sculpture (viz, Spiral like a Snake, but without Distinction of

Head and Tail) as the fore-mentioned Stone at the Entry and the Cave . . . They found several Bones in the Cave, and part of a Stag (or else Elks) Head . . . the rude Carving at the Entry and in the Cave seems to denote it a Barbarous Monument . . . it should follow, that it was some Place of Sacrifice or Burial of the Ancient Irish.[19]

The spiral carvings that Lhwyd described are now, along with other megalithic carvings for the nearby passage tombs at Knowth and Dowth, considered to be the most significant of their type in Europe. Important among Lhwyd's description of the tomb was that, apart from the heavily sculpted entrance stone, other carvings with their 'barbarous sculpture' were located deep inside the tomb. The range of carvings in these tombs is impressive. All are abstract, geometric forms. Forty per cent of the carvings at Brú na Bóinne are in passage tombs at Knowth, and these are 30 per cent of the entire megalithic art in Europe. Not only are most of the carvings inside the tombs, but they are on the underside of the large stone slabs, so turned to face inwards. The range of art is extensive. While the spring-like spirals are iconic, there are also smaller, simpler circles. Some circles encompass radiating lines carved in a star-like pattern. In others the circles contain radiating petals. There are extensive zig-zag motifs and semicircular fan-like carvings, complete with either radiating lines, or with a series of concentric lines. What is apparent for each of these major types of carvings is that most correspond very closely in their features to the fossils that were buried in the passage tomb at Ballycarty and which occur commonly in rocks in and around Brú na Bóinne.

These carvings have been interpreted in many ways: as the passage of the Sun and stars; or of the seasons. Some have seen them as maps:

maps of the area; or of the afterworld; or of the stars. Others see them as visions that shamans had when under the influence of mind-altering substances, eaten or smoked. None of these explanations, though, are able to be substantiated. They are mere conjecture. Rock carvings (petroglyphs) by Neolithic and Palaeolithic people in other parts of the world, such as the extensive Aboriginal rock art in the Burrup Peninsula (Murujuga) in the Pilbara region of Western Australia, reflect the artists' experience of nature – of the world around them and of the world of which they are a part. Mostly their carvings, as with their paintings, are of the animals they hunted or saw on a day-to-day basis, or which formed an integral part of their belief systems and of themselves. But they are all artworks inspired by nature. Would the Neolithic people of Ireland have been any different? Rather than drawing their inspiration (as it were) from the living fauna and flora, could they have been inspired by the variety of shapes of fossils that they would have seen in the rocks with which they built their homes, made their tools and constructed their tombs?

Very little has been written concerning the influence of fossils on the evolution of human art. One of the few researchers to examine this question, and to argue for its importance, is John Feliks. Writing in 1998, Feliks argued strongly that what he called 'creative substitution' described how early people sometimes replaced either fossil or living shells, or other types of fossils, with an 'artificial' artistic substitute.[20] Feliks points out that there was an apparent increase in fossil-collecting activity during the Middle and Late Palaeolithic, just before the Aurignacian began carving animal figurines in earnest. These fossils, he argues, were the inspiration for these three-dimensional art objects. Feliks highlights how some 34,000-year-old Aurignacian ivory beads were carved to resemble the gastropod shells that occurred in the same layers at the site at La Souquette in

France, even down to details of the ornamentation. These gastropod 'sculptures' pre-date the famous human and mammal figurines by about 2,000 years. Feliks suggests that the presence in a number of Late Palaeolithic sites of both living and fossil gastropods indicates that the collectors were quite cognisant of a biological relationship between the two. Gastropods seem also to have inspired some larger scale sculptures carved out of rock.[21] In a Neolithic 'temple' in Malta fossil gastropods and limestone carved into the image of a gastropod, as well as clay models of the shells, have been found.[22]

The rocks in the vicinity of Brú na Bóinne are primarily Carboniferous limestones and shales and, like the rocks at Ballycarty, contain rich fossil faunas, dominated by brachiopods, corals, crinoids, gastropods, bivalves and nautiloids. Could it be that rather than place the fossils in the passage tombs, as at Ballycarty, the talented artists at Brú na Bóinne were inspired to replicate the patterns they saw in nature in the artworks they created and which they placed in the underworld? The iconic spiral motif at Brú na Bóinne closely resembles the spiralling form seen in many of the fossils found in these Carboniferous rocks: in gastropods, in nautiloids and in goniatites. John Feliks recognized the similarity between these spiral carvings and fossils. However, he suggested an inspiration from the large, spiralled foraminifer *Nummulites*. These fossils, though, are not present in rocks in this part of Ireland.

To some Neolithic people across the water in what is now the southern Cotswolds in southwest England, the spiral form was also significant. But rather than carve their own, in their megalithic construction they used what nature left lying around. About 5,500 years ago these people constructed a chambered tomb that we now call Stoney Littleton Long Barrow in which to house their dead. Thirty metres (98 ft) long and 3 metres (9.8 ft) high, the barrow was constructed of limestone quarried from nearby outcrops. With a central gallery aligned towards the midwinter sunrise, the opening is flanked by two large, flat stones. One is covered by a sea of shells – the bivalve *Gryphaea*, known as devil's toenails. The other sports just a single fossil – a spiralling, dinner-plate-sized ammonite. A sentinel, perhaps, to guard the dead during their journey into the long sleep.

One of the most stunning carved stones at Knowth has not only a gastropod-like spiral, but a fan-shaped carving that looks just like a spiriferid brachiopod. It has the same shape as the shell, with a straight hinge line and, from a centrally placed hole on this line (in the shell there is also a hole called the foramen), a series of fine radiating lines. It is a very good representation of one of these brachiopods.

Stone engraving from Neolithic Knowth passage tomb at Brú na Bóinne, Co. Meath, showing spirals, reminiscent of fossil gastropods, nautiloids and goniatites; fan-shaped engravings very similar in form to spiriferid brachiopods; and small circles looking like isolated crinoid ossicles. All of these fossils occur in local Carboniferous limestones and have been recovered from passage tombs. Nature inspiring art?

Aerial view of the Neolithic megalithic site at Knowth during excavation.

It has been suggested that this carving functioned as an elaborate sundial. Whether it did or not, I believe that its shape was directly inspired by the brachiopods that these artists were seeing every day. And on this carved block at Knowth, surrounding this 'brachiopod' and the spiral, are a number of smaller circles. The Carboniferous limestones contain the debris of destroyed crinoids. The long stems, made up of a series of circular ossicles, disintegrate at death and often make up much of the material in these limestones. On a broken weathered surface of the rock they appear in cross-section simply as circles. Interpreted this way, the Knowth slab stops being an array of random, abstract patterns and becomes a not unreasonable artistic representation of a slab of Carboniferous limestone and the fossils that it contains.

As I have pointed out, the only fossil found at Newgrange is a solitary rugose coral, broken transversely to reveal the radiating pattern of the septa. This pattern is represented in a number of carvings at Knowth of radiating petals enclosed in a circle. Some brachiopods, notably the productids, have poorly developed radiating ribs. They do, though, often have distinctive growth lines. Carvings at Knowth also occur with just this same pattern. Some even have large, often paired, circular structures within them, looking for all the world like paired muscle scars often prominent on this type of brachiopod.

Feliks also suggested that further petroglyphs were inspired by fossils. A 28,000-year-old 'abstract' fan shape from Kostienki is like a fossil brachiopod.[23] A rock carving at a 17,000-year-old site at Ussat-les-bains in France resembles a bivalve.[24] A spiral engraving on a reindeer horn of similar age is perhaps inspired by a gastropod. A heart-shaped engraving also of this age from Les Eyzies, France, looks like a type of brachiopod or the common heart urchin *Micraster*. Feliks thought radially symmetric ivory beads from a 28,000-year-old site in Sungir, Russia, were reminiscent of a crinoid ossicle.

If there is any merit in the interpretation of the Brú na Bóinne megalithic art and these other examples as having been inspired by the natural world of fossils, then it suggests great spiritual reverence for the fossils that shared their world. At Ballycarty they were important enough to be carefully collected and buried with the cremated remains of the ancestors. At Brú na Bóinne I think they inspired a community of artists to create their own versions of the fossils in rocks, and likewise placed them deep back into the earth in the passage tombs. Turned away from this world they faced into the afterlife, to where the spirits of their ancestors were inexorably travelling.

SIX

SAVING THE SOUL

For more than 400,000 years people have collected fossils. They
treasure them in their stone tools. They wear them around their
necks and wrists, and in their clothes. They inspire the creation
of sculptures from stone and bone, and carvings of images on
rock for their tombs. And they offer them to their gods. So
important in this life, fossils must also be taken into the next
– and buried with the dead.

Written in Stone

Palaeolithic hunter-gatherers of fossils seem to have been possessive
of their prized finds – once found, always kept, as far as we can judge.
With some fossils they spent time modifying or adapting them or
the rocks in which they were preserved. Then, about 7,000 years
ago, the archaeological record provides intriguing pointers to the
idea that people did something that, on the surface, seems a little
strange. They started giving their fossils away. What drove them
to do this? Had altruism finally evolved? One explanation is that
many societies began to regard fossils as high-value objects with
great symbolic importance. Far from fascinating baubles, fossils

became integral parts of these peoples' belief systems, thought to possess powers to enable the possessor to curry favour with the gods, or with the spirits of the rocks, the streams or the forests. To do this it was necessary to present them as votive offerings – gifts to ensure well-being in this life and in the next. They had, in effect, to be given away.

This behaviour coincided with the time when many societies passed from primarily leading a hunter-gatherer way of life to living in semi-permanent or permanent settlements and domesticating a variety of animals and plants – what we call the Neolithic. Buildings were constructed that would last longer than the average person's lifespan. Some were erected as temples for performing rituals, including receiving votive offerings, such as fossils. Fossils were given away in other ways. They were offered up to shrines that honoured the dead. They were also placed with the deceased in their graves.

While the archaeological record provides evidence of this altruistic behaviour via the context in which the fossils occur, the question remains: why were people doing it? We can engage in conjecture. We can arm wave. We can speculate. If only somebody thousands of years ago had taken the time to write down something to give future generations an inkling of some of their ideas about fossils. Well, guess what ...

In 1903 the Italian archaeologist Ernesto Schiaparelli began a series of excavations in archaeological sites in Egypt. Working at various classic locations, including Hermopolis Magna, Asyut, Aswan and Heliopolis, and the Valley of the Queens, Schiaparelli discovered the tombs of the sons of Ramesses III, Khaemwaset and Amenhirkhopshef, and the tomb of Queen Nefertari, one of the principal wives of Ramesses II. Among the spectacular objects he uncovered, there is one that seems insignificant, yet really piqued his interest – a fossil sea urchin. The fossil, the size of a small potato, is a cassiduloid sea urchin, called *Echinolampas africanus*. Across its high, domed surface sits a five-pointed star – the urchin's ambulacra – five paired lines of tiny holes. Surprisingly, this unprepossessing object sheds a direct light on the perceived spiritual dimension of fossils.

Is there any wonder that Schiaparelli was intrigued by this fossil? First, he would have seen the urchin's pentagonal mouth punching a hole in the centre of a flat, oval surface. From this radiated five smooth grooves in the pattern of a five-pointed star. But what likely intrigued Schiaparelli was the presence of twelve carefully engraved hieroglyphs, each about 1 centimetre high, running around the fossil's edge. Somebody, thousands of years ago, had written on the fossil. It is, by far, the oldest written comment about a fossil and is a key to our understanding of what people long ago thought about fossils.[1]

Fossil sea urchin *Echinolampas africanus*, collected by Ernesto Schiaparelli during excavations between 1903 and 1906 at Heliopolis in Egypt. The lower surface shown here is inscribed by hieroglyphs documenting who found the fossil and where he found it. This is thought to have been done as far back as during the Old Kingdom (4,180–4,710 years before present).

It was to be another forty years before the hieroglyphs were translated by Ernest Scamuzzi.[2] For those of us who have spent much of our lives curating museum specimens, the writing on the fossil gladdens our heart, for it spells out the curatorial maxim – always record where the specimen was found and by whom. Whoever inscribed the hieroglyphics was telling future generations, according to Scamuzzi's translation, that the fossil was 'Found south of the stone quarry of Sopdu by the "Father-of-God" T-nofre'.

Scamuzzi felt that the names Sopdu and 'T-nofre' indicated when the urchin had been found and inscribed. For 'Father-of-God' read 'priest'. He argued that the spelling of the name Sopdu (an early Egyptian god) is similar in style to that found in the Sinai mining area, particularly from the reign of Amenemhat III and Amenemhat IV in the late 12th Dynasty. This would place the fossil as having been found and written on about 3,750 years ago. More recently, Inke Schumacher, in her book on the god Sopdu,[3] reinterpreted the hieroglyphs. They are best translated as 'Found in the south of the quarry of Sopdu by the god's-father Tja-nefer'.[4]

So, the fossil was found not south of the quarry, but within it. The exact location of the quarry where Tja-nefer the priest found the fossil is not known. The fossil, though, clearly must have been of great importance to him, as he both recorded the details of his finding on the fossil and also took it with him back to the holy centre of Heliopolis. When Scamuzzi studied the hieroglyphs he believed that clues to the location of the quarry where the fossil was

Hieroglyphs on the fossil sea urchin that read: 'Found in the south of the quarry of Sopdu by the god's-father Tja-nefer'. Transcription by Inke Schumacher.

found come from its association with Sopdu, the god honoured together with King Sneferu of the 4th Dynasty and with the goddess Hathor in inscriptions in the Sinai mining area, and spelt in the same way as on the fossil. Here, Sopdu was called Smiter of Asiatics, and Lord of the East, as well as Master of the Easterners.

So, who was Sopdu, and what leads can he provide to unravel the significance of fossils to these people? Sopdu was one of a triad of gods, the son of Sah and his partner Sopdet (Sirius to the Greeks and Sothis in the Graeco-Roman period). These were old gods of Heliopolis, and paralleled Horus, Osiris and Isis, respectively. Sah was Orion, as we know it today; Sopdet was the star Sirius (the 'Dog star').[5] Offspring of the two stars, Sopdu was also seen as a star himself, and was sometimes known as the 'Morning Star'. As Sah spoke in the Pyramid texts: 'My sister is Sothis, my offspring is the Morning Star.'[6]

But if Tja-nefer found the fossil in the quarry of the 'Morning Star', Sopdu, what was so special about it that he kept it and took it back to Heliopolis? And just what was Tja-nefer doing there in the first place? Was it because he knew it was somewhere that such strange stones could be found? Or was it merely by chance? To Tja-nefer, could his find have been ordained by the stars? The fossil must have been of significance to him if he went to the trouble of engraving it with both his name and the place where it was collected.

What probably appealed most to Tja-nefer was that here in the hot, dry Sinai desert, he found, engraved on a rock, perfectly symmetrical five-pointed stars. Of all pre-Christian peoples, it was the early Egyptians who appear to have been most taken by the symbol of the five-pointed star. They called it *seba*. This pattern became synonymous with the stars in the sky. The sky was a celestial ocean that encircled the world. Here, in death, mortals could be reborn as circumpolar stars. The womb of the sky goddess Nut was the underworld, into which the Sun disappeared each night through her mouth. It was then reborn the following day. And her body was swathed with stars. The night sky was known as the Duat – the world of the afterlife. Its hieroglyph was a five-pointed star set within a circle – the very image of a fossil sea urchin. Were the Egyptians also interpreting the five-pointed star which they were seeing on the fossils as symbolic of the human form?

Nut can be seen stretching over the 3,200-year-old sarcophagus of the pharaoh Merneptah in the Egyptian Museum in Cairo. Clothed only in a constellation of five-pointed stars, she spreads herself over the deceased pharaoh so that he might become one of the imperishable stars and gain eternal life. In the same way, she arches across the entire ceiling of the elaborate tombs of the pharaohs Seti I (1294–1279 BC) and Ramesses VI (1143–1136 BC) and others in the Valley of the Kings. Flanking her outstretched body is a celestial aura of five-pointed stars. Even in Heliopolis the chief priest wore a cloak covered in symbolic stars, as if festooned with fossil sea urchins.[7]

The chambers in the pyramids of Saqqara show just how important five-pointed stars were to the early Egyptians. The ceilings of many burial chambers are crowded with vivid constellations of five-pointed stars. More than a thousand crowd together on the chamber ceiling within the Unas pyramid. On the ceiling of the burial chamber of the pharaoh Merenre, the stars are so closely packed together that they almost overlap. Our knowledge of the beliefs, rituals and spirituality of early Egyptians, including the significance of stars, derives from the Pyramid Texts that were carved on the internal walls of ten of the pyramids at Saqqara.[8] Many contain allegories concerning stars. The most important is the strongly held belief that the dead pharaoh would be reborn in the heavens as a star: 'the King is a star in the sky among the gods'. (Utterance 586A, PT 1583); 'my bones are iron and my limbs are the Imperishable Stars. I am a star which illuminates the sky.' (Utterance 570, PT 1455)

Critical in the rebirth ritual was the ritualistic act of mummification. Through this the dead pharaoh was reborn, his soul rising to join Sah, the father of Sopdu, in the constellation of Orion, as a star. There are many images of Sah-Orion in ancient Egyptian drawings. One of the oldest on the capstone of the pyramid of Amenemhat III shows Sah striding forth carrying a large, five-pointed star. Crucial to the significance of the fossil, and where it came from, was that in life pharaohs believed themselves to be the reincarnation of Sopdu. When the pharaoh, as Sopdu, died he was confident in the knowledge that he would be reborn in the afterworld of the Duat. Tja-nefer's interest in the fossil urchin found in the quarry of Sopdu now becomes much clearer: the balance of evidence suggests that the fossil he found represents Sopdu, the morning star, son of Sothis, who was the star Sirius, and Sah, the constellation Orion. The motif of a five-pointed 'star' became symbolic of the star in the sky. The fossil, with its five-pointed star, was playing a crucial role in the Egyptians' belief system.

Offerings to the Gods

Timna, north of the Gulf of Aqaba, to the east of the Sinai Peninsula, has been a centre for copper mining for at least 7,000 years. And it was not far from where Tja-nefer found his fossil. As well as evidence of extensive mining activity in this region, certain structures have been found during archaeological excavations that have been interpreted as sites of worship – temples and shrines. One of these is called the Shrine of Hathor, named after an Egyptian deity who was the goddess of mining. Built about 3,400 years ago, close to the time when Tja-nefer founds his fossil nearby, this 15-metre-square (49.2 ft) shrine was found to contain thousands of artefacts when it was excavated. Many are thought to have been gifts to Hathor. There were sculpted figurines of gods, people and animals; jewels, minerals, shells and beads. There were also fossils: two fragmentary bivalves, a pair of fossil sea urchins (specimens of both species, *Heterodiadema* and *Coenholectypus*, having been found in a number of archaeological sites in Jordan); and three internal moulds of helically spired gastropods.[9] These too were all votive offerings to the goddess Hathor.

Hathor was a versatile deity. Adopted by the Egyptians from the Mesopotamian goddess Ishtar, she was the partner of Sopdu-Horus, he of the inscribed fossil. In addition to being the goddess of mining, Hathor was one of the underworld deities and also a goddess of the night sky. 'Mistress of the Stars', she, like the goddess Nut, was thought to give birth to the Sun each morning. In this guise Hathor was a goddess of fertility. To those wanting children, votive objects were propitiated to her. Crucially, she also helped deceased souls be reborn. She would lend them her outer robe to grant them safe passage through the dangers they might face on their unknown journey into the afterlife. Placing star-crossed stones with the deceased became a widespread practise in many societies for thousands of years.

In her role at Timna as goddess of mining, she provided inspiration in the search for new deposits of minerals and metals. The Sinai region has, for thousands of years, been a source of the precious stone turquoise. So Hathor was also known as the 'Mistress of Turquoise'. Votive offerings were made at Hathor's shrine as a means of finding new mineral deposits. Central to this was the important ritual of oracular dreaming to foretell the future. Stones were erected as memorials of the dreams and as tokens of a sacred place.[10] The dreaming was important in the search for turquoise. To propitiate the Mistress of Turquoise at her shrine, offerings and sacrifices were lavished upon the goddess in this place of dreaming.[11] Among these were fossils – bivalves, sea urchins and gastropods. She requited these offerings by revealing the locations of new sources of turquoise to the priests in their dreams. The discovery of these fossils along with a host of other artefacts interpreted as votive offerings strongly suggests that they were used in much the same way.

There is even firmer evidence that fossils played an important role in the spiritual belief systems of many cultures. This is based on the observation that rather than place the fossils in pre-existing edifices constructed upon the surface of the Earth, which were used for other purposes, they were returned from where they came – back into the Earth in structures constructed specifically for that reason. Much planning and effort would have gone into making these structures, built for the sole purpose of placing a fossil – almost like the world's first museums to house specially collected natural objects. Yet these proto-museums contained just a single specimen.

Three such sites are known in western France. All are barrows (tumuli) – structures excavated in the earth to receive objects, which were then covered in a mound of the rock and soil displaced from the initial excavation. Usually barrows contain bodies, or their cremated remains. However, the Neolithic Tumulus de la Fourcherie at Juick in Charente Maritime contains no human remains. All that was found when it was excavated was a single fossil sea urchin. A younger, early Bronze Age barrow made about 4,000 years ago, at Coatmocum-en-Brennilis in Brittany, likewise contained just a single fossil sea urchin, protected by three flat stones.[12] This fossil must have been brought to the site from at least 200 kilometres (124 mi.) away.

Even more impressive is the Tumulus du Poiron in Deux-Sèvres.[13] This barrow, 20 metres (66 ft) in diameter and reaching 4 metres

(13 ft) to the sky, was constructed from layers of schist over which soil and rocks had been piled to make the mound. Within was a box: slightly smaller than an egg carton, it had been carefully made from six sheets of shale. And inside the box, like the last egg left abandoned in an almost-empty carton, a single fossil sea urchin. There seems little doubt that barrows like these, called remembrance barrows, highlight the profound spiritual attachment that people must have had for these fossils over many thousands of years.

Usually, though, fossils were not reburied in the earth alone. They were often accompanied by a corpse.

Dream Stones

On Sunday 16 January 1797, the *Bristol Mercury and Universal Advertiser* reported on strange events that had occurred eight days earlier:

> as two young men were pursuing a rabbit in Burrington Combe, they observed it take shelter in a small crevice of the rock. Desirous of obtaining the little animal, they with a pick-axe enlarged the aperture, and in a few minutes were surprised with the appearance of a subterraneous passage leading to a large and lofty cavern, the roof and side of which are most curiously fretted and embossed with whimsical concreted forms. On the left side of the cavern are a number of human skeletons, lying promiscuously, almost covered in stone.[14]

Whether the animal was caught and ended its days as a rabbit and mustard casserole is not recorded, but the rabbit hunters had discovered a burial site containing more than fifty skeletons of Mesolithic hunters and gatherers who had lived and died here about 10,500 years ago. During detailed excavations of the cave (which came to be called Aveline's Hole) in the first decade of the twentieth century, fossils, described as a 'nest of seven ammonites cases', were found associated with skeletal remains.[15] The particular significance of the find was that the fossils were discovered with skeletal remains – part of a human cranium and a jaw. They had been placed by, or maybe underneath, an individual's head. This has echoes of Pliny's account of the legend of placing an ammonite under a sleeping person's head to enable them to see into the future.

There can be little doubt that the ammonites were placed in the cave on purpose. The caves were formed in Carboniferous limestone (about 350 million years old). But the ammonites, today called *Arnioceras bodleyi*, are much younger, of Jurassic age, about 200 million years old. The closest localities in which these fossils naturally occur are about 15 kilometres (9 mi.) from Aveline's Hole.[16] Somebody, more than 10,000 years ago, collected them and brought them into the cave.

Of the seven ammonites, none are complete. Rather, they all resemble segments of an orange. All are of similar size, nearly the length of a little finger. With transverse ribs and a ridge running along the keel, the ammonites also appear to have been artificially modified. At least one has smoothly rounded ends that have been coated with an unknown substance.[17] Rather serendipitously, this shows up because the specimens were burned in a fire: in November 1940, during the Blitz, when the Luftwaffe bombed the University of Bristol Spelaeological Society (UBSS) Museum. Six of the seven ammonites survived. It can be assumed that these were not the Luftwaffe's intended target.

Given their purposeful placement in the cave, it seems likely that the ammonites had a magical or spiritual significance to the

A Jurassic ammonite
with nacreous shell
preserved.

Mesolithic hunters and gatherers. They had not been long in this
part of Europe. When the glaciers and tundra began to recede north
as the planet started to escape from the great global chill, colonizing
plants and animals were spreading out of central Europe. Among
these were the Mesolithic people who lived and hunted around
what we now call the Mendips, in Somerset. Recent DNA analysis
reveals that they were dark-haired, blue-eyed and dark-skinned. One
thing they brought with them was a fascination for fossils, and for
the magical powers that they perceived were bound up with these
little figured stones.

Pliny's suggestion that ammonites can somehow help the sleeper
foretell the future might seem far-fetched. Yet the discovery of
ammonites by the heads of these Mesolithic hunters hints at an
intriguing ancient lineage for this legend. There is further archaeological evidence to suggest this legend was widespread in time and
space. The Swedish archaeologist Carl Bernhard Salin (1861–1931)

recorded two Anglo-Saxon period graves in which 'a large ammonite [was] found beneath the head of a child at Ennery on the Moselle and another beneath the head of a woman at Hailfingen in Württemberg.'[18] Perhaps it was thought that in death the woman and the child, resting eternally on an ammonite, could look forward into their future lives. If there was, indeed, a link between Pliny's account of ammonites as dream stones and these two burials, it would imply an adherence to a legend giving magic powers to ammonites that extended from the Mediterranean region through to northern Europe, for at least 10,000 years from the Mesolithic through to Anglo-Saxon times, just a thousand years ago or so.

Placing ammonites in graves during Anglo-Saxon times was not, it would seem, an unusual pastime. When a seventh-century grave in Wrotham, Kent, was excavated, the goods therein included an ammonite, along with iron spearheads and a gold pendant. Gold jewellery in a grave suggests that the person who accompanied it was of reasonably high social status. Patterns begin to emerge from this and other ammonite-bearing graves. The occupants, where the sex is known, were invariably women, and their grave goods point to them being part of the social elite. The Pagan Lady of Peel was one of these. A tenth-century Norse grave on the Isle of Man showed that she left the world wearing a necklace that consisted of more than seventy glass, amber and jet beads, of Scandinavian, eastern or Mediterranean and English origins. Around her waist was a woven belt, ornamented with a pair of amber beads and an ammonite fossil.[19] She was laid to rest not on an ammonite but on a down-filled pillow, as she headed into the deep sleep. Of the more than twenty other Norse burials on the Isle of Man, hers is the only one of a high status female.

Fifteen hundred years earlier, in the southern German early Iron Age site at Heuneburg, another woman of very high social standing was buried on the banks of the River Danube. With her was an astounding assortment of grave goods. The early Iron Age (Hallstatt) settlement of Heuneburg was one of the largest in central Europe, covering a good kilometre square. Within the settlement area one of a number of burial mounds was excavated in 2005. Known as the Bettelbühl necropolis, excavation followed the discovery of a gold-plated bronze fibula (a brooch that fastens a garment). Frequently flooded by a stream that flows into the River Danube, the excavation revealed a richly furnished grave of a child, possibly a girl aged between two and four years. But this was not the sole burial. It was secondary to a much larger one. A trial excavation by archaeologist Dirk Krausse and colleagues exposed burial chamber timbers that had survived due to frequent emersion in water. A decision was taken that the entire burial chamber should be dug out. So, a block measuring $6 \times 7 \times 1$ metres (around $20 \times 23 \times 3$ ft) and weighing some 80 tonnes was removed and transported to the Archaeological State Office in Baden-Württemberg for detailed examination and excavation.[20]

The burial chamber had a wooden floor measuring 4.6×3.8 metres (15×12.5 ft), made from nine oak and silver fir planks. Dendrochronological (or tree-ring dating) analysis of the timbers revealed that they were felled in 583 BC. Given that the wood appears to have been used in its 'green' state, the burial can be pinpointed with an amazing degree of accuracy to the year in which the trees were felled. Within this wooden tomb the remains of two bodies were found, both female. One had few grave goods. The other, however, about thirty to forty years old at her time of death, was adorned with a wealth of gold, amber, and other items. Gold and amber fibulae rested near her shoulders, clasps, no doubt, for the fine cloak she would have been buried in. Gold filigree spheres, 26 tubular gold beads and many made of amber, formed an elaborate necklace. A large amber pendant lay near her hip, and a leather and bronze belt wound around her waist. On her forearms were seven bracelets made of jet. Solid bronze rings clasped her ankles. She was, undoubtedly, a woman from the upper echelons of Iron Age society.

More unusual among her grave goods were a pair of wild boar tusks, their bases encased in bronze. From strips of metal attached between the curving tusks hung bronze bells. This, Krausse and his colleagues concluded, was part of an elaborate horse tack. Objects interpreted as amulets also accompanied the woman – fragments of rock crystal, a heart-shaped piece of the yellow-brown iron mineral goethite, a red hematite ball and other polished stones. Among all these precious items there were also fossils – an ammonite and a fossil sea urchin.[21] The urchin had been greatly modified. Clearly, these were important items to the Bettelbühl woman during her life. Yet how did she suppose they could help her in death? The key may lie not with the ammonite, but with the sea urchin. This little

Oblique view of the fossil sea urchin found with burial of a high-status early Iron Age woman at Heuneburg, Germany, along with an ammonite. The sea urchin has been extensively altered. The groove on the left of the photo is a natural feature of the fossil, but has been artificially enhanced. The grooves in the foreground and on the right have both been artificially made. The fossil, a type of heart urchin, may have been so altered in order to fit onto a staff or the pommel of a sword.

fossil, carrier of the five-pointed star, has been found in burials from the Mesolithic to medieval times throughout much of Europe, accompanying many in their journey into the afterlife.

Soul Stones

It is a time of fragile emotions. A time of grief. The grave is filled with the soil and rock that has been dug from the hole and now returns to enshroud the body. If it contained a fossil in the first place, then it would be returned from whence it came. It's so easily done. An unknowing act. There's always that chance.

But sometimes, just sometimes, it was intended – a fossil placed carefully, lovingly, with the deceased. How can we know, though, of the intention of this action carried out thousands of years ago? Well, it is all a matter of context. If a grave contains hundreds of fossils, it is unlikely they are there by chance. And if the skeletal remains are clutching a fossil to their bosom, they clearly wanted to take it with them into eternity.

Though only a few bones of her right hand survived the ravages of time, they were tightly clasping a stone. She rested in a grave, one of 65 discovered during housing construction at Westgarth Gardens in Bury St Edmunds, Suffolk, in the early 1970s. Her grave goods were meagre. Just a blackened pot and the stone. Around her throat, a necklace of 22 glass beads; a pair of brooches on her shoulders and some blue beads around her waist. The stone nestled snugly in the palm of her hand was a flint sea urchin.[22] Part of it had broken, no doubt long before it came into her possession. Not the most attractive of fossil sea urchins, but what it plainly carried on its surface, and probably appealed to her, were five sets of incised rows of pinholes. They delineated a five-pointed star – the human form splayed across the stone. There are echoes of a similar funereal behaviour in a number of thirteenth-century graves in Donegal in Ireland, where many of the bodies have been found with stones clasped in their hands.[23]

Fossil sea urchins are by far and away the most common of all palaeontological grave goods. In a survey of the archaeological literature published in 2001, François Demnard and Didier Néraudeau recorded nearly 150 examples.[24] And in many, like the grave of the Westgarth Gardens woman, the fossils seem to have been placed quite deliberately in the graves. Often they were placed by specific parts of the body. A sixth-century AD woman buried at Stössen, Germany, for instance, had a fossil sea urchin carefully placed between her knees;[25] and a third-century AD grave at Frilford, Berkshire, contained a woman with urchins placed carefully by the joints of her skeleton.[26] The practice of positioning these fossils by a particular part of the body has a long heritage, extending back more than 7,000 years to the Mesolithic of northern Europe. In one of the earliest known cemeteries at Skateholm, Sweden, excavated over many years by Lars Larsson and his colleagues from Lund University, two graves were found to contain fossil sea urchins with the human remains. Dated at about 7,220 years before present, and being part of the so-called Ertebølle culture, these women had had fossils placed in their graves next to a particular part of the body. This points to what the fossils must have meant to members of the society at that time. In both graves the fossils were situated at the base of the pelvis, between the thighs, as though they had just been born. There are echoes here of the meaning of these fossils to the Egyptians thousands of years later – the ritualistic rebirth of the individual after death. These fossils, and the ones at Skateholm, were, to all intents and purposes, soul stones.

Not all soul stones were fossils, though. In many European Iron Age burials, egg-shaped pebbles, frequently white in colour, have been found with interred bodies. Usually the pebbles are made of milky quartz or quartzite. Like the fossil sea urchins, these rocky soul stones would be placed at specific sites on or by the body – the head, the waist or groin, and the feet. And like the fossils, they were usually interred with women or children.[27] A number have been found in burials around the Heuneburg hillfort in southern Germany. It has been proposed that these egg-shaped stones may also be linked symbolically with either fertility or rebirth.[28]

There are, then, many parallels with the fossil sea urchins. Those fossils found in chalk country are often white (though not always – some are preserved in flint and are grey or brown). They are also sometimes egg-shaped. The fossil sea urchins may well have been another form of soul stone, placed with the body in an attempt to help smooth its journey into the afterlife. The custom of placing fossil soul stones in graves appears to have transcended social status, if the accompanying grave goods are any indication.

A high-status Anglo-Saxon woman buried at Edix Hill near Cambridge, who probably died of leprosy, was accompanied by an extensive suite of grave goods – silver rings, knives, a sword, a wooden box, a comb made from an antler. Some items appear to have been in a bag that she held in her lap, including a fossil sea urchin. Unusually, and a sure indication of her position as a member of the social elite, was the fact that she was buried lying on her bed.[29]

Her situation starkly contrasts with two much older Neolithic burials at Whitehawk causewayed enclosure in Brighton. Archaeologist Cecil Curwen, who excavated the site in 1933, commented on what he thought was the appalling way in which the bodies had been buried. One grave held the remains of a young woman. All that

Neolithic skeleton of a woman and child excavated by Cecil Curwen in 1933 from the Whitehawk causewayed enclosure near the Brighton racecourse. Buried with them were two fossil sea urchins (*Echinocorys*) and two pieces of chalk with holes in them, and part of an ox bone.

was buried with her was a fossil sea urchin. According to Curwen, 'It looked as if she had been flung into the ditch with the other refuse, for she was lying there half on her face with one arm thrown out behind her and her knees doubled up, with no sort of prepared grave.'[30] And the fossil had just been thrown in with her.

The other human remains found by Curwen were of another young woman. But this one was accompanied by a small child. Their grave goods were a pair of fossil sea urchins (the holasteroid urchin *Echinocorys*), presumably one for each person, two pieces of chalk with holes through them and an ox bone.[31] These were hastily arranged burials of low-status members of the community. But even so, somebody had thought that the least they could do was to

A recent reconstruction of the Whitehawk woman who had been buried with a child and two fossil sea urchins.

provide each of the bodies with a fossil. Insurance, perhaps, to ease their transition into the next life. But if you really want that sort of insurance, why stop at just the one fossil?

March 1887: Worthington George Smith has been summoned to inspect some bones. Smith had cut his archaeological teeth on early Palaeolithic gravel deposits in London, discovering most of the significant sites himself. This cool spring day he was closer to home – the chalk hills of the Chilterns, above Dunstable, where he lived. A friend of Smith's, the farmer Frederick Fossey, had ordered two of his workers to lower a mound in one of his fields, the remnant of an early Bronze Age barrow that had been largely levelled in the

1850s. This was in order to make the land easier to plant crops. As soon as the workers began digging up the chalky soil, bones appeared. Fossey told the men to stop, and he sent for Smith. For two days Smith painstakingly extracted the many shattered bones. The skeleton, he concluded, was that of a young woman.[32] Smith felt that he needed to give her a name. Maud came to mind. Though he never explained why, it is tempting to speculate that Smith might have been thinking of one of Tennyson's more famous poems: 'Dead, long dead,/ Long dead!/ And my heart is a handful of dust.'

As Smith carefully picked over the bones he realized that Maud was not alone in her grave. Like the woman at Whitehawk, she had been buried with a young child. What really surprised him, though, were other objects that tumbled out of the 4,000-year-old grave. As the collection of bones began to accumulate he started finding fossils. Again, fossil sea urchins. In this case, however, there was not just one for each body. There were more. Far more. On initial digging, twelve were found – a mixture of the heart urchin *Micraster* and the helmet-shaped holasteroid *Echinocorys*. But this was not the end of it. As Smith and his helpers continued excavating the grave, fossil urchins were flipped out of the soil like a crop of potatoes. Astonishingly, a further hundred fossils were recovered. But the men still were not done. Raking over the rest of the area where the barrow had once stood, even more appeared. As Smith recalled: 'On repeated shovelling and raking over the earth from the entire tumulus, 200 or more were found and most of these, undoubtedly, originally belonged to the girl's grave, as none were found in the other graves.'[33] Smith's subsequent engraving of Maud and her child shows the pair encircled by 147 of the fossils, like a shroud protecting them in death, or an insurance for them to pass safely from this world into the next.

There seems to have been something of a fashion for being buried with huge numbers of fossils at this time. In 1949 an excavation was carried out by Elsie Clifford in Gloucestershire. Among the grave goods she uncovered while excavating the Ivy Lodge round barrow,[34] near Woodchester, was a 'nest' containing an astonishing 121 pebble-like fossil terebratulid brachiopods. These had been covered by a layer of red clay.[35] The palaeoanthropologist Kenneth Oakley believed they were in the barrow because they had some unknown symbolic significance. Their placement in the grave took place around the time Maud was being showered with fossil sea urchins, with other items excavated from the mound indicating that it had been constructed in the early Bronze Age, about 4,000 years ago. The pebble-like form of these fossils is very suggestive of the egg-shaped pebbles of quartz favoured by some people at the time as soul stones.

But the prize for the most fossils in any one burial must surely go to a good Bronze Age soul whose skull lies in a grave at Mont-Vaudois in Haute-Saône, France. In the grave of the dear departed were deposited not only a large, artificially worked bone and a cup made from a red deer antler, but a staggering pile of fossil sea urchins, said to have been some 2–3 metres^3 (70–105 ft^3).[36] It has been calculated that this represents something in the region of 20,000–30,000 fossils. Insurance indeed.

Do not think for one moment, though, that for a soul to be sent forth with a cache of fossils it had to be popped, holus bolus, into a hole in the ground. A cremated body deserved its quota of fossils just as much.

Twelve barrows stand high on the chalky ridge of Ashey Down on the Isle of Wight. Excavated by the aptly named Benjamin Barrow in the mid-nineteenth century, they contained evidence of a series of cremations. The first he dug into, one of the largest, yielded

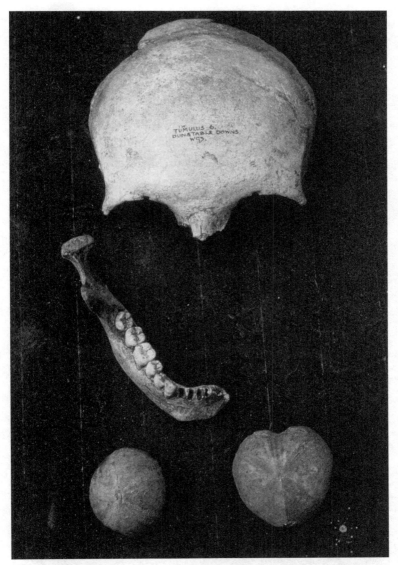

All that remains of the Bronze Age skeleton found near Dunstable, named 'Maud' by her discoverer, Worthington G. Smith: an incomplete cranium and mandible, and just two of the hundreds of fossil sea urchins originally buried with her.

burned bones and charcoal. The funeral pyre would have been a spectacular sight on the hill-top, visible from kilometres away, and from the sea, to the north, east and west, fire licking to the heavens which 'swallowed the smoke'.[37] The only other things Barrow found in the remains of the pyre that burned some 4,000 years earlier were some broken shards of pottery and iron pyrite – and a fossil sea urchin. Only five of the barrows contained cremated human remains. In four of these, single sea urchins were found. One had been placed in a small cremation urn, along with an animal's tusk and a piece of iron pyrite. The fossils' significance as soul stones was clear.

While fossil sea urchins and ammonites used as grave goods seem to have been reserved just for women and children (when we can tell their gender), there is one type which seems to have been placed in burials irrespective of gender: belemnites. These fossils have been frequently discovered in late Neolithic burials in Bulgaria. For

Bronze Age barrow at Ashey Down, Isle of Wight. This is one of twelve of which four each contained a single fossil sea urchin, along with cremated human remains.

instance, of 23 graves excavated at the necropolis of Polyanitsa, most contained belemnites.[38] Sometimes they had been placed near the deceased's head and invariably just one per grave. Some of the belemnites had been sharpened artificially into points, turning them apparently into arrows. This resonates with more recent Bulgarian folklore in which these fossils are called *gramotevichni streli* – literally 'thunder arrows'. There are echoes here of the northern European interpretation of belemnites as 'thunderstones'.

The thunder arrows were believed to have magical powers that gave good luck to the possessor. They were also thought to have special healing powers and may have been used in rituals or worn as amulets to bring success in hunting or in battle. And though it might not have worked the first time, if the fossil was buried with the slain warrior the magic might just work when they passed into the afterlife.

For thousands of years, then, fossils seem to have played a singularly important part in people's rituals in death. They helped ensure a smooth progression for the soul into the next life. In this life, also, some fossils were bestowed with great power – to protect the owner from a swathe of misfortunes and to bring success, especially in hunting. Without them, the hunt might fail and the people then starve. Hunting the fossil became as important as hunting the dinner.

SEVEN

PROTECTING THE BODY

Fossils, it was thought, were magical objects. As amulets, they could protect you from misfortune, from the evil eye and the destructive forces of nature, like lightning.[1] And from evil spirits in all their nefarious guises. Even from the Devil himself. They could also protect your house, your possessions and animals. But as well as throwing up this protective shield they could also be used as charms to help your well-being. On the simplest level they could bring you luck and good fortune, and make life just that little bit more bearable. At the other extreme they could project great power to ensure success in some of the more important facets of life – like hunting. This brought social prestige to those who possessed the power of the fossils. And with this came the ability to wield their own personal power – over other people.

The Magic of the Hunt

In the summer of 1921 Samuel Barrett, in his first year as Director of the Milwaukee Public Museum, was in Niitsitapi (Blackfoot) country, in the Great Plains of Montana. His aim, which he successfully achieved, was to collect ceremonial objects for the museum from the Native Americans who inhabited this part of the Great Plains prairies. One, in particular, intrigued him, to such an extent that he was inspired to write an article describing its importance and ritual significance to the Niitsitapi.[2] These were *iniskim* – buffalo calling stones – fossils bundled within a pouch of buffalo hide. We call them ammonites. The Late Cretaceous deposits of the northern Great Plains, particularly the Pierre Shale, contain rich deposits of these fossils, usually beautifully preserved with iridescent shells. They often occur, like three of the specimens in Barrett's acquisition, as the standard complete, coiled ammonites. But some *iniskim* were ammonites with straight shells. These are so-called heteromorph ammonites called baculitids. Some *iniskim* were complete shells, but many were just the lithified infillings of the ammonites' internal chambers.

The ammonite shell consists of two parts: an outer body chamber, in which the squid-like animal lived, and an internal chambered section which contained gases that could be transferred between chambers to aid the living ammonite in adjusting its buoyancy in the water. A frequent occurrence during the fossilization process was that these inner chambers became full either with sediment (which cemented together) or mineral calcite. As fossilization progressed, the walls of the chamber would dissolve, leaving a spiral of loosely interlocking, infilled chambers. Because of irregularities in the chamber walls, these chamber infills had the appearance of a

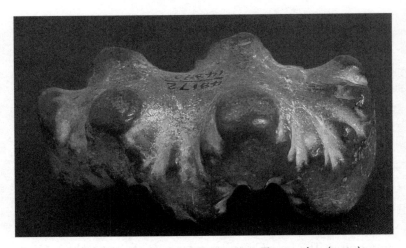

'Buffalo' stones or *iniskim*, from Rock County, Wisconsin. This 6-cm-long (2.4 in.) chamber infill of an ammonite bears an uncanny resemblance to a tiny buffalo and was used as a totem in the buffalo hunt by Niitsitapi (Blackfeet) Native Americans.

resting mammal, particularly one with which the Niitsitapi were very familiar: buffalo. Sometimes broken *iniskim* would be mended. A Niitsitapi specimen in the Milwaukee Public Museum collections consists of two halves of a coiled ammonite that have been glued together with resin, then bound with plant fibres and the whole covered in ochre.

To the Niitsitapi, fossil ammonites were most closely associated with rituals involving the capture of buffaloes. When wrapped with buffalo hair and other ritualistic objects, the *iniskim* were considered to have power to help the owner to corral the buffaloes they hunted. Properly sanctified, *iniskim* were objects of sacred power and played a fundamental role in Niitsitapi religious practices.[3] As well as collecting the *iniskim*, Barrett also collected a story of the origin of this sacred ceremony and its importance to the Niitsitapi in their buffalo hunts. The story that Barrett collected, involving the use of ammonites as hunting charms, shows many similarities to another story collected at the turn of the nineteenth century by Clark Wissler and David Duvall:

> At a place known as Elbow-on-the-Other-Side, in Canada, at a site by the river called Place-of-the-Falling-off-without-Excuse, a poor woman known as Weasel-Woman was picking berries. Hearing a noise, she followed the sound. It came, she realised, from a rock that was lying on a piece of buffalo hide and sage grass. It was talking to her, telling her that it was very powerful and that it would teach her the songs that were associated with its power, especially ones that could charm buffaloes. Returning to her camp with her stone, the iniskim,

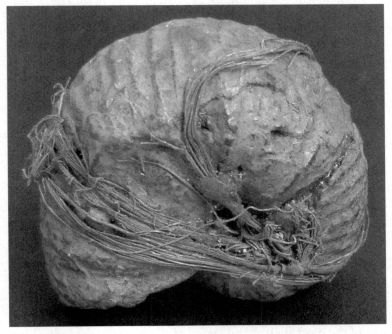

An entire scaphitid ammonite bound in plant fibre and used as a 'buffalo stone' (*iniskim*) by Niitsitapi (Blackfeet) Native Americans.

she told her husband, Chief-Speaking, about what she had found and how she could teach him and the other men the songs and the rituals of using the iniskim.

That night the song was repeatedly sung. 'There are plenty of buffalo which we are going to have, for I am the powerful buffalo medicine.' After singing more songs, she brought forth the ammonite from her dress, showing it to the people of the tribe for the first time. The rest of the day was spent preparing for the big buffalo drive. The buffalo were corralled towards the cliff as incense was burned. The hunters then chased more than one hundred of them over the cliff to their deaths.[4]

From then on the ammonite, as a buffalo stone or *iniskim*, resting on matted buffalo hair, was found in every painted lodge of the Niitsitapi people. Along with the sacred red and black paints, rattles and fire tongs, it formed part of the sacred buffalo bundle, used in buffalo-hunting rituals. It was not just anybody who had the privilege of possessing *iniskim*. This honour only went to the medicine men who played an important role in ensuring the tribe had plentiful supplies of meat. The medicine man who prepared the ritual would begin at about noon on the day before the hunt, and continue with the ceremony until news came that the buffalo had been driven over the cliff and the hunt was at an end. For his efforts, the medicine man received the buffalo tongues and some of the other best cuts of the meat.[5]

The Niitsitapi also treasured ammonites as sources of more personal power,[6] in particular medicinal, providing good health and long life, as well as good luck, even success in war.[7] *Iniskim* were one of the most ancient and sacred of all objects to the indigenous peoples of the Great Plains. And not just to the Niitsitapi. Other

Native American tribes also valued ammonites. These include the Tsuu T'ina, the Hidatsa and the Atsina (who called them thunderstones, as did the Assiniboine).[8] The Arapaho called ammonites 'centipedes'. They painted them red and kept them in a bag of incense to be brought out during their Sun Dance. The Crow used them as buffalo stones to help not only in the hunt, but in medicine, as they appear more regularly in personal bundles related to functions other than the hunt. Eleven Great Plains archaeological sites contain fossil ammonites, indicating that the use of *iniskim* as charms or amulets has a long heritage, at least as far back as the Old Woman's Phase (1,250–650 years before present).[9]

The use of fossils as hunting charms was not confined to North America. It reached also to Australia. In the late 1960s the Australian anthropologist Kim Akerman was given a number of items by Aboriginals in the western Kimberley region of northwestern Australia. These were all charms that had been used for different sorts of magic. As well as quartz crystals, there was a tooth from the extinct diprotodontid *Zygomaturus*, attached with resin to a hair string, some belemnites and a cache of fossilized kangaroo teeth.[10] The former two sets of fossils were used in projection magic while the latter were used, like *iniskim*, in the hunt.

The four fossilized teeth belonged to the extinct short-faced kangaroo *Procoptodon browneorum* and were kept in a small feather wallet. The teeth, one premolar and three molars, came from a Worara man at the Mowanjum Community near Derby, in the southwest Kimberley region, who used them for 'kangaroo increase' ceremonies and as magical objects to help with hunting prey. *Procoptodon* was one of the largest of all kangaroos. A significant part of the Australian Pleistocene megafauna, it reached up to 3 metres (10 ft) in height and weighed a quarter of a tonne. Like other large members of this megafauna, it is thought to have become extinct about 40,000 years ago, after the arrival of humans in Australia.

Due to their large size, it is thought they were unable to hop. More likely they had a gait similar to that of humans. And like us they had a pair of forward-facing eyes. Their feet were horse-like, most toes having been reduced, apart from one large, hoof-like digit. There are no known fossil deposits anywhere in the Kimberley region that contain the remains of *Procoptodon*. Relatively common in late Pleistocene fossil deposits, their remains have only been found in the most southerly part of Western Australia and South Australia. The closest fossil locality known to have yielded this species is some 2,500 kilometres (1,550 mi.) away to the south. While it is possible that unknown deposits containing the remains of this short-faced kangaroo could occur close to the Kimberley region, what is known about their ecological requirements and their known biogeographical distribution suggests this will prove unlikely. More probably the teeth were either carried or traded over an extraordinarily great distance. It also means that they were probably in use as charms for a very long time. Culturally significant natural history objects are known to have been traded by Australian Aboriginals across huge distances. Shells from the Pacific Ocean have been found in the Pilbara and northern Goldfields regions of Western Australia, again suggesting trade over many thousands of kilometres.[11]

The question has been raised as to whether the *Procoptodon* teeth and the *Zygomaturus* tooth charm had been collected by Aboriginals from animals when they were still alive. This would imply that they had been kept as culturally important items for tens of thousands of years, which seems unlikely. Moreover, both sets of teeth have red matrix adhering to them, indicating that they had been recovered from geological deposits. Undisputed evidence of associations between Aboriginals and the megafauna is rare.[12] There is some evidence from an upper incisor of the largest of the diprotodontids, the rhinoceros-sized *Diprotodon optatum*, from southeastern Australia, which has been engraved. The tooth has been dated at 19,800 ± 390 B.P.[13] The engravings on the tooth consist of 28 incised grooves. These appear to have been made while the tooth was still fresh, rather than on the tooth after it was fossilized.

Warding Off Evil

The tree is beautifully crafted from silver. It stands the height of a respectable wine glass. At its base a figure reclines languidly on a bed of silver rocks around which slides a snake. From an overhanging canopy of leaves hang six silver branches. From each droops, like a frozen dagger with a hilt of gold, a fossil shark tooth – *Isurus*, it is now called. Crowning the tree, and dwarfing the dangling fangs, is a huge tooth from the maw of the extinct giant great white shark, *Carcharocles megalodon*. And seated somewhat incongruously beneath it is Mary with baby Jesus resting in her lap. Now in the collections of the Staatliche Kunstsammlungen in Dresden, this astonishing work of art is called a *Natternzungenbaum* (adders' tongue tree) and was created in Nürnberg, Germany, at the beginning of the sixteenth century. It is one of the very few still in existence. Standing resplendent on a *credenza*, or special sideboard, it fulfilled a vital function in the courts of the royalty and nobility of Europe from the thirteenth to the sixteenth centuries. It was insurance against being poisoned.

Fossilized shark teeth were known at the time as *glossopetrae*, or tongue stones. They were first recorded as such by the Roman naturalist Pliny. He understood that they fell from the sky during a lunar eclipse:

Glossi-petra resembleth a man's tongue and groweth not upon the ground but in the eclipse of the Moon falleth from heaven and is thought by the magitians [*sic*] to be very necessary for pandors and those that court faire women: but we have no reason to believe it, considering what vain promises they have made otherwise of it; for they bear us in hand that it doth appease winds.[14]

During the Middle Ages in Europe, *glossopetrae* were thought to be petrified snakes' tongues that had the ability to cure snake bites with sympathetic magic. In German they were called either *Schlangenzungen* (serpents' tongues) or *Natternzungen* (adders' tongues). As well as the belief in their power to cure snake bites, the *glossopetrae* were considered to have other magical properties, in particular effective apotropaic powers to protect against the evil eye.[15] They could also, it was thought, ease cramp and the pain of childbirth.[16]

But it was the perceived wisdom that they were powerful magic against poison and this made them so important, especially during medieval and Renaissance times. In this period in Europe, poisoning

Natternzungen-Kredenz crafted from gold-plated silver and *glossopetrae* (fossil sharks' teeth). One of few remaining examples, it was crafted in the early 16th century. It is in the form of the tree of Jesse, the father of David (who is lying at the base of the tree with a snake flanking him). The branches of the tree are drooping flowers out of which emerge fossil shark teeth (the genus *Isurus*). Mary, holding Jesus (a descendant of Jesse), rests against the huge tooth of the extinct shark *Carcharocles megalodon*.

was the nobility's favoured, albeit somewhat unsavoury, means of assassination. Murder was seen as a potent political tool. It was carried out so effectively, and so often, that the deaths of popes, cardinals and kings were rarely attributed to natural causes. At this time, somewhat surprisingly, fossil sharks' teeth rose to importance as amulets to protect against being poisoned. Various poisons were used, including snake venom, aconite, belladonna, strychnine and, probably the assassins' poison of choice, arsenic. Soluble in hot water and tasteless in food, it was seen as the best poison to dispatch the unwary, troublesome victim.

The family who are said to have most used poison as a tool of murder, raising it almost to an art form, were the Borgias, the most notorious family in Renaissance Italy. Prominent in the political and ecclesiastical machinations of the fifteenth and sixteenth centuries, the Borgias counted two popes among their number, Calixtus III and Alexander VI, along with Alexander's two illegitimate children Cesare and Lucrezia. The Borgias were said to be past masters at disposing of nobles, cardinals and bishops, as though participating in some Machiavellian game of chess. They were fascinated with different types of poisons and were even said to have had the most exotic and powerful poisons laid down in their cellar, like fine vintage wines.[17]

The best poisons were those hardest to detect, reliable and preferably slow acting yet strong enough to kill. Arsenic was the Borgias' favourite. But not in its usual white form of arsenic oxide. They are said to have experimented with making a far more toxic form called *cantarella* after having discovered that mixing arsenic with organic material made for a much more efficient poison. And what better material to add to the arsenic than a rotting pig.

There are differing accounts of how exactly *cantarella* was made, but all involve using a dead, or dying, pig. In one, the pig is slaughtered then disembowelled and the entrails sprinkled with arsenic. This slowed but failed to stop the putrefaction. After some days the rotting flesh was squeezed and the resulting liquor, more potent than any other form of arsenic, flasked for future murderous uses. It has also been said that *cantarella* was made by hanging a pig up by its hind legs after it had been poisoned with arsenic. The drool that dripped from the unfortunate dying beast's mouth was collected and bottled. Either way, the Borgias produced a poison of great potency. Ironically, both Alexander VI and his son Cesare are said to have accidentally imbibed some *cantarella*. While Alexander died in agony, his son, it is said, survived by climbing into the body of a dead horse.

So, how to counteract such a poison if there is no convenient recently expired horse nearby? Well, use a fossil, of course. Strict precautions had to be taken to prevent such assassinations, especially at prominent feasts throughout medieval and Renaissance

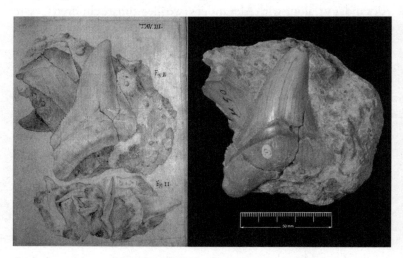

Original pencil drawing by Agostino Scilla for Plate 3 of his *La vana speculazione disingannata dal senso* (1670), showing *glossopetrae* or 'tongue stones' and the original specimen upon which Scilla based his drawing. He argued vehemently that these were the fossilized teeth of sharks.

European courts of royalty and the nobility. A food and drink taster was employed who, despite the inherent lack of job security, undertook their role at the beginning of a feast with great pomp and ceremony. The food and drink to be tested was placed on the ceremonial *credenza* on which had been placed the *Natternzungen*, the dangling fossil sharks' teeth glinting in the candlelight. The more elaborate the *Natternzungenbaum*, the more the guests would be impressed. The gold- or silver-mounted fossil shark's tooth would then be carefully placed into the goblets of wine in order to nullify the effects of any poison that might have been slipped into the drink. Whether or not it worked, history does not record.

The sharks' teeth had another trick up their sleeve, though. Without even dipping them into a glass it was thought that if they sweated or changed colour it indicated that the food and drink nearby had been poisoned. However, the Italian naturalist Ulisse Aldrovandi (1522–1605) pointed out that the fossils could also sweat in the presence of food that was hot, whether or not it was poisoned. More than just being antidotes to poison and snake bites, fossils were also sometimes used as more generalized protective amulets – as protection against those who might want to kill you by less subtle means than using arcane poisons.

Although he was a banker, Frank Beckwith's real passion was not the pecuniary interest of the good folk of Delta, Utah, where he lived, but exploring the local geology and lifestyles of the Pahvant, the Native Americans who inhabited the area. In the 1920s, at a Native American burial site just outside of town, Beckwith made a discovery that combined both of his interests. While excavating a human skeleton, he found, lodged within the rib cage, a solitary fossil trilobite.[18] The trilobite, a Middle Cambrian species called *Elrathia kingi*, occurs very commonly in the area, particularly in the House Range, 60 kilometres (37 mi.) to the west of where the body had been found. A small hole had been drilled through the trilobite's head, presumably so that a cord could be threaded through to be worn as a pendant. The cord had long since rotted away.

While the date of the burial is not known, Beckwith asked a friend, a member of the Pahvant tribe, what he knew about the fossil. 'Timpe khanitza pachavee' was the name he gave to it – 'little water bug like stone house in'. Beckwith then asked his friend's brother about the trilobite: 'shugi-pits napa t'schoy' ('lizard foot bead things'), he called it. The first name was one used for a trilobite preserved on a piece of rock, the other for an isolated fossil, like that Beckwith had found in the burial. When he asked what trilobites were used for, he was told:

The Cambrian trilobite *Elrathia kingi* from the Wheeler Amphitheater, House Range, Utah, in a contemporary silver setting.

'body defendancies, Beckwith; help diphtheria, sore throat, lots of sickness. Old timers wore 'em in necklace – no get shot while have 'em on – at least it work for a time.'[19]

Beckwith also recorded an account he was given of a group of Native Americans who, fearing reprisals after stealing horses from some European pioneer settlers, went to the House Range to collect trilobites 'to keep them from being hurt by the white man's bullets'.[20] Today trilobites are quarried in the House Range at Wheeler Amphitheater for sale as curios, and sometimes as pendants. There is certainly a resonance between the trilobite Beckwith found with the body and the pierced 17,000-year-old trilobite from the Grotte du Trilobite in France. Could it also have been worn as a pendant – not just as a personal ornament, but as an amulet – to ward off evil?

Lucky Charms

The rare fossil trilobites with holes punctured into them are one thing. But a fossil that comes with a premade hole, courtesy of a boring worm's activity a hundred million years ago, is quite another. It is almost crying out to be slipped onto a cord and slung around the neck. And that is what people have been doing with this type of fossil, possibly for hundreds of thousands of years. The worm that so kindly constructed the hole through the sponge on the Cretaceous sea-floor was a sipunculid, or 'peanut worm'. The dead sponges through which the worm bored are called *Porosphaera*. The fossilized remains of this sponge look for all the world like a Malteser – spherical, brown and the diameter of, well, a Malteser, those chocolate-coated, crunchy confections. *Porosphaera* fossils with attendant holes have turned up frequently in archaeological deposits throughout much of northern Europe.

Preserved usually as siliceous spheres, they can be found anywhere there are accumulations of flint, weathered out of chalk deposits. And what better place to find a small, pebble-shaped flint fossil than on a beach where there are millions upon millions of flint pebbles – like Brighton Beach. In 1932 Herbert Toms, when recording some of the Sussex folklore associated with fossils, reported on a woman in the mid-nineteenth century who had sold 'lucky necklaces' on Brighton Beach made from these *Porosphaera* fossils. It was commonplace at the time for women in Brighton to wear a solitary *Porosphaera* on a string or tape around the neck 'in order to ensure good health'.[21]

Three thousand years earlier, in the Bronze Age, a woman was buried in a stone-lined grave at Higham Marshes near Rochester in Kent. Around her neck was a necklace made of 79 *Porosphaera* beads.[22] These fossil beads are particularly common in Anglo-Saxon graves, either as complete necklaces, such as one found in Kent at Reculver, or as single beads.[23] One, from Howletts in Kent, was a centrepiece in a necklace accompanied by sixteen other beads made of glass and amber.[24] Whether they were being worn just for aesthetic reasons or as amulets, or both, is unclear.

Fossil *Porosphaera* have turned up in an archaeological context other than graves. In many of the Anglo-Saxon huts at West Stow Heath in Suffolk *Porosphaera* fossils have been found that indicate a prolonged period of occupation of the site.[25] This began between AD 400 and 500, extending through to AD 650. In two of the older huts, four fossils were found. In two of the younger ones, built over the older dwellings, six were found. By the sixth century, nine huts contained nineteen of the fossils, the most being nine in one hut. Of the youngest huts to hold fossils, two contained fifteen. None were found in the remaining younger huts. These were occupied during the

Specimens of the Cretaceous sponge *Porosphaera globularis* threaded on cord to make a necklace. The specimens were derived from a Bronze Age burial site at Higham in Kent, and acquired by Herbert Toms in 1928.

conversion of the local inhabitants to Christianity and it has been suggested that at the end of the pagan period there would have been no further use for such holed stones to bring luck.

There is tantalizing evidence that people were making use of these holed fossil sponges as necklaces hundreds of thousands of years ago. Worthington George Smith, who uncovered Maud and her coterie of fossil sea urchins in 1887, spent most of his efforts as an archaeologist prior to this discovery excavating early Palaeolithic gravels in London. After moving to Dunstable, he set about discovering Palaeolithic deposits in the area, some up to 400,000 years old.

In 1880, while working on a site at Bedford, he discovered his first cache of fossils in what he thought was an archaeological context – more than two hundred *Porosphaera* fossils.[26] These occurred with flint implements and worked flakes of the Palaeolithic type. Given that these globular fossils all had holes running through them, Smith was firmly of the opinion that they had been artificially perforated. Now that we know the holes were probably naturally worm-made, it brings into question whether or not the fossils had actually been collected by Palaeozoic people. Smith argued, not unreasonably, that they were all found together in river gravels. It is unlikely that they would accumulate in such a way naturally. Moreover, many of the sponges showed evidence of abrasion around the openings. Not only that, but some contained black material that Smith suspected was organic and derived from decayed cord upon which the fossils had been threaded. He even commissioned two chemists to analyse the material. And his suspicion was confirmed – organic material.

There has been much debate in the past decade about whether or not these fossils and other similar examples were actively collected and used by early Palaeolithic people as personal ornaments hundreds of thousands of years ago.[27] If, as many have argued, this is the case, it has enormous significance for our appreciation of the cognitive abilities of these pre-*Homo sapiens*.[28] It means they had a well-developed sense of self, a structured society and an aesthetic sense, just like the good Victorian ladies of Brighton.

In much of northern Europe, as well as fossil sponges the other fossils always thought to be lucky charms were fossil sea urchins. During his long summers spent cycling around southeast England in the 1920s, Herbert Toms recorded as much of the fossil folklore that still persisted as he could. In Sussex, Wiltshire and Dorset he found that some people still believed that the fossil sea urchins they came across in ploughed downland fields would bring them luck. The fossils, some shaped like a heart, others like miniature cakes or loaves of bread, would be carried home and usually placed either on a windowsill or by the front door. This was for the same reason that people put horseshoes and stones with holes in them near the door – not only as a charm against witchcraft and a protection against the Devil, but because they would bring luck to the inhabitants of the house.

One of the 'luck' myths associated with fossil sea urchins was that if they were kept in the house there would never be a shortage of bread, perhaps in allusion to their shape.[29] They would also ward off evil spirits. In Suffolk, 'fairy loaves', as fossil sea urchins were sometimes called, were thought to be lucky charms, so they were placed by the brick oven in bakeries to ensure the bread would rise.[30] Fairy loaves were also useful in dairies, as they were thought to prevent milk from going sour, an idea that must have persisted well into the twentieth century, given observations of their emplacement on windowsills in dairies in southern England. Not only will your milk stay fresh, the cream will be creamier and you are sure to have (as they say) better butter.

Seventy years ago, Herbert Toms photographed ten fossil sea urchins of the genus *Echinocorys* lined up on the windowsill of a cottage at Patching in West Sussex.[31] This was not a lone example. At least sixteen cottages in the area were observed to have had these fossils on their windowsills around the same time.[32] Fossils could also provide luck away from the home, by functioning as protective worn amulets. In the first millenium AD it was common practice to have a fossil sea urchin bound with metal clasps, perhaps worn hanging from a belt. The presence of these so-called fossil-bound pendants in graves attests to their importance both in life and in death.

Fossil sea urchins (*Echinocorys scutatus*) photographed by Herbert Toms in 1928 on the windowsill of a cottage in Patching, West Sussex. According to his notes: 'Mr Ruff found the crowns in position when he took possession of the cottage in 1923. They were placed on the sill by a former occupant ... about 1909. Regarded ... as curiosities; but the custom is evidently a survival from the time (about fifty years ago) when nearly every local cottage sill had its full complement of "crowns" which were then regarded as lucky.'

And what of the other fossil thunderstones, belemnites? In East Anglia, a strongly held folk belief was that fossil belemnites could protect the owner and bring them good luck. The arrow-like shape of belemnites lent them another term, 'prehistoric arrow', and they were associated with fairy darts or elf-arrows, which had once been thought to be the cause of diseases in both people and cattle (see Chapter Nine). Like the fossil sea urchins, they were more often considered to have magic power, to stave off lightning, or to be used as a charm to bring good luck.[33]

In addition to both fossil belemnites and sea urchins being associated with the thunderstone myth, the two types of fossils were also linked in their association with fairies. In southern Sweden fossil belemnites are called *vätteljus*. This name derives from *vättar*, a term in Swedish folklore used for creatures that are part elf or part fairy and partly souls of the dead. There are two kinds: those who are good-natured, and those who are just plain evil. The strong magic power of the *vätteljus*, or belemnites, was a protection against evil, especially at Christmas when the more nasty *vättar* were about. Again, they were seen as powerful amulets that could protect the house against malicious intent. There is a more contemporary view of the *vättar* as cute little creatures somehow related to Father Christmas. In this belief, belemnites are thought of as candlelights used by the *vättar* to illuminate their underground dwellings.[34]

Protecting the Home

As well as being antidotes to poison or snake bites and amulets to protect the individual, as well as their loaves of bread and milk, it was thought that fossils also had the power to protect the home against misfortune. In particular, there is a rich folklore tradition concerning the apotropaic powers of thunderstones, both fossil sea urchins and belemnites. Much of the source of this information comes from the early twentieth-century folklorist Christian Blinkenberg, who lived in and collected folklore of Denmark. Blinkenberg's appeal to the public through newspapers not only unearthed details about exactly what sort of natural and artificial objects were thought of as thunderstones, but brought forth valuable information about what people thought were the protective 'powers' of these objects. Writing to Blinkenberg, Andre Jensen, the headmaster of Flemming School, told him that:

> Thunderstones were fossilized sea-urchins. I never heard other stones called thunderstones. At the strike of lightning such a stone, in a glowing state, fell down and brought the fire with it. Only when a crashing thunderclap followed the lightning did we think that a stone had fallen, and it was precisely its fall and great speed which produced the crashing sound. In all other cases the stone remained in the thundercloud. Such a stone acted as a protection against lightning (the thunder would not strike where it was). The stones were therefore collected and carried home. They were put everywhere as safeguards, both in the house and the out-houses, in a window or on a shelf, on a beam or in a corner, but they were not made much of and in most cases were covered by dust and cobwebs. Notably large and fine specimens were laid on a chest as a decoration. One often carried a small stone about, as a protection, when out in a storm. I myself carried a couple of stones in my pockets and felt fairly safe in a thunderstorm; I did this even after I had learned at school what the stones really were.[35]

So whether a thunderstone that had fallen from the sky during thunderstorms, especially during lightning strikes, was a fossil urchin, a belemnite or even a stone axe, the perceived powers they possessed were the same. As a protective charm, the thunderstone was thought to have possessed special abilities, protecting the finder and their house against the devastating power of lightning. Sometimes they were hidden in a wall or laid under the floorboards. At other times they were placed high up in the dwelling, such as on top of a four-poster bed, or even on the roof – closer to the source of destruction.

Mr Clemens Sönnichsen of Ballum told Blinkenberg that:

> The thunderstones (fossilized sea urchins) were believed to avert lightning; they were put on top of the clock and in various places about the house – even in the loft under the roof. The house was shielded and we felt fairly safe and well protected with them near us while the storm lasted. When these stones were damp (when they 'sweated' as we said) it was always a sure sign that a storm was coming on, and as long as the stone 'sweated', we children were if possible kept at home.[36]

It is interesting that, like the fossil snakes' teeth, the thunderstones were thought to sweat in the presence of potential misfortune. A similar folklore was present in England in the early twentieth century.[37] Sometimes the fossils were placed on windowsills to give warning of when it was going to rain, because the fossils were thought to 'sweat' before rain came. Perhaps, because they were preserved as flint, they would cool quicker than the surrounding area, so any excess atmospheric moisture would condense on the flint fossil.[38]

Thunderstones were multi-purpose charms that were thought to possess many other powers. They could keep trolls and other unpleasant creatures such as witches from the house. Indeed, they had the power to keep all evil away from the home and bring good luck. A fossil sea urchin in the Pitt Rivers Museum in Oxford, purchased in Sussex in 1911, has a label with it that reads: 'Shepherd's Crown placed on window ledge outside to keep the Devil out'. If your child had yet to be christened, no worries. Just place a thunderstone or two in the house to prevent the child from being 'changed' – in other words, to stop it from being stolen and replaced by a fairy child imposter. Concerned about your horse having nightmares? No problem. Simply bed it down with some thunderstones. Want to stop cattle in the barn contracting a nasty disease? Place thunderstones on window ledges or over stable doors – anywhere will do the trick.

The archaeological record provides evidence that such beliefs in the power of fossil sea urchins to protect buildings have existed for thousands of years. Excavations were carried out in the 1960s at Studland in Dorset of cottages and huts that had been occupied for about four hundred years, from the mid-first century through to the fourth century AD. In six of the dwellings, fossil sea urchins were recovered.[39] In one of them the fossil had been placed beneath a stone that had been wedged against an inner post, indicating deliberate burial. At other stratigraphic levels fossils were found directly on top of ones that had been placed there at earlier times, suggesting a ritualistic placement of the fossils. Interestingly, all the fossil sea urchins were *Echinocorys*, the helmet-shaped urchin that closely resembles the shape of the huts within which they had been placed.

Incorporating fossils into a building was another way to ensure its protection against evil. One of the most fascinating examples is the church of St Peter's in the little village of Linkenholt in northwest Hampshire. Set high on chalk downland the church, like many in chalk country, is made from flint collected from the nearby fields. The current church was rebuilt in 1871, though its predecessor had stood for almost seven hundred years. When the Victorians rebuilt it they chose, presumably for sentimental reasons, to retain a small number of items from the original medieval church. Among these was a very simple, round-headed window, little wider than the span of my hand. Tucked away on the dark, damp north side of the building, it is so small that in the twilight zone of this side of the church very little light can penetrate through to the interior. So why did the church rebuilders keep it?

Maybe it wasn't the window itself. It may have been what surrounded it. Placed with great care around the window in a pattern like a top hat were 22 fossil sea urchins. Ten are set horizontally along the top of the window. Five extend vertically down each side, the last having another placed next to it. They are all the same species, the helmet-shaped *Echinocorys scutatus*. Although they have been rather worn by the ravages of the weather over the centuries, each has been set around the window to ensure that the prominent five-rayed star of the animals' ambulacra are showing.[40]

The retention of fossil sea urchins in the fabric of the church when it was rebuilt suggests that these fossils were of special significance to the local inhabitants for at least seven hundred years. One possible reason for such a 'pagan' symbol set around the window in medieval times may be because it was located on the north side of the church adjacent to a small door. When the church had originally been built, such doors, set into this northern wall, were known as 'Devil's Doors'.[41] In early Christian churches people who were hedging their bets and still clinging to some of the old pagan beliefs were allowed to enter the church through this door. The identification of the door with the Devil relates to the link that the early Christian Church

Medieval window inset into the north wall of St Peter's church, Linkenholt, Hampshire. It is surrounded by 22 flint fossil sea urchins, all of the genus *Echinocorys*, set there, perhaps, to keep the Devil out.

made between its views and the old pagan ideas, which they wished to suppress. The 'Devil's Door' also played an important role during baptisms. It was left open so that any evil spirit lurking within the baby could be lured outside. The door would then be quickly closed, preventing the spirit from returning to the church and re-entering the baby. The widespread belief in the apotropaic powers of fossil sea urchins as symbolic of the triumph of good over evil is reflected in the fossils being placed near such a door, so as to prevent the Devil from ever re-entering the church.

Even more intriguing, when the church was rebuilt in 1871 other fossil sea urchins were incorporated into its walls. Immediately to the left of the rebuilt old medieval doorway is a window much like the medieval one on the north side. When it was rebuilt, a veritable cache of fossil sea urchins, shepherds' crown, were set around the window, 25 in all. Apart from a single example of the heart urchin *Micraster*, all are the helmet urchin *Echinocorys*, prominently displaying their five-pointed stars on their convex dorsal surfaces.

Why the nineteenth-century rebuilders of the Linkenholt church continued this practice undertaken by their medieval forebears is not known. Maybe they just thought them attractive oddities. Or perhaps it was because these fossils, frequently found in the local fields during ploughing, had been such an integral part of the folk culture of the village for so long. This idea is supported by the presence of fossil sea urchins in the wall of another building in the village. Following the rebuilding of St Peter's, a small one-room school was built adjacent to the church. Its architecture is a mirror of the church to such an extent that it too has an arched window to the left of the door, around which 46 fossil sea urchins were placed. And even in the last few decades, fossil sea urchins found in the fields would be collected and placed by the front door of the finder's home.[42] When asked why the fossils were placed in this particular place, like a faded memory mirroring habits that have been taking place for probably thousands of years, the answer was very simple: Well, it's just something you do, isn't it?

EIGHT

CURING THE BODY

Fossils provided protection against evil, brought good fortune in life and solace in death. But at some stage in human evolutionary history people thought they would be good to eat. Not for their culinary qualities, but for medicinal reasons. They swallowed them whole or ground them up, mixing them with the likes of ashes of burnt scorpions and hares, wrens and parsley to cure all manner of ailments. Dragons' teeth might be able to sort out a bad case of liver disorder, but imbibing a good dose of ground fossil sea urchin spine spiked with goat dung and crocodile fat was thought to work wonders against snake venom. While the archaeological record may be largely silent on the medicinal merits of fossils, folklore overflows with efficacious remedies.

The Enigmatic Charm of Toadstones

The workmen could hardly believe their luck. It was 18 June 1912 and they were breaking up the floor of an old building, one of three, on Cheapside, just around the corner from St Paul's Cathedral in London. The buildings had outlived their usefulness and were long overdue for demolition. The floor barely gave a shudder as one of the pickaxes slammed straight through it, sending debris tumbling into a void. A long-forgotten cellar had found the light of day again. No doubt there would have been the usual banter about what they were going to find in the musty, damp space below. A box of treasure, perhaps. Widening the hole and clambering down, that is exactly what they found.

Sitting on the chalky floor of the cellar was a wooden box. It didn't take long for the workmen to break it open and out poured hundreds upon hundreds of exquisite, glittering pieces of jewellery. The Cheapside Hoard, as it became known, was being seen by human eyes for the first time in more than 250 years. Gems and jewels were stuffed into pockets, wrapped in handkerchiefs and piled into caps. But what to do with it all? They knew. Take it to Stony Jack, of course. He would buy the pieces. Otherwise known as George Fabian Lawrence, an antique trader and pawnbroker, he was the go-to man for any historical or archaeological objects found during building or excavation work in central London at the time.

Many years later Lawrence boasted that he had cultivated the men who worked on these sites: 'I taught them that every scrap of metal, pottery, glass, or leather that has been lying under London may have a story to tell the archaeologist, and is worth saving.'[1] Having been made inspector of excavations for the fledgling London Museum in the same year the hoard was found, Lawrence was in an ideal position to recover many of the gems and jewels and ensure their retention as a discrete public collection. Much now resides in the Museum of London and a small amount in the British Museum.

Over a number of weeks, parcels were brought to the shop and soon Lawrence had acquired nearly five hundred pieces of spectacular Elizabethan and Jacobean jewellery. Research in recent times suggests the collection had been squirrelled away, probably by a jeweller, between the early 1640s and 1666.[2] Evidence of fire damage and records of the original wooden building having been consumed in the Great Fire of London give an upper date for its storage. The area where the collection was found was the centre of jewellery trade and manufacture in the seventeenth century and given that the English Civil War was raging in the 1640s, it is likely it was hidden in the cellar some time between 1642 and 1649.

The collection contains an astounding range of pieces – agate cameos of Elizabeth 1 and an ancient Ptolemaic queen (possibly Cleopatra) made nearly 2,000 years previously, sapphires, rubies, diamond rings, exquisite salamander and floral brooches made of emeralds and amethysts, and perhaps the most stunning piece of all, a pocket watch crafted from a Colombian emerald. But there was

Gold and toadstone ring made in the 14th century in Italy.

also something else, more obscure perhaps, but greatly prized at the time – a cache of toadstones.

Many medieval writings spoke of a small, round, smooth stone with countless virtues. The size of a fingernail, it was sometimes black, but more often than not shades of brown: this was the toadstone. Writing in 1657 the Polish physician Johannes Jonstonus observed that:

> Toads produce a stone; with their own image somtimes [*sic*] … Amongst the other vertues it is observed that it hath very great force against malignant tumours, that are Venomous, Cholerick or Erisipelas, Apostems, and Bubos; and for Cattel that are betwitched. They are used to heat it in a bag, and to lay it hot, without any thing between to the naked body, and to rub the affected place with it. They say it prevails against Inchantments [*sic*] of Witches, especially for great bellied Women and Children bewitched. So soon as you apply it to one bewitched, it sweats many drops. In the Plague it is laid to the heart to strengthen it. It draws Poyson out of the

Part of the jaw of the Jurassic ray-finned fish *Gyrodus* showing the typical battery of circular crushing teeth, long interpreted as 'toadstones' or 'serpents' eyes'.

heart, and out of Carbuncles and Pestilent sores. It consumes, dissipates and softens all hardnesse, Tumours, and Varices.[3]

Most toadstones are, in fact, fossils of the crushing teeth of primitive, ray-finned fishes commonly found in Jurassic and Cretaceous rocks such as *Lepidotes*. The toadstone or serpents' eye is the smooth, round cusp that sits on the crown of the tooth. It was seen as the multi-purpose cure-all. It was said to help dispel poisons associated with malignant tumours, infections, bubonic plague, carbuncles, sores, malaria, fevers, labour pains, fits, scrofula, diarrhoea, bladder stones and epilepsy.[4] But toadstones had one particular virtue that made them indispensable to those who were in particular need of watching their backs: they were believed to provide protection against being poisoned. Often set into quite elaborate rings, the cool toadstone rested against the skin. One is said to have graced the finger of Elizabeth I.[5] Not to be outdone, Mary, Queen of Scots, kept one in a silver bottle.[6] In his poem 'De laudibus divinae sapientiae', Alexander Neckham (1157–1217), foster brother of Richard I, wrote that despite being 'an animal of horror', the toad served mankind in producing the toadstone that 'drives away poison'. As Shakespeare expounded in *As You Like It* (1599):

> Sweet are the uses of adversity;
> Which, like the toad, ugly and venomous,
> Wears yet a precious jewel in his head
> (II.I.12–14).

The earliest documented reference to the toadstone is in the magico-medical Greek work *Kyranides*, written in the fourth century. It was thought to have been compiled by Harpocration of Alexandria and Kyranos, king of Persia. As the work was based not on the teachings of Galen or Hippocrates but on folklore it was regarded as an unreliable text in the Middle Ages. However, a Latin translation was produced by Gerard of Cremona (*c.* 1114–1187) in which the origin and 'virtues' of the toadstone were discussed:

> The earth toad, called saccos, whose breath is poisonous, has a bone in the marrow of its head. If you take it when the moon is waning, put it in a linen cloth for forty days, and then cut it from the cloth and take the stone, you will have a powerful amulet. Hung at the girdle, it cures dropsy and the spleen as I myself have proved.[7]

Original pencil drawing by Agostino Scilla of Plate 2 of his *La vana speculazione disingannata dal senso* (1670), showing 'toadstones' or 'serpents' eyes'.

The original specimen of the jaw of an Atlantic wolf fish whose teeth, Scilla argued, were the same as the fossil 'serpents' eyes' upon which Scilla based Plate 2 of his *La vana speculazione disingannata dal senso* (1670). Specimen in Sedgwick Museum, University of Cambridge.

Toadstones came with a variety of other names, in addition to serpents' eyes. They were also called *Bufonius lapis*, bufonites, borax, nosa, crapondinus, crapaudina and chelonitis. Extricating them from a toad was a tricky business. In his book *The History of Four-footed Beasts*, published in 1658, Edward Topsell pointed out how this was done and some of the long-held views about toadstones:

> There be many late Writers, which do affirm that there is a precious stone in the head of a Toad . . . for there be many that wear these stones in Rings, being verily perswaded [*sic*], that they keep them from all manner of gripings and pains of the belly and the smal guts. But the Art . . . is in taking of it out, for they say it must be taken out of the head alive, before the Toad be dead, with a piece of cloth of the colour of red. This stone is that which in ancient time was called Batrachites, and they attribute unto it a virtue . . . for the breaking of the stone

in the Bladder, and against the Falling-sicknesse. And they further write, that it is a discoverer of present poyson, for in the presence of poyson it will change the colour.[8]

As well as being worn in rings for therapeutic purposes, toadstones were also taken by mouth in an attempt to cure a range of ailments. Albertus Magnus (1200–1280) suggested that 'if swallowed this is said to cleanse the bowels of filth and excrement'.[9] The supposed advantage of this was that the stone could be reused – a number of times. Leonardus records in 1502 how it 'rolls about the Bowels, and drives out every poisonous Quality that is lodg'd in the Intestines; and then passes thro' the Fundament and is preserved'.[10]

But it is the toadstone's use against poison that so impressed medieval and earlier writers. In his book *Batman uppon Bartholome, His Booke De Proprietatibus Rerum* (1582), Stephen Batman records that 'in presence of venimme, the stone warmeth and burneth his

Woodcut of how to collect a 'toadstone' from the head of a toad, as interpreted in Johannes de Cuba's *Ortus sanitatis* (1491).

finger that toucheth him'.[11] It worked a treat against snake bites and, as Batman writes, 'creeping worms'. Others noted that it helped cure the bites of spiders, wasps and rats.[12] With the realization in the seventeenth century that, far from being the great wonder drug, they were just another fossil fish tooth, toadstones faded from fashion. But there were, and are, other fossil teeth still used for a range of medicinal cures: dragons' teeth.

Dragons Revisited

In *Children of the Yellow Earth* (1934), Johan Andersson described how Chinese pharmacopoeia ascribed a wide range of curative powers to dragons' teeth (*lung ku*) and bones (*lung chi*).[13] The teeth and bones of a menagerie of fossil vertebrates have long been dug up in China. They have been used in folk medicine to cure a range of ailments, such as dysentery, gall-stones, fevers, convulsions in children at the breast, internal swellings, paralysis, 'women's diseases' and malaria. The oldest medicinal work, *The Herbal*, by the 'red emperor' Shen Nung (2838–2698 BC), father of Chinese medicine and pharmacology, said that dragons' teeth (that is, the teeth of hyenas, tapirs, elephants and rhinos) drive away spasms, epilepsy, madness and twelve types of convulsions in children. Others say they can appease 'unrest of the heart' and 'calm the soul', cure headaches, melancholy, fever, madness and attacks by demons, but especially liver diseases.

A more detailed example of how dragons' teeth were used was provided by Hsu Shu-wei in 1133. He recounts meeting a man called Tung who was suffering from 'restlessness', or what we would now categorize as a psychological disorder. Every time the man lay down his *hun*-soul would fly about, and he would wake and realize that his *hun*-soul had not returned to his body.[14] Hsu Shu-wei came to the conclusion that the disorder arose in the man's liver, as this was where the *hun*-soul resided. Treatment was pills prepared from ground mother-of-pearl of the black-lip pearl oyster *Pinctada margaritifera* mixed with powdered dragons' teeth. The man, Hsu Shu-wei reports, was cured within a month. This shows that one of the ways to understand 'folk' attitudes to fossils, such as those used in Tung's pills, is from early written records, like Hsu Shu-wei's, or more generally from their incorporation into myths that were passed down the generations orally.

Dragons' bones and teeth were included in the *Shen Nong Ben Cao Jing* (*Herbal Classic of Shennong* or *The Divine Farmer's Materia Medica*) of circa AD 200–250, which mainly describes the agricultural and medicinal value of plants. The fossils were especially valued for their treatment of spirit disorders:

> Dragon bone is sweet and balanced. It mainly treats heart and abdominal demonic influx, spiritual miasma, and old ghosts; it also treats cough and counterflow of qi, diarrhoea and dysentery with pus and blood, vaginal discharge, hardness and binding in the abdomen, and fright epilepsy in children. Dragon teeth mainly treats epilepsy, madness, manic running about, binding qi below the heart, inability to catch one's breath, and various kinds of spasms. It kills spiritual disrupters. Protracted taking may make the body light, enable one to communicate with the spirit light, and lengthen one's life span.[15]

In contemporary Chinese medicine, dragons' bone is classified as being sweet, astringent and mild. When taken internally it is said to neutralize nervousness, calm the mind and reduce sweating. Taken externally, rubbed on to the skin, it is believed to promote

tissue regeneration and reduce boils, as well as settle uprising yang –
a syndrome that causes hypertension, stroke, menopausal hot flushes
and various mental disorders. Dragons' teeth, on the other hand, are
classified as being astringent and cool. They are said to stop palpita-
tions, and are used to treat epilepsy and to calm the mind. Because
of this they are used in the treatment of manic-depressive psychosis,
hysteria, anxiety, irritability and insomnia. Dragon bone, however,
works in ways that dragons' teeth do not. It can 'anchor the liver yang
to treat liver yang rising, which manifests as dizziness, tinnitus, head-
ache, and dream-disturbed sleep. Second, it can stabilize the leakage
of the essence and body fluids'.[16]

In South America, some fossils are used for medicinal purposes.
Quarry workers who find fossil turtles in Cretaceous deposits in
Ceará, northeastern Brazil, grind up the shell and administer it
orally as a sedative to very energetic, vigorous children to calm
them down. This is presumably thought to act as a sympathetic
medicine because of the slow life habits of the fossil's terrestrial
counterparts.[17]

Some southern Indian traditional medicines even today still
make use of fossils in the preparation of curative powders. In particular, fossil crabs. Known as *Nandukkal*, they are part of Siddha
medicine, one of the oldest medicinal systems in the world, practised by people in the Tamil region of southern India and Sri Lanka.
Ground fossil crabs are used for a variety of disorders: urinary, mental,
musculo-skeletal, dermatological, gastro-intestinal, opthalmological,
and for venereal diseases, general fever and to treat toxins.[18] The fossils are combined with different ingredients to combat different
conditions. So to sort out urinary problems the fossils are ground
with radish juice and the juice of sirupeelai (mountain knotgrass,
Aerva lanata). The mixture is then dried and taken internally.

Belemnites and Lynx Stones

From the first brachiopod that he collected that cold winter's morning in 1690, John Woodward's collection of rocks, mineral and fossils grew over the years to almost 10,000 objects. Among them were many specimens of a type of rock (or was it a mineral, or maybe a fossil?) that had confused people for centuries. While belemnites were often still known under their folk name of 'thunderstones' or 'elf darts', the learned men of the sixteenth and seventeenth centuries who had long pondered their origins had no idea what they were. In the catalogue of his collection published posthumously in 1728 and 1729, Woodward recorded many specimens of belemnites that he collected from around southern England. He even collected one close to where he found his first fossil, in Sherborne. It was a typical belemnite, shaped like a bullet, but made of what Woodward called 'spar' (in fact, calcite). In a block of rock, along with fragments of shell, Woodward observed that: 'There is lodg'd in it a Piece of a Belemnites.'[19] He catalogued it as specimen *d.24.

Woodward catalogued all his specimens meticulously – giving them numbers (still showing on many of the specimens today) and recording in catalogues where they were found and what with. In 1696 he even published the first book that documents how natural history objects should be curated.[20] Many of his precepts are still assiduously followed today. With *d.24 he also noted some other comments. However, these observations were not about the belemnite itself, but concerned how people in the countryside used them. 'In this country the Farriers use the *Belemnites*, finely powdered, in watery Affections of the Eyes in Horses. The common Pharmacologists recommend it inwardly in Nephritic Cases.'[21]

The use of ground-up belemnites appears to have been rife in Scotland in the eighteenth and nineteenth century. On Skye:

The *Velumnites* [*sic*] grows ... in these Banks of Clay, some of 'em are twelve Inches long, and tapering towards one end, the Natives call them *Bat Stones*,[22] because they believe them to cure the Horses of the Worms which occasion that Distemper, by giving them Water to drink in which this Stone has been Steept for some Hours.[23]

Belemnites were also thought to be effective in curing bewitched cattle.[24] Robert Plot, first Keeper of the Ashmolean Museum, wrote that belemnites were used to cure bladder stones, 'exsiccation of Wounds' and 'Ocular Distempers in Horses, in all parts of England'.[25] These is evidence, too, of them being used to treat ailments in children. Two belemnites are displayed in the Pitt Rivers Museum in Oxford. One, from Oxfordshire, carries a label saying that powder scraped from it was given 'mixed with water, to children suffering from eruptive diseases'. The other, from Dorset, was 'preserved as a thunderbolt used as a charm'. Against what, the label does not relate.

In his 1728 attempt to classify belemnites, John Woodward, believing they were not, on balance, of organic origin, pronounced that they belonged with 'native fossils' – that is, rocks and minerals. He grouped them with the minerals selenite (calcium sulphate), 'spar' (calcite), 'muscovy-glass' (white mica), stalactites and stalagmites, among others. In doing so he noted that belemnites were '*Lapis Lyncis* which probably was the *Lyncurinus* of the Antients'.[26] That is, he thought they were what had long been known as lynx stones.

First described in the third century BC by Theophrastus, lynx stone was a yellow or brown crystalline material whose medicinal properties were widely discussed in classical literature in relation to its medicinal powers. The earliest recorded medicinal use of lynx stone is said to have been by the magician Damigeron.[27] A Roman centurion, Licinius Frontinus, having presented gifts to Evax, king of Arabia, on behalf of Emperor Tiberius in the first century AD, received, in return, a document called *De virtutibus lapidum* (The Virtue of Stones). Within it was 'everything there is in the world about all kinds of remedial stone'.[28] According to Damigeron: 'The stone Lyngurus or Lynguris [lynx stone] is the best stone for safety at home, and keeps pregnant women and children from being afraid. Worn, or ground up in wine and drunk it also keeps the King's Evil away.' The King's Evil is a condition also called scrofula, a form of tuberculosis, that kings were said to be able to cure by the laying on of the hands. The lynx stone was long considered to be congealed lynx's urine. But some classical writers, notably Pliny the Elder and Dioscorides (~AD 40–*c*. 90) were far more sceptical, the latter writing: 'But that [urine] of the Lynx, which is called Lyncurium, is thought as soone as it is pist out, to grow into a stone, wherefore it hath but a foolish report.'[29]

Hildegard von Bingen (1098–1179), abbess, writer and composer, writing on the medicinal uses of stone, suggested soaking lynx stone in wine, water or beer for fifteen days.[30] Taken after breakfast, the stone was thought to be an effective cure for stomach ache. Because it was thought to be mineralized urine, lynx stone was often consumed to help cure bladder problems, such as dysuria. Hildegard stressed that because the lynx stone was so powerful in these two cures, if it was put to any other use it would stop the patient's heart and shatter their skull. The idea that lynx stone was really petrified urine persisted into late medieval times. This is illustrated in a version of Johannes de Cuba's *Hortus sanitatis* (1521),

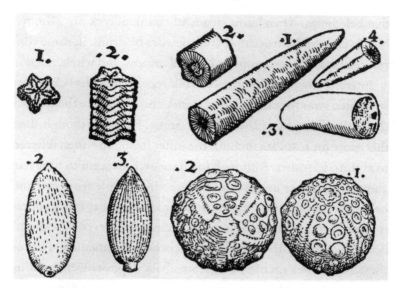

Woodcuts from Conrad Gesner's *De rerum fossilium, lapidum et gemmarum*, published in 1565. The 'star stones' (two top left) are parts of the column of an isocrinid crinoid. The four to their right are 'elf darts' or belemnites. Numbers 2 and 3 on the bottom row are *Lapis judaicus*, radioles of the cidaroid sea urchin *Balanocidaris*. The two fossils bottom right Gesner called *ovum anguinum* or 'snake's eggs'. These are cidaroid sea urchins.

beneath a woodcut of a lynx, where it is written: 'his pisse baketh in ye sonne and that becommeth a ryche stone'.

While it is possible that some lynx stones were amber, the fossilized tree resin, other early geological writings identified them with belemnites. The first book to elucidate belemnites was Conrad Gesner's (1516–1565) *De rerum fossilium* . . . , which was published the year he died of the plague. Gesner classified belemnites with geological material that resembled artificial objects, in this case darts.[31] Significantly he observed that they were used at the time as *Lapis lincis* to treat bladder stones. Anselmus de Boodt in 1644, on the other hand, saw them as petrified lynx urine, noting their often yellow colour and crystalline nature.[32] Moreover, he argued that belemnites when burnt frequently stank of lynx piss. Thomas Nicols observed in 1652 that 'if its powder be drunk in some convenient liquor, it will prohibit Lustfull dreams, and witchcrafts.'[33]

Interestingly, John Woodward, while recognizing that belemnites were often synonymous with lynx stones, also referred to them under their other folk name, 'The Thunder-Stone'. He never, though, used this name for fossil sea urchins, the other fossil type often referred to as thunderstones. Although fossil sea urchins seem to have had a myriad of other uses, such as protecting people from evil and helping the dead as they moved into the afterlife, they rarely appear to have been used in traditional medicines. However, Woodward does make one of the very few references to the medicinal use of these fossils. Sea urchin fossil from chalk deposits were used by seamen in England as they were considered to be 'one of the finest remedies for subduing acrid humours of the stomach':

Those who frequent the Sea, and are not apt to vomit at their first setting, fall frequently into Loosnesses, which are sometimes long, troublesome and dangerous. In these, they find *Chalk* so good a remedy that the experienced Sea-Men will not venture on board without. They chiefly make use of that which is contain'd in the Shells of Echini Marini; which indeed is usually very fine and pure. These are dug up commonly in the *Chalk-Pits* on each side of the River, of Purfleet, Greenhyth and Northfleet, where the Chalk-Cutters drive a great Trade with the Sea-Men, who frequently give good Prices for these Shells, which they call Chalk-Eggs.[34]

While sea urchin shells may have had limited medicinal virtues, their protective spines were quite another story.

The Jews' Stone and the Sea Urchin Spine

Two sea urchins, both alike in carrying a star-crossed pattern, but different in so many other ways: these somewhat prosaic 'irregular' heart and helmet urchins covered with a coat of tiny hair-like spines ploughed their way through the milky chalk Cretaceous seas, much as many still do today. Some, over time, were fossilized. Millions of years later a few were found by humans, kept for a while, revered then returned to the earth into graves like Maud's. The other, 'old-school' regular echinoids live a very different life. They have wandered the sea floor, the shallow reefs and rock pools for more than 200 million years, bristling with a defensive armour that would make a knight jealous. Some, such as cidaroid urchins, goad potential predators with a baroque array of protective spines, spikes, clubs and jousting sticks.[35] Yet these urchins do not fare as well in the fossilization stakes. Unlike the burrowing irregulars which live and die in their muddy tombs, all ready to be fossilized, the regulars roam the surface of shallow, wave-swept sea-floors and once dead are subject to destruction by scavengers and storms. Their shells disintegrate and their protective spines and spikes break free. But these are stout, hardy structures made of a dense meshwork of calcite that fossilize more readily than the isolated plate fragments of the shell. And often the only evidence in the fossil record of the past existence of these urchins is the spines.

One cidaroid urchin, *Balanocidaris glandifera*, which lived in Jurassic seas in what is now the Mediterranean region, sported 'spines' that have long intrigued humans. This is probably because they occur commonly as fossils but mainly because many of them are shaped rather like a swollen phallus. Fossils of these spines, found at two levels in the sediment of a rock shelter called Ksâr'Akil, 10 kilometres

Regular cidaroid sea urchin *Tylocidaris clavigera* showing swollen spines (radioles) similar to those referred to as *Lapis judaicus*.

(6 mi.) northeast of Beirut, were collected and placed there at least 40,000 years ago.[36] The rocks that the shelter is set in do not contain these fossils, so they must have been brought in from elsewhere. This was a site for habitation prior to the last glacial maximum, the remains of countless shellfish – good eating then, as now – having been found in the cave deposits. But why collect the fossil spines? There is evidence from the debris left by Gravettian mammoth-hunters that sea urchin spines may have been collected to sew into their clothing. Were the occupants of Ksâr'Akil similarly collecting them for aesthetic purposes, or were they also being consumed?

The swollen *Balanocidaris* spines have a long history of collection in the eastern Mediterranean region and beyond. Even today they are widely collected and sold in markets in Jordan, Iran, Iraq, Afghanistan, India and Pakistan.[37] This is because of their perceived medicinal powers. They have been used for this purpose for at least 2,500 years, extending back at least to the 26th dynasty in Egypt around 650 BC.[38] In European medieval medical treatises, the fossils are called *Lapis judaicus*, usually anglicized to 'jew stones', for the simple reason that they had long been found in Judea. In Persian they are called *Sang-e-Jahudan* and in Arabic *Hajarul Yahud*. Because of their perceived phallic shape, they were used primarily for treating bladder ailments, especially bladder stones or urinary calculi.

The first detailed reference to *Lapis judaicus* being used medicinally is in *De materia medica*, likely written by Pedanius Dioscorides, a first-century AD Greek surgeon and botanist in the army of the Roman emperor Nero.[39] His recipe was first translated into English by John Goodyer in 1655:

> But ye Judaicall stone grows in Judea, in fashion like a Glans, white, of very handsome form, having also lines answering one another as if made by turning. Being dissolved, it yields no relish in ye taste. But a Cicer-like bigness (thereof) being dissolved like a Collyrie on a whetstone with three Cyathi of warm water & drank, is of force to help Dysuries & to break ye stones in ye bladder.[40]

In other words, the fossil was ground into a powder, dissolved in water and then drunk in order to help cure difficulties in passing urine or in helping in the dissolution of bladder stones. In his extensive study of the many recipes in medieval and early modern medical works, Chris Duffin has shown that *Lapis judaicus* was often considered to work most effectively in combination with a mixture of other ingredients.[41] One typical recipe published by Gualtherus Bruele in his *Praxis medicinae* in 1632 exemplifies this:

> A Cataplasme of the flowers of Camomile, Mellilot, meale of Linseede, Fengreeke, Wheate and Lupines. *Lythontripon*, with Turpentine, washed, or with the decoction of the roots of *Gramen* and Fennell. *Elect. Justinum*, of the ashes of Scorpions, *Dialacca*. The decoction of the wood *Guajacum*. The ashes of a Scorpion, the jaw of a Pike, Eg-shelles when the Chickens are hatched. The great conserve of our description is a good preservative against the stone. Conserve of the roots of Parsley, Radish, water-Cresses, Turpentine burnt upon a hot Tile, the stones of Peaches, and Cherries. Hot Goats-blood, that it may not curdle in the belly, a little of the *Coagulum*, or seed of the Goate must be added. The powder of a hare with the skin dried in the fornace; the fruits of *Alkekengi* bruised, and strained, when they have been steeped in Wine. *Lapis Judaicus*. A Wagtaile, Sampier, seeds of Saxifrage, Burnet, *Ruscus*, Fennell, Parsly, Radish, *Milij solaris*, Broome ... The rinds of the most sharpe and biting Radish bruised, and macerated in white wine. The flowers of Broome, steeped in the oyle of Camomile, and so set in the Sunne. Oyle of Cherries and the simple oyle of Scorpions; let him use these medicines, when he takes that doe breake the stone.[42]

In his *General Practise of Physicke* (1617), Christopher Wirtzung described a recipe that not only offered relief against bladder stones, but was a prophylactic, perhaps due to the addition of the elytra of the beetle *Lytta vesicatoria*, otherwise known as Spanish fly, to the mix.[43] Other items, along with the *Lapis judaicus*, included 'ashes of burnt Scorpions', 'Bucks blood', 'Hares ashes, ashes of Wagtayles', along with a range of herbs including caraway, saxifrage, hollyhock seeds, pepper, mallows, maidenhair and roses.[44]

In England, well into the nineteenth century, *Lapis judaicus* continued to be used to cure bladder ailments.[45] So many of these fossils were imported into the country during the reigns of Elizabeth I and Charles II that an import tax of one shilling per pound weight was imposed on the fossils.[46] In the Near East during medieval times they were used to cure not only bladder and kidney stones, but bowel bleeding, wounds, sting and snake bites.[47] Their use as an antivenin was described by Moses Maimonides in 1211. To powdered *Lapis judaicus* he suggests adding a number of other ingredients, including crocodile fat, pigeon and duck excrement and goat dung, along with onions and honey. The mix was kneaded into a plaster and placed on wounds as a poultice to draw out poison.[48]

It was not until the late seventeenth century that the true nature of *Lapis judaicus* was revealed. In 1670 Agostino Scilla demonstrated that fossils in Malta similar to *Lapis judaicus* were sea urchin spines. However, it was specifically John Woodward who claimed that he was the first to identify *Lapis judaicus* as fossil sea urchin spines. In his published catalogue he describes a set of specimens of *Lapis judaicus* in his collection and describes how he interpreted their true nature in his inaugural lecture at Gresham College in London, after being elected professor of Physick:

A great Number of Spines of Echini [sea urchins] of different Sizes & Figures; brought from Syria under the name of *Lapis Judaicus*. These Bodyes are by Naturalists ever reputed meer Stones; but in a Lecture that I red publiquely in Gresham

College May 19, 1693, I demonstrated them to be Spines of Echini to the full Satisfaction of the Auditory.[49]

The beautifully handwritten catalogue, held in the archives of the Sedgwick Museum in Cambridge along with his others, and which was copied for the printed version in 1729, contains more information to this entry. A pencil line has been drawn through it, presumably by Woodward, to indicate to the typesetter that it was not to be included in the published book. That was because of allegations Woodward made suggesting that his idea had been plagiarized without due acknowledgement. The redacted section reads:

Among others were present – John Osborn Esq of Darby, Walter Moyle Esq of Cornwall, Dr Tancred Robinson, Dr H. Brooks & Dr Northcote. Some Months after came forth Mr Dales Pharmacologia: in which page 90, he saies, they seem to be petrified Spines of a Sea Echinus, *Echini marini Spinulae petrifactae esse videntur*. It is certain Dr T. Robinson held a constant Correspondence with him during the Time of his composing that Book, of which he makes some Acknowlegement at the End of his Praeface . . . But whether Mr Dale had the Intimation from him, or from some other Person present, or whether it it came to him finaly [*sic*] from the Rumour & Talk of those, who being curious in these Things attended these Lectures, the Design of which were to assert the true Origin of these & other analogous Bodyes, I cannot tell.

Robinson, in Woodward's eyes, was the villain; Dale, the unwitting stooge; Robinson and Woodward were forever at one another's throats.[50] Had he lived past the year 1728, Woodward might have found some comfort in knowing that the 1739 reprint of Dale's book acknowledged Woodward's interpretation of the true nature of *Lapis judaicus.*[51]

In a world that is today dominated by Western medicine, one could be forgiven for thinking that all these 'folk' or traditional remedies that use fossils to cure an assortment of ailments were quaint, misguided and just plain nonsense. But in 2013 and 2014, articles were published in the *Journal of Ethnopharmacology* and the *Pharmacognosy Journal* describing chemical analyses of *Lapis judaicus* and details of clinical trials of its use in Iran to cure kidney stones that suggest its efficacy.

In the first study, a number of specimens sold as *Sang-e-Jahudan* in Iranian markets were purchased to make a study of the possible curative nature of these fossils.[52] Interestingly, a range of fossils were obtained. While many were, indeed, *Balanocidaris glandulifera*, there were also a few fossil sea urchin tests and rhynchonellid brachiopods. The aim of the analysis was to establish what effect ground-up *Lapis judaicus* could have on inhibiting the growth of calcium oxalate, a major component of bladder and kidney stones. The study showed that finely ground powder of *Lapis judaicus* reduced the size of calcium oxalate stones by 35.1 ± 7.9 per cent after two days and by 58.2 ± 1.64 per cent after five days.

In the second study sixty patients suffering with kidney stones were selected.[53] Of these, thirty were given placebos, the remainder were given 2 grams of ground *Lapis judaicus* a day for ten weeks. In those who had received the ground fossil, the size of the kidney stones was reduced significantly and in nine completely dissolved. The likely reason for the effective use of the fossil powder is that echinoderm calcite is magnesium rich, and this played a significant role in the dissolution of the stones. Maybe Dioscorides, Goodyer,

Wirtzung and the many others who wrote about the efficacious use of *Lapis judaicus* or who consumed it were not so misguided.

The last word should, I think, go to the polymath Sir Thomas Browne (1605–1682). In his *Pseudodoxia epidemica* (1646), this metaphysical writer, physician, naturalist and wit succinctly put paid to many purported medicinal (one of the many words coined by Browne) and magical benefits of fossil and minerals:

> He must have more heads than *Rome* had hills, that makes out half of those vertues ascribed unto stones, and their not only Medical, but Magical proprieties, which are to be found in Authors of great Name.
>
> The *Lapis Lasuli* hath in it a purgative faculty we know ... that *Lapis Judaicus* [is] diuretical, *Coral* Antipileptical, we will not deny. That *Cornelians, Jaspis, Heliotropes*, and Blood-stones, may be of virtue to those intentions they are implied, experience and visible effects will make us grant. But that an *Amethyst* prevents inebriation; that an *Emerald* will break if worn in copulation. That a *Diamond* laid under the pillow, will betray the incontinency of a wife. That a *Saphire* is preservative against inchantments; that *Crysoprase* makes one out of love with Gold; as some have delivered, we are yet, I confess, to believe, and in that infidelity are likely to end our dayes.[54]

NINE

THE DARK SIDE

There is little doubt that to most people fossils look good. They are great to collect and keep. And on top of that, for thousands of years people believed that they could protect you from a myriad of misfortunes and bring their bearers plentiful good luck. Not to mention cure bodily ills. But for all the numerous benefits that possessing fossils seem to have had, sometimes, just sometimes, an ugly face was turned upon those who removed them from their comfortable geological settings. For fossils also had their dark side, often a very dark side – they were playthings of evil spirits, of the Devil. And of a variety of sprites – elves, faeries, pixies. These creatures of the dark side were thought to imbue fossils with powers to bring misfortune on others. Some were certainly less than benign. In fact, some could be downright dangerous. Human imagination was again running riot.

Projection Magic

Fossils could be weapons. When I lived in Sussex long ago, I heard an apocryphal story that fossil sea urchins had been used as sling-shots in the Battle of Lewes in 1264 between the rebel barons, led by Simon de Montfort, and King Henry III's army. Unfortunately, I could never find a source to corroborate this rumour. However, there is evidence that some fossils have been used to inflict injury in a slightly more subtle manner. Australian Aboriginals believed that certain fossils could be imbued with dark magic and attain the power to create havoc, cause injury and even death. Other fossils were believed to be able to cause direct physical harm by being shot at the unwary. Among the fossil charms from the Kimberley region of Western Australia that anthropologist Kim Akerman had been given in the 1960s were two types that he was told had been used for projection magic. To certain Australian Aboriginals projection magic is a form of sorcery whereby a power believed to be invested in an object, such as a fossil, or a pointed bone or crystal, is sent with the sole intention of causing as much damage and suffering as possi-ble to the intended victim, either to harm them in some way, or even to kill them.[1] Sometimes this magical power is believed to pervade the object. More often, this power can be loaded into the object by the use of spells. These may be parts of songs that relate to evil spirits. The most well-known of all projection magic is bone-pointing.

One of the charms given to Akerman was a tooth that had been mounted in gum and attached to 'a rather frayed 19 in. length of hair string', for it was to be worn as a pendant.[2] Given to Akerman by an Aboriginal man from Mount Hart, it had, according to him, been used for projection magic. It was known as *Tjagola*, though this term was also used for other objects used in such magic, for example, unusual stones, bones, shells or teeth.[3] The tooth gifted to Akerman was a fossil that had once sat in the mouth of a wombat-like diprotodontid called *Zygomaturus trilobus*. This was a buffalo-sized marsupial that became extinct about 40,000 years ago and which had been part of the Australian Pleistocene megafauna. The tooth clearly had been derived from a fossil deposit as it had red matrix adhering to it. What is particularly intriguing is that, like the *Protemnodon* teeth that had been used as hunting charms, it turned up in the southwest of the Kimberley region in Western Australia, far from its known fossil occurrence. The closest known natural source of this species is in the Murchison region, some 2,000 kilometres (1,240 mi.) to the south.

While other fossil deposits containing diprotodontids have been found closer to the Kimberley region, these all represent the larger,

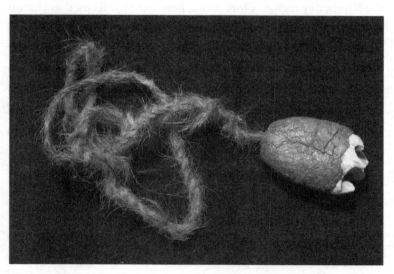

An Aboriginal charm used for projection magic made from the fossilized tooth of the extinct diprotodontid *Zygomaturus trilobus* mounted in gum and attached to 'a rather frayed 19 in. length of hair string' so as to be worn as a pendant; from Mount Hart, Kimberley region, Western Australia.

rhinoceros-sized *Diprotodon*. However, the fossil record indicates that *Zygomaturus* occupied the more humid regions of southwest Australia. *Diprotodon* remains occur in more arid and northern areas.[4] The implication must therefore be that this fossil tooth, purveyor of destructive magic, had travelled thousands of kilometres from where it had first been found. Clearly it was an object of great cultural significance to its owners.

The other fossils from the Kimberley region given to Akerman, and which he was told were also charms used in projection magic, were belemnites. Again, they appear to have been carried or traded from far away, for to date belemnites have never been found in this part of Australia. The nearest occurrence in Western Australia is far to the south, in a rock type called the Windalia Radiolarite in the Carnarvon Basin, nearly 2,000 kilometres (1,243 mi.) to the south of the Kimberley region. Once more, here were fossils used as charms that had been carried over vast distances and probably used for evil purposes for a very long period of time. What Akerman was never told was whether these charms just projected magic, or whether they were also physically projected. For in much of Europe even though belemnites were used for positive medicinal purposes, they also had a dark side – a belief that involved using them as darts or arrows to inflict pain or bring disease.

The Inconvenience of Being Elf-shot

For people living before the Enlightenment, during the Middle Ages in Europe, the causes of sickness, illness and bodily harm were largely a mystery. We know from some Anglo-Saxon charms used to try and help cure people that it was believed a likely cause were evil spirits. But how did they invade the body? Elves. A widespread belief in the

Middle Ages was that some illnesses and unexplained pains in humans, as well as in cattle and horses, were caused by the malevolent actions of elves or other supernatural creatures. The terms 'elves' and 'fairies' (or 'fayries') were largely interchangeable. These were not the cute Tinkerbells of more recent fiction, but generally malicious beings. A sudden or mysterious pain meant that you had been 'elf-shot'.

In his British Academy lecture of 1919, Charles Singer wrote:

> a large amount of disease was attributed . . . to the action of supernatural beings, elves, Æsir, smiths or witches whose shafts fired at the sufferer produced his torments. Anglo-Saxon and even Middle English literature is replete with the notion of disease caused by the arrows of mischievous supernatural beings. This theory of disease we shall, for brevity, speak of as the doctrine of the elf-shot. The Anglo-Saxon tribes placed these malicious elves everywhere, but especially in the wild uncultivated wastes where they loved to shoot at the passer-by.[5]

To cure the effect of having been attacked by a host of marauding elves, charms were intoned. The most famous is the (possibly) late tenth-century *Wið færstice* (Against a Sudden Stab).[6] In her masterly *Anglo-Saxon Amulets and Curing Stones*, Audrey Meaney provides a literal translation:

> Loud were they, lo loud, when they rode over the burial mound,
> Were fierce when they rode over the land.
> Shield yourself now, that you may be saved from this enemy.
> Out, little spear, if you be in here!
> [I] stood under the lime-wood, under the light shield,

There where the mighty women concentrated their might,
And, yelling, sent forth spears.
I will send another back against them,
A flying arrow in opposition to them.
Out, little spear, if it be in here!
A smith sat, struck out a little knife
. . .? An iron weapon wounded greatly
Out, little spear, if in here.
Six smiths sat; they made war spears.
Out, spear; not in, spear!
If in here be a piece of iron –
The work of witches – it shall melt.
If you were shot in the skin, or were shot in the flesh
Or were shot in the blood (or were shot in the bone)
Or were shot in a limb, never would your life be touched.
If it were the shot of gods, or if it were the shot of elves,
Or it were the shot of witches, I will help you.
Fly there, on the mountain top.
Be you healthy. May the Lord help you. Take then the knife;
    put it in liquid.[7]

In Scotland, where the concept of being elf-shot persisted into the nineteenth century, cattle that had been attacked by warble flies, which cause a hole in the animals' skin, seemed proof of physical elf attack. In his *Tour in Scotland* published in 1774, Thomas Pennant wrote that:

Elf-shots [that is,] the stone arrow heads of the old inhabitants of this island, are supposed to be weapons shot by Fairies at cattle, to which are attributed any disorders they have: in order to effect a cure, the cow is to be touched by an elf-shot, or made to drink the water in which one has been dipped.[8]

Their weapons were small darts – 'elf-darts', elf-shot', elf-arrows', 'elf-spurs', 'elf-bolts' or 'fairy-darts' – and one type of object interpreted as such was belemnites. The name 'belemnite' derives from the Greek *belemnon*, meaning 'dart'. Robert Plot pointed out in 1705 that in Oxfordshire they were called thunderbolts and were 'in the form of arrow heads and thought by the vulgar to be indeed the darts of Heaven'.[9] As Meaney points out, the terms 'elf-arrows' and 'thunderbolts' are compatible concepts. 'To be thunderstruck', as she says, 'was one way of being elf-shot'.[10]

Sir Thomas Browne, writing in his *Pseudodoxia epidemica* of 1658, also pointed out the evil connotations of both belemnites and fossil sea urchins:

Terrible apprehensions and answerable unto their names, are raised of *Fayrie* stones, and *Elves* spurs found commonly with us, in Stone, Chalk, and Marl-pits, which notwithstanding are no more than *Echinometrites* and *Belemnites*, the Sea-Hedg-hog, and the Dart-stone.[11]

Browne was not fooled and figured out the 'true' nature of fossils, perhaps the first person in England to do so in print. But as he pointed out, when it comes to fossils being associated with 'terrible apprehensions' you also had to keep an eye open for fayrie stones.

On Fairies and the Naming of Fossils

Browne, perceptively for his time, realized that his 'fayrie stones' were '*Echinometrites* ... the Sea-Hedg-Hog', or fossil sea urchins. And these particular fossils seem to have acquired a veritable lexicon of names associated with fairies – 'fairy loaves', 'fairy weights', 'fairy sugar loaves', 'fairy hearts' and 'fairy faces'.[12] The name 'fairy loaf' was particularly common in Suffolk, Essex, Berkshire and Surrey even until the 1940s, especially relating to the helmet urchin *Echinocorys*. In Suffolk sea urchins are known to have been placed on mantelpieces not merely as decorations, but in the belief they would ensure a constant supply of bread in the house. So too in the bakery. Here it was placed by the brick oven and used as a charm. The loaf-like shape of the urchin *Echinocorys* was a guarantee that the bread would rise.[13] This preoccupation with food led to them being called 'sugar loaves' in Kent and Sussex.[14] Bread and sugar were combined in north Norfolk in naming the fossil urchins *Echinocorys* and *Micraster* 'fairy sugar loaves'.[15]

It is tempting to suggest that calling the fossils 'fairy loaves' could have derived from a belief that fossil urchins may simply have once been believed to be tiny loaves of bread made by fairies. Other fairy names were used for fossil sea urchins. Some were called 'fairy heads' in Dorset in the 1870s. Gideon Mantell in 1844 recorded that some cidaroid urchins were sometimes called either 'fairies' night-caps' or 'fairies' turbans'.[16] As we have seen, the landlady in the hedge ale-house in Oxfordshire had her own 'fairy night-cap' in the form of a conical stone that, in all likelihood, was the helmet urchin *Echinocorys*. In the Isle of Wight fossil sea urchins were known as 'fairy weights',[17] probably a corruption of 'wight'. In medieval England, this word meant 'man' or 'creature'. Parts of fairies' anatomy could, it was believed, be fossilized. In Dorset early Jurassic and chalk belemnites were called 'fairies' fingers'. Their culinary appliances provided a name for rows of fossil fish vertebrae – 'fairy saltcellars'.[18] Sometimes fossil crinoid stems (what Woodward and his contemporaries called *entrochi*) were known simply as 'fairy stones'. In the catalogue of his collection, Woodward records that specimens of 'Entrochi', numbers xd.56 and 57, were collected 'out of the Brook call'd the *Fairystone Brook, at Stickland head, Westmorland*'.[19]

A different form of the fairy was the pixy. In the nineteenth century fossil sea urchins were also called 'colepexies' heads'.[20] 'Pexy' or 'colepexy' was another word for 'pixie'. Another corruption of 'fairy' was the word 'phairisee'. In Suffolk the 'fairy loaf' was sometimes called a 'pharisee loaf', the word deriving from 'fairisee'. This was corrupted further to 'Paris loaf', or at other times to 'farcy loaf'. Farm horsemen were said to have kept these fossils in their pockets as a charm against a disease in horses called 'farcy' or 'glanders'. In his book on the folklore of East Anglia in England, *The Pattern Under the Plough* published in 1966,[21] George Evans suggested that the word 'pharisee' evolved from 'ferrisheen', which itself derived from the Gaelic term 'fer-sidhe' (pronounced 'far-shee'). This means 'man of the hill', basically a male fairy.

Fairies, it was believed, inhabited a mystical, enchanted world – an Otherworld. It was,

> the most delightful land of all that are under the sun; the trees are stooping down with fruit and with leaves and with blossom. Honey and wine are plentiful there; no wasting will come upon you with the wasting away of time; you will never see death or lessening. You will get feasts, playing and drinking; you will get sweet music on the strings; you will get silver and gold and many jewels.[22]

It was a magical world accessible through caves and lakes, but mostly through Neolithic and Bronze Age barrows. Those who lived in these mounds were the fairies, known in Irish as the *sidhe* (pronounced 'shee'). The place under the hill was also known as the *sidhe*. In Anglo-Saxon it was called *biorh* (pronounced 'berr'). Here, it was believed, lived the *sidhe*-folk, gods and goddesses of the Otherworld that over time morphed into fairies of folk belief. Spirits of enchantment, they were notorious for interfering in human affairs. They were responsible, it was believed, for sudden, unexplained illnesses in people and animals, and could change weather patterns to affect farming.[23] They were also adept at stealing children, and so were creatures to be very wary of. Consequently, any unexplained object that was found, such as a strange fossil, must have belonged to the fairies.

Living in the Otherworld, fairies never grew old, nor suffered pain or sickness. In the *biorh* there was a magic cauldron producing endless supplies of food that had the power to restore the dead back to life. For the Otherworld was also the land of the spirits of the dead, of those still trapped between this world and the next awaiting their chance to return to mortal life. Given the frequency with which fossils, in particular fossil urchins, are found in barrows from the Neolithic onwards, and have names associated with fairies, they appear to have been part of the Otherworld myths. Moreover, the tradition of placing fossils with the dead indicates they may have been there to help the spirits of the dead on their passage into the Otherworld. Could it be that 'fairy loaves' were, perhaps, seen as spiritual food to ensure the deceased person's immortality?

Of all the folk names associated with fossil sea urchins, perhaps the most enigmatic is one that has been most commonly used in southern England – 'shepherds' crown'. Although some people think the fossil looks a little like a medieval hat, shepherds are unlikely to have come across many of these fossils in their everyday work, as the majority were found by those who ploughed the land. I have suggested elsewhere that I think this name has nothing to do with shepherds. More likely it is another linguistic corruption, deriving from the Celtic word *sidhe*. The barrow within which the *sidhe* (fairies) lived was the *biorh*. It seems possible that *sidhe biorh* (the fairy home) could have been transformed over thousands of years into 'she-pherd'. It may be no coincidence that the shape of the domed *Echinocorys* is very similar to that of a barrow. But the association with the word 'crown' is a mystery.

Speak of the Devil

I suppose my interest in trying to unravel the fossil-collecting habits of our ancient ancestors, and follow their quest to understand the meaning of fossils, is partly my own attempt to understand why I also inherited the fossil-collecting gene. The fossiliferous chalk country of Sussex where I was brought up was an ideal place to rummage in chalk quarries, or stumble through ploughed fields of ankle-wrenching flints looking for enticing fossils. Whenever I did this, the Devil was not far away. I don't mean in the sense of fossil collecting being an evil pursuit. Even though in the Middle Ages fossils might have been thought of in some quarters as spawn of the Devil, set there, perhaps, to confuse the unwary, it was more how the Devil's name was used to explain what to most people was the unexplainable. Especially when it came to geological features or objects.

In my youth, long ago, when not collecting fossils, I went to football matches involving Brighton and Hove Albion. While they now ply their trade in a spanking new stadium (which coincidentally sits on former muddy fields where I had to endure school cross-country running), they used to play at the Goldstone Ground. Goldstone was not a commercial sponsor, but a huge sarsen stone the size of a car that squats toad-like in a nearby park. Sarsens are very hard, dark-brown, coarse quartz sandstones of early Cenozoic age, 45–50 million years old, that formed when the Earth was much warmer, CO_2 levels in the atmosphere much higher and weathering of rocks more intense. The result was that the groundwater became enriched in dissolved silica and iron compounds, and these acted as powerful cements to form this hard sandstone. Blocks of sarsen litter southern England. The large pillars and lintels of Stonehenge are sarsens. More than 60 per cent of the stone used to build Windsor Castle is sarsen.

The story I heard tell was that the sarsen called the goldstone had been put there by an enraged Devil. In an attempt to rid the countryside north of the South Downs of Christian churches, he decided to dig a trench one night through the South Downs to the sea in order to flood the land. Unfortunately, at least from the Devil's point of view, a woman came out of her cottage carrying a lantern to find out what was making such a dreadful noise. Mistaking the light for the rising Sun, the Devil was so annoyed he kicked the sarsen stone over the hill to its final resting place. His unfinished trench became known as Devil's Dyke. In reality it is one of the most impressive of coombes – steep-sided valleys carved out of the chalk by the erosive action of water flooding out of the melting permafrost at the end of the last glacial maximum. It would seem that natural forces, in effect, did the Devil's work, though a little earlier than Christian times.

While the Devil left his mark in Sussex geomorphologically, palaeontologically he left either his footprints or parts of his anatomy or possessions scattered across the lands. On the dry flanks of Roccamonfina volcano, near Rome, are mammal track-ways, including three sets made by humans 385,000 to 325,000 years ago. Locals called them 'Devil's trails'.[24] Given the Devil's usual dwelling place, it was believed that only he could have walked on the hot volcanic surface. The trails lead away from the vent, heading downslope. The Devil was also thought responsible for footprints in the 'Holy Cross' Mountains in Poland. Three-toed footprints, probably made by a small theropod dinosaur, were thought by locals to have been evidence of the Devil passing through. Having made a bet with an angel that he could jump across the Kamienna River valley, the Devil did so in a huge leap. However, he landed so hard that he left his footprints in the rocks. Other dinosaur footprints in the area have been considered to be of the Devil's making, as he set off to occult gatherings or to Satanic temples.[25] In Malta, the Devil rather miraculously left his footprints on the fossil sea urchin *Schizaster*, the five sunken star-like ambulacra known locally as either 'Devil's footprints' or 'Devil's footsteps'.[26]

The Devil left many parts of his anatomy in the rocks. Fossil bones found in a cave in Kolozs County, Romania, were thought to be his bones.[27] Likewise, fossil bones found in Jurassic rocks near Scarborough in Yorkshire were thought to be the remains of fallen angels – those who had followed Satan when he rebelled against God.[28] The most well-known part of the Devil's anatomy found in rocks are his toenails. Various species of the early Jurassic oyster *Gryphaea*, with their thick, hooked valves, have long been known as Devil's toenails in many parts of southern and western England, though in Warwickshire they were the Devil's thumbs. Belemnites of the same age were regarded as his fingers. In Hungary the tere-bratulid brachiopod *Coenothyris vulgaris* was known as 'Satan's

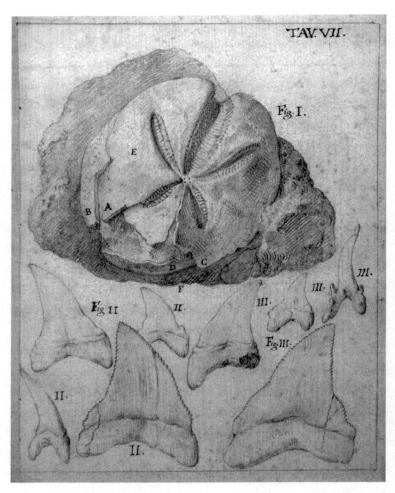

Original pencil drawing by Agostino Scilla for his Plate 3 of his *La vana speculazione disingannata dal senso* (1670), showing the irregular spatangoid sea urchin *Schizaster*, interpreted on Malta as 'Devil's footprints' or 'Devil's footsteps'. Below this specimen are a range of 'serpents' tongues', interpreted by Scilla as sharks' teeth.

The early Jurassic fossil bivalve *Gryphaea dilatata* (known colloquially as 'Devil's toenail'). Specimen from the collection of John Woodward.

buttons'.[29] The Devil also seems to have spread money around the countryside. The large coin-like foraminifer *Nummulites* is known as *Monnaie du Diable* (Devil's money) in France; *Teufelspfennige* or *Teufelsgeld* in Germany; *Duivels munt* in Belgium; and *az ördög tallerjai* (Devil's thalers) in Hungary.[30]

Despite this frequent association of fossils with the Devil, few demonic traits have been associated with their possession. As I hope I have shown, having any type of fossil is usually thought to be a positive experience. However, there are always exceptions to this rule . . .

Be Careful What You Wish For

In 1565, shortly before he died from the plague, the Swiss zoologist, botanist and lexicographer Conrad Gesner's book *De rerum fossilium, lapidum et gemmarum* was published. This book, written by arguably the greatest natural historian of the sixteenth century, has been considered as playing a pivotal role in the development of palae-ontology as a science.[31] Gesner was one of the first to argue that some fossils represented the remains of once-living organisms. Significantly, Gesner's book was the first to provide illustrations in the form of woodcuts of the most common fossils. Gesner was proud of these drawings, saying that 'he always experiences a feeling of delight in the contemplation of the forms and shapes in which the Creatress Nature has expressed herself pictorially as it were with the brush of a painter'.[32]

He classified fossils such as pecten and other sea shells as resem-bling forms now living in the sea. Isocrinid crinoid stems were in a group of forms like heavenly bodies, because of their star-like pat-tern. Belemnites, as 'elf-darts', were grouped with what Gesner called his 'artificial' group objects. Fossil sea urchins fell into three groups. One was the *Lapis judaicus*, the spines of cidaroid sea urchins, which he placed in a group that were like trees, or the parts of trees; another was the thunderstone, or omnia and brontia, which he placed in his category of objects fallen from the sky. These were the irregular sea urchins. One type of regular sea urchin, though, he placed in quite another group – those forms resembling insects and serpents. Ammonites were placed here. But so too was something which since Roman times had been known as *ovum anguinum* (snake's egg). The quality of the woodcuts in his work is so good that it is clear the object to which Gesner was referring was a fossil sea urchin. But rather than being a shepherds' crown or a thunderstone (in other words, a burrowing irregular sea urchin), it is a particular type of regular urchin called a cidaroid. What characterizes these urchins are the blister-like tubercles that run in irregular rows on the side of the spherical shell. The function of these tubercles is to provide an attachment site for long, thick spines (the *Lapis judaicus*), articulating in a ball-and-socket joint. Insinuating themselves between the tubercles like little snakes, five ambulacra wind round. In naming these fossils *ovum anguinum*, Gesner was harking back to Pliny, reflecting common folklore.

Gesner's interpretation of *ovum anguinum* was supported by other contemporary naturalists. Michele Mercati, in his 1574 book *Metallotheca vaticana*, also illustrated fossil cidaroid sea urchins and similarly called them *ovum anguinum*. Likewise, in France at the time they were known as *les oeufs des serpents*. In Wales *ovum anguinum* were sometimes known as adderstones or *glain nadir*. The question is, why were these fossils identified with snakes' eggs and what power was attributed to them? One possibility in Britain at least is a link between snakes and Druids, who were also sometimes

A typical Jurassic fossil cidaroid sea urchin, typified by its prominent tubercles on its interambulacral plates, the two rows being separated by sinuous, serpent-like rows of small tubercles. Such fossils were often called *ovum anguinum*.

known as *naddred*, or adders. This alluded to the supposed rebirth undertaken by initiates casting off the skin of their old life and then being reborn.

Robert Plot, in his *Natural History of Oxfordshire*, published in 1677, thought the link between urchins and snakes was the sinuous nature of the five ambulacra that course over the spherical test. He observed that:

> By Boetius and Gesner, and all the old *Authors*, they are called *Ova anguina*, Serpents eggs; perchance because from the basses there issue as it were five *tails*, of *serpents*, waved and attenuated toward the upper part of the stones. They tell us also a story of its being engendered from the *salivation* and *slime* of *snakes*, and cast into the Air by the force of the *fibulations*, where if taken, has effects as wonderful as its generation, and therefore of great esteem amongst the *French Druids*. But I care not to spend my time in *Romance*, and therefore proceed.[33]

In all likelihood, it was just such a fossil sea urchin at the centre of one of the most peculiar decisions undertaken by Emperor Claudius (10 BC–AD 54). Recounted by Pliny the Elder in his *Natural History*, Claudius's action showed that a misused fossil can have a distinct dark side:

> Over & besides, I will not overpasse one kind of eggs besides which is in great name and request in France, and whereof the Greek authors have not written a word: and this is the serpent's egg, which the Latins call Anguinum. For in Summer time yerely, you shall see an infinite number of snakes, gather round together into an heape, entangled and enwrapped one within

another so artificially, as I am not able to expresse the manner
thereof: by the means therefore, of the froth or salivation which
they yield from their mouths, and the humour that commeth
from their bodies, there is engendered the egg aforesaid. The
priests of France called Druidae, are of opinion, and so they
deliver it, That these serpents when they have thus engendered
this egg do cast it up on high into the air, by the force of their
hissing; which being observed, there must be one ready to
latch and receive it in the fall again (before it touch the ground)
within the lappet of a coat of arms or soldiours cassocks. They
affirm also that the party who carrieth this egg away, had need
to be well mounted upon a good horse and to ride away upon
the spur, for that the foresaid serpents will pursue him still, and
never give over until they meet with some great river between
him and them, that may cut off and intercept their chase. They
add moreover and say, that the only mark to know this egg
whether it be right or no, is this, That it will swim aloft above
the water even against the stream, yea though it were bound
and enchased with a plate of gold. Over and besides, these
Druidae (as all the sort of these magicians be passing cautelous
and cunning to hide and cover their deceitful fallacies) do
affirm, That there must be a certain special time of the Moon's
age espied, when this business is to be gone about, as if (for-
sooth) it were in the power and disposition of man to cause the
moon and the serpents to accord together in this operation
of engendering the egg aforesaid by their froth and salivation,
I myself verily have seen one of these eggs, and to my remembrance, as big it was as an ordinary round apple: the shell thereof
was of a certain gristly and cartilaginous substance, and the
same clasped all about (as it were) with many acetables or

concavities representing those of the fish called a Pourcuttle, which she hath about her legs. And it is the ensign or badge that the Druidae doe carry for their arms. And they hold it a soveraigne thing, for to procure ready excess unto any princes, and to win their grace and favour; as also to obtain the upper hand over an adversarie in any suite and process of law, if one do carry it about him. But see how this vanitie and foolish persuasion hath possessed the minds of men! for I am able upon mine own knowledge to avouch, that the Emperor *Claudius Caesar* commanded a man of arms and gentleman of Rome, descended from the Vocantians, to be killed for no other reason in the whole world, but because he carried one of these eggs in his bosom, at what time as he pleaded his cause before him in the court.[34]

If we accept that the *ovum anguinum* was indeed a fossil sea urchin, then Pliny's description in his *Natural History* is the first written attempt to explain the nature of fossil sea urchins. Pliny recorded that to Celtic Druids *ovum anguinum* was a powerful magic object. It had a number of attributes. It could be used as an antidote against poison. It had the power to ward off illnesses. *Ovum anguinum* was undoubtedly a magical object that had the power to ward off evil. How could it, then, be part of the dark side of fossils? For the Vocontian knight wanting to plead his case before an emperor renowned for his highly unpredictable behaviour, to base his case purely on a small, cold stone was, clearly, foolhardy. The Vocontian lost not only his case – but his life.

It is possible that Claudius was not being totally irrational. The Romans are known to have despised Druids. Any link with them, such as the use of an *ovum anguinum* in a lawsuit, might have infuriated

Woodcut, *c.* 1497, based on Pliny the Elder's account of the *ovum anguinum*; somebody stealing a 'serpent's egg' leaping high over a seething mass of serpents, tossing the egg in the air and then catching it in a cloth as they did so. If dropped it would lose its magical powers.

Claudius. Even though they themselves were renowned for their bloodthirsty practices, the Romans were horrified at some Druidic practices. The Roman author Diodorus Siculus wrote in his *Histories*:

> When they [the Druids] attempt divination upon important matters they practice a strange and incredible custom, for they kill a man with a knife-stab in the region above the midriff, and after his fall they foretell the future by the convulsions of

his limbs and the pouring of his blood, a form of divination in which they have full confidence, as it is of old tradition.[35]

Even to Claudius, divining the future from the death throes of a human sacrifice was beyond the pale. What annoyed him was what he perceived was the Druids' perceived mockery of a noble pursuit: the Romans' own practice of sacrificing animals and reading the future in their entrails – the sacred ritual of *haruspices*. The Druids had to be destroyed. While dispatching the Vocontian knight so maliciously may just have been a typically irrational and barbaric Claudian act, it may have been more than that. Perhaps it was distaste for Druidic belief systems as a whole and a response by a succession of Roman emperors to annihilate such Celtic sacrificial practices once and for all. Then again, maybe Claudius just didn't like fossils.

TEN

A JOKE OF TIME

What an hallucination to affirm that it was all due to chance, or
to some subtle generative virtue composing Nature's jokes and
shutting them up in rocks! What piffle! These shellfish lived in
water and then rotted: a joke of time, not of Nature.
(AGOSTINO SCILLA, 1670)

The superstition and the folklore of fossils. Their myths and
legends. All begin to waver as ancient Greek philosophers
ponder their true meaning. A medieval Arabic mathematician
and a Renaissance polymath, renowned in particular for
his paintings and daring to explain the mysteries of human
anatomy, suggest there may be more to some fossils than being
mere sports of Nature. These are the first tentative attempts at
empirical explanations for these figured stones.

It takes a mid-seventeenth-century artist living on an island
in the Mediterranean to really crack the true meaning of fossils.
With a flourish of his pencil, he hammers the last nail into the
coffin of fossil folklore, legend and myth. A suite of exquisite
drawings reveal a wondrous world of animals petrified in rock
for, as was to transpire, an unimaginable period of time.

There is a group of small islands that, some 5–10 million years ago, rose from the sea. Piles of sediments, the granulated debris of shells of countless marine invertebrates that lived and died in and upon the sea-floor, were thrust up by tectonic forces to form this new land. Locked within these gold and grey limestones is the story of the animals that had inhabited a warm, shallow sea 10–20 million years ago. Sharks, some much larger than any living today, cruised the waters. A kaleidoscope of sea urchins – flat and portly, prickly and hairy – ploughed on and in the sea-floor. Scallops snapped over them and other bivalves, while gastropods crawled slowly and obliviously. All left their calling cards in their fossilized remains.

When people first settled the islands it was hard for them to miss these aquatic fossils scattered through the rocks. Eight thousand years ago people came here to farm, but soon exhausted the soil's fertility. The next settlers were the builders of spectacular megalithic structures, temples to honour the dead, built between 5,500 and 4,500 years ago. Not only did the builders collect fossils and place them in their temples, but they even carved their own versions. Later societies on the islands weaved their own stories about the fossils. These were sucked into their myths and new legends were created that leaked through to the present day. Eventually, these intriguing fossils piqued the imagination of a Greek poet, but his musings were largely ignored for more than 2,000 years. It took a curious artist living in Sicily – who, exactly 350 years ago, made beautiful drawings of them and pondered about this fossilized menagerie – to tell the world exactly what they were, these fossils of the Maltese islands.

Builders of Temples and of Ideas

About 5,500 years ago there settled on the Maltese islands people with not only great construction skills, but a vision to build mighty monuments to the dead. In Malta and the neighbouring smaller island of Gozo, over a period of about 1,000 years, they erected some twenty groups of stone-built temples or monumental shrines, along with two underground mausolea. Symmetrical in construction, the huge blocks were hewn from the fossiliferous limestones of the islands. With a concave, high stone facade, a narrow entrance led to lobed inner spaces.[1] Within some, altars or shrines were created. They were also sanctuaries for the dead. One, the Hal Saflieni Hypogeum, was an underground temple within which up to 7,000 bodies were discovered by archaeologists in the early twentieth century.[2]

The community that built these remarkable structures lived in an isolated island world that was coming under increasing economic and environmental stress.[3] Their temples became larger and more complex. Building them had become a societal obsession. The ritualized cult of the dead came at the expense of building domestic dwellings of any significance, and ultimately the society collapsed. Yet what it left behind were some of the greatest Neolithic megalithic structures in Europe. And within, countless offerings to the gods, including the fossils that peppered the rocks from which the temples were built.

These master builders are intrigued by the fossils they find in the rock they are using for their monumental buildings. They cannot resist collecting the strange objects and placing them in their temples. Some are shiny shark's teeth, as big as a man's hand. Grey as tarnished pewter, and with a serrated edge as keen as the sharpest knife, they are unearthed by twentieth-century archaeologists in five of the nine temples in which the megalith builders placed their fossils. What did the temple builders make of these fossils? Did they peer inside the maw of a dead shark to see the resemblance? They collected other unusual figured stones that piqued their imaginations: scallop and cone shells, bivalve shells, including one that looks like a large date turned to stone. Into this one they drilled a hole at one end, to hang it from a cord. Disc-like fossilized shark's vertebrae were found and placed with care inside the temples. To modern eyes, these fossils resemble pieces from a draughts board, turned to stone.

Some fossils were important enough to be placed in special places within the temples. In the five interconnected temples at Tarxien, they placed an astonishing collection of artefacts, many, if not all, votive offerings. Some of the columns and pillars of the temples revealed during the excavations were intricately carved with bulls and spiral decorations. Within one column are five shallow recesses, easy to access, just above ground level. They were places perhaps for worshippers or priests to deposit their votive offerings. Some placed dark, polished stones. Someone placed two fossil sea urchins.[4] In another temple someone placed a fist-sized, domed fossil sea urchin, resplendent with its incised, five-petalled floral emblem, the tiny rows of pores looking like they have been fashioned with great care by a pin.

These fossils are not in the temples by chance. They have not just fallen passively from the rocks used to build the temples. Many are from rock types other than those used in the temples' construction. They have been carefully collected, transported and placed in the temples as votive offerings, amulets, cult objects or propitiatory items for the dead. Perhaps possessing these objects granted a feeling of power to the guardians of the elaborate ceremonies of the temples.

The fossils also inspired art. Oversized limestone and clay models of gastropods were carefully crafted – inspired, perhaps, by the natural, helically spired internal moulds of fossil gastropods in the Upper Coralline Limestone. Unwittingly the Natufian artisans of Jordan are mimicked by the carving of a conical piece of stone which they incise with longitudinal grooves. It 'resembles more than anything else a fossil sea urchin.'[5] Their artistry also extended to using some of the fossils themselves as creative tools. In two temples, Ghar Dalam and the Tarxien Cemetery, teeth of the extinct great white shark *Carcharocles megalodon* decorate clay pots, the serrated edge of the tooth having been pressed into the soft, unbaked clay to produce a pattern of gently curving rows of tiny holes. The sharp end of the tooth is used to make rows of fine parallel incisions.[6] They applied these same techniques to strange human figurines that have huge, circular, flattened torsos.[7]

We have no way of knowing what these temple builders made of all the fossils they collected and kept. Later inhabitants of the islands conjured up their own imaginative folklore. But 2,000 years after the last temple rose from the island's limestones, a wandering Greek poet and philosopher began to the consider the ways of the fossils he saw in Malta.

The poet and philosopher Xenophanes was born in 570 BC in Colophon, an ancient Greek city in Ionia, in what is now present-day Turkey. Xenophanes is said to have lived to a ripe old age, dying in his nineties between 478–475 BC. At 25 years old, when the Persians invaded his homeland, Xenophanes set off on a journey that was to last a lifetime, as he spent nearly seventy years travelling through much of the ancient Greek world. He is known to have lived for some time in Italy and in Sicily, just a stone's throw from

Malta (well, about 80 kilometres (50 mi.)). Although most of the writings of Xenophanes are lost, his work 'on nature' was summarized by the Roman theologian Hippolytus (AD 170–235). According to Hippolytus, Xenophanes believed that most things were incomprehensible. He did, however, suggest that the Sun is born each day from gatherings of small particles of fire, and that the Earth is boundless and surrounded by neither air nor heaven. He also postulated that there are innumerable suns and moons. But it is the significance of the presence of fossils in rocks, and his recognition of them as being the remains of once-living organisms, that makes Xenophanes arguably the earliest person to infer the true nature of fossils. And it was, in part, the fossils he saw on his travels in Malta that played a crucial role in the development of his ideas:

> And Xenophanes opines that there was once a mixture of earth with the sea, and that in time it was freed from moisture, asserting in proof of this that shells are found in the centre of the land and on mountains, and that in the stone quarries of Syracuse were found the impress of a fish and of seals, and in Paros the cast of an anchor below the surface of the rock and in Malta layers of all sea-things. And he says that these came when all things were of old time buried in mud, and that the impress of them dried in the mud; but that all men were destroyed when the earth being cast into the sea became mud, and that it again began to bring forth and that this catastrophe happened to all the ordered worlds.[8]

Other Greek writers, such as Xanthus of Sardos (mid-fifth century BC), shared the view of Xenophanes. Xanthus wrote of the fossilized mussels and other shells he saw far inland in Armenia and Phrygia.

From this he deduced the area must, in the past, have been covered by the sea, and that the fossils were the remains of formerly living animals. But others, like Theophrastus (326–284 BC), thought differently. On finding buried ivory and stones shaped like huge bones, he conjectured that they had grown in the Earth through some spontaneous unknown force at work in Nature.[9] This view, that fossils merely fortuitously resembled once-living animals and plants, permeated Western thought for the following two millennia, greatly influenced by the go-to source for all things natural history, Pliny the Elder's *Natural History*. There were a few lone voices against this idea, notably the Persian polymath Ibn Sina (AD 980–1037), known by his Latinized name Avicenna. He argued for the organic origin of fossils:

> If what is said concerning the petrifaction of animals and plants is true, the cause of this is a powerful mineralizing and petrifying virtue which arises in certain stony spots, or emanates suddenly from the earth during earthquakes and subsidences, and petrifies whatever comes into contact with it. As a matter of fact, the petrifaction of the bodies of plants and animals is not more extraordinary than the transformation of waters.[10]

Important as these philosophical musings were, they had no impact on the inhabitants of Malta. They created their own, quite distinctive folklore to explain away these enigmatic figured stones. And in the process created a thriving overseas business.

An Island Fossil Folklore

A good part of Maltese fossil folklore is, somewhat ironically, based on a significant Christian figure: St Paul the Apostle.[11] On his way to Rome from Jerusalem, with more than two hundred other prisoners, Paul was shipwrecked off the Maltese coast. Legend has it that, to make matters worse, after struggling ashore he was bitten by a snake. Even though it was said to have been a viper, he apparently suffered no ill effects. For the snake's temerity, Paul promptly, it was said, deprived all snakes on the island of their venom. Some maintained that St Paul's cursing of the snakes meant that they also lost their tongues and their eyes. These body parts ended up in the rocks as 'serpents' tongues' (*glossopetrae*) or as 'serpents' eyes' (elsewhere, toadstones). Because the Maltese people treated him so well, St Paul repaid their kindness by blessing the rocks and the fossils. He also imbued them with anti-poison properties, as well as the ability to regenerate and produce wonderful 'figured stones'.[12] As a consequence, the 'serpents' tongues' in particular were believed to have miraculous magical properties, all thanks to St Paul. Other islanders preferred to call them *Ilsien San Pawl* or 'St Paul's tongues'. They believed each fossil to be an image in stone of the saint's tongue, which he had used to convert their heathen forebears to Christianity. Some even believed that the power of his teaching was so forceful that his tongue actually penetrated the solid rock.[13]

A commonly held view in Malta, espoused by the surgeon Giacomo Buonamico (1630–1680) in a manuscript dated 1667, was that the tongue stones on the island, whether they were serpents' tongues or St Paul's tongues, 'grew spontaneously' in the rocks.[14] Few people had any concept of the organic nature of these fossils. No link was made with the dentistry of the sharks that cruised around the island. The view of spontaneous growth was supported by local historian Count Gio Antonio Ciantar in his *Malta Illustrata*, published in 1772. He wrote that over time the tongues grew larger and larger.[15] Buonamico thought that imperfect or broken fossils were formed by 'incomplete generation'. He also believed that they bore offspring, interpreting the small lateral denticles attached to the root of many shark teeth as offspring not yet separated from their parents.

The magical powers of the serpents' tongues were manifested in different ways. When powdered and added to wine or water, they were believed to be a powerful antidote to poison. Alternatively, they could be dipped whole straight into the drink, as this would nullify any poison present. The fossils could also afford protection by being worn round the neck. They were also used as amuletic aids to obstetrics, being placed with a woman about to give birth. This was to hasten the child's delivery. Moreover, in hospitals in Malta in the mid-1700s, fossil sharks' teeth, in powdered form, were used in more than thirty medical prescriptions.[16]

There was also a strong belief in the power of serpent's eyes to ward off the effects of poison. Most powerful were cups carefully manufactured from rocks and fossils blessed by St Paul. These were poison cups or *Contra-veleno* cups. The special feature of these vessels was that they were made from ground-up limestone derived from St Paul's Grotto.[17] This is the cave where St Paul was said to have spent three months in enforced residence on Malta following his shipwreck. According to local tradition the rocks here were suffused with St Paul's power to protect against poison. To make the cups, powdered rock from the cave was soaked in plantain water then filtered. The resulting paste was shaped into a cup and left to dry in the sun. Known as *Terra sigillata melitensis*, or 'Maltese sealed earth', it was moulded into cups, vases or medals. But to ensure even more effectiveness to one made into a poison cup why not also add a protective fossil?

In the Hans Sloane collection in the British Museum is a poison cup from Malta.[18] All that remains is the base and part of the side. It is decorated on its outer base with snakes and on the inside is the impression of a seal that authenticates it as a true *Terra sigillata melitensis*. It bears the inscription: 'PIETRA D.S. PAOLO, CONTRA-VELENO'. To make this cup an even more potent antivenom receptacle, its inside is studded with seven fossils. Only five have survived: three serpents' eyes – the fossilized teeth of a ray-finned fish – and two isocrinid crinoid ossicles. While there appears never to have been any folklore linking crinoid ossicles to protection against poison, just the fact that they came from Maltese rocks blessed by St Paul might have been enough reason to add them.

Somewhat surprisingly, in the Middle Ages there was a flourishing trade in fossils from Malta. This was because the main source of the tongue stones used in Europe at the time as antidotes to poison were from the the Cenozoic limestones of Malta. Not only are they such a common component of the fossil assemblage, but Maltese tongue stones were regarded as being the most efficacious. What may well have made them the preferred fossil of choice in *Natternzungenbaum* in Europe could have been their link to the legend of St Paul. As a result, a very active export trade took the fossil teeth to apothecaries and jewellers throughout Europe. Nicolas Steno (1638–1686), a pioneering geologist and one of the first to realize the true nature of tongue stones, observed in 1664 that hardly any ship would leave the island without a consignment of the fossils. This was the case even until well into the eighteenth century.[19]

St Paul, according to local legend, left his mark on other Maltese fossils. As well as leaving multiple copies of his tongue in the Maltese limestones he also left other, rather surprising, parts of his anatomy. Consider finding a small, flattish, rhombic plate in the rocks, barely the size of your little fingernail, out of which brazenly protrudes a nipple. Its resemblance to a mammalian nipple is uncanny. What could be succoured by such objects in the rocks? Whose nipple could it be? For some strange fancy, having scattered his tongue many times through the island's rocks, the first thought that seems to have come to some people's minds is that man again. It must be the maker of miracles – St Paul.

In a sermon that he gave on the laying of a foundation stone at Valetta on 28 March 1566, the Augustinian monk Padre Spirito Pelo Angusciola talked about the *Vestigie di San Paolo*, the representations of St Paul's body embedded in the rocks of the island. As well as the tongues (*Lingue*) and his breasts (*Mammelle*), there were his footprints (*Pedate*) and, most notably, his 'stick' (*Bastoncino*). This name was applied to the long rod-like fossils, some reaching the length of a little finger. While the reality is that they are nothing more than fossil sea urchin spines which attach by a ball-and-socket joint to the nipple-like tubercles of the *Mammelle di San Paolo*, the often phallic-shaped *Bastoncino di San Paolo* led to their suggestive anatomical assignation. Perhaps this is best left to a limerick recounted by Kenneth Oakley:

> There was a man from Rossal
> Who found a remarkable fossil.
> He could tell by the bend
> And the knob at the end
> It was the tool of St Paul the Apostle.[20]

Original pencil drawing for the frontispiece to Agostino Scilla's *La vana speculazione disingannata dal senso* (1670). Sense is vainly trying to convince wraith-like 'vain speculation' that the fossils on the ground were once living organisms, like the sea urchin he is holding in his hand. On Sense's neck is the all-seeing eye.

Into the Light

It takes an artist to see through the miasma of superstition and cant surrounding fossils. A man with an eye for shape. For form. For colour. He can see it as clearly as when he peers into a calm, transparent sea. A sea pulsating with life. With fishes and dolphins. With sea urchins and scallops. And on land he sees the petrified morsels of St Paul's anatomy, the toadstones and tongue stones. But he sees them all for what they really are – battered remnants of past life, trapped for eternity in rocky tombs. All he wants to do is to grab wraith-like 'vain speculation' by the scruff of his neck, shove a rotting sea urchin under his nose and force him to look at its petrified counterpart on the ground. So, this he does, and creates a stunning frontispiece to his book. A book that shatters the myths and superstitions of fossils and marks the birth of modern palaeontology. Agostino Scilla (1629–1700) is the artist. A Sicilian, he painted the usual subjects of his time – religious themes and portraits of august gentlemen. But he was also adept at painting the natural world – animals, fruits, shells and scenery – with great accuracy.[21] He also wrote a book. He called it *La vana speculazione disingannata dal senso* (Vain Speculation Disabused by Sense).

It all started with a box of fossils from Malta that piqued his interest:

> I chanced to see a small box of tongue-stones excavated from the mines of Malta, and this made me eager to possess some of them, either to confirm what I believed about them or, by making more leisured observations of other things, to embrace the contrary opinion. Among these tongue-stones I saw a little piece of rock containing the tooth of a dogfish and one half

of a shell, along with some fish vertebrae lacking their lateral bones. That convinced me that no one with any brains could be content to see, or (to put it better) capable of seeing, them as anything save true and mighty miracles of Nature; that no such person could believe that she has a shortage of such miracles, or that they cannot be accounted for by reasoned speculation, and so attempt some terrible, repugnant, novel and thoroughly perverse way of explaining them.[22]

He wanted to see more of these fossils, so he wrote to his friend, the Sicilian botanist Paolo Boccone (1633–1704) 'with my usual impetuosity . . . asking him kindly to procure me some tongue-stones mingled with other things that are excavated from the mines of Malta. Instead, he struck me with a sudden flash of lightning.' Somewhat mischievously, I suspect, Boccone asked the Maltese surgeon Giacomo Buonamico to reply to Scilla on his behalf, undoubtedly aware that their opposing views on the origins of fossils were as chalk is to cheese. Thanks to Boccone, what this thunderbolt sparked in Scilla was the creation of a series of 28 exquisite pencil drawings of fossils from Malta and Sicily, and an accompanying 163-page answer in response to Buonamico's reply. This, after all, was the man who argued that fossils were merely figured stones that grew in the ground, a view that, frankly, Scilla found risible. Scilla's extensive and copiously illustrated reply was written with coruscating wit, combined with rational, analytical interpretations, drawing heavily on his artwork and on the fossils that Buonamico sent him from Malta.

To Scilla, there was no questioning that tongue stones fell from the mouths of a range of different fishes. 'Please believe that Malta's tongue-stones are fragments of animals,' he wrote to Buonamico. He

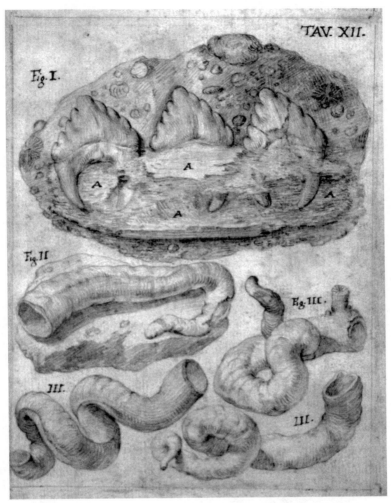

Original pencil drawings for Plate 12 of Scilla's *La vana speculazione disingannata dal senso*, showing part of the jaw with three teeth of the extinct dolphin *Squalodon melitensis* and a number of serpulid worm tubes, known colloquially in Malta as *Serpe petrificato* ('petrified snakes').

was greatly influenced by their variability in shape and size, arguing that they derived from different kinds of fishes, including sharks. He carefully observed how they varied in their preservation: 'I will show them to whoever may wish to see them: tongue-stones corroded, eroded and mostly decayed in the root, tongue-stones which never had a crust, tongue-stones broken and tongue-stones whole; but all very similar to, indeed identical to, the teeth of Sharks, Dogfish and the like.' He was certainly not the first to argue for the organic origin of tongue stones or *glossopetrae*. Guillaume Rondelet (1507–1566), the anatomist, naturalist and Regius professor of medicine at the University of Montpellier, and Fabio Colonna (1567–1640), a botanist and naturalist, were both intrigued by tongue stones. Rondelet, having observed the similarity between *glossopetrae* and sharks' teeth in Mediterranean fish markets, suggested in his book *Libri de piscibus marinis*, published in 1554–5, that they grew not in rocks but in sharks' mouths. In 1616 Colonna, writing in his short work *De glossopteris dissertatto*, thought that 'nobody is so stupid that he will not affirm at once at the first insight that the teeth are of the nature of bones, not stones.'[23] At the time these men were lone voices shouting against a hurricane of superstition and their views gained little traction.

Where Scilla stands head and shoulders above others is in the sheer detail and range of fossils that he not only described in careful detail, but drew so carefully and with such accuracy. Combined, they made his arguments more compelling. Scilla thought it was only necessary to use one's eyes and brain to see fossils for what they truly were:

All this, together with the evidence previously mentioned, compels me to believe that the Shells, Sea Urchins, sea

Original pencil drawings for Plate 14 of Scilla's *La vana speculazione disingannata dal senso*, showing a range of fossils: sharks' teeth, brachiopods, corals, gastropods and barnacles. All, Scilla believed, were once living animals.

Porcupines, Teeth (called Tongue-stones), Vertebrae, Corals, Sponges, Crabs, Sea Potatoes, Turbinate shells and countless other bodies, which some people believe to be generated from pure stone as Nature's idea of a joke, were once animals: not only that, but animals that absolutely belonged in the sea, carried inland through some accident along with the material that contained them (which we now see raised up into hills and mountains, made of pure sand or marl, tufa or rock).

Scilla also turned his mind towards the toadstones that peppered the Maltese limestones. By sticking his head (metaphorically speaking) inside the mouth of a wolf-fish, Scilla was able to show the world the true nature of toadstones. Scilla knew these fossils as *Occhi di Serpe*, snakes' eyes. 'It is manifestly wrong', he wrote in *La vana speculazione*, 'to claim these "snakes' eyes" as jewels or precious stones fashioned on Malta by Nature.' He had no doubt of their origin:

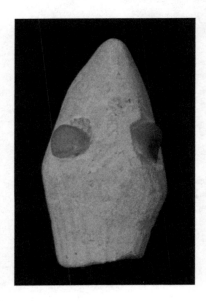

A small block carved into the shape of a snake's head into which two *Occhi di Serpe* (snakes' eyes) have been inserted. From the collection of Agostino Scilla, acquired by John Woodward in 1717. A reflection, perhaps, of Scilla's sometimes humorous take on matters. The specimen is now in the Sedgwick Museum, Cambridge.

'The little stones called snakes' eye are quite obviously fishes' teeth.' They came neither from the head of a toad, nor from the head of a snake, but, in Scilla's opinion, from the head of a fish – a wolf-fish. Like a number of other fishes that feed by crushing up molluscs, echinoderms and crustaceans on the sea floor, the Atlantic wolf-fish (*Anarhichas lupus*) has a mouth lined with batteries of small, round, peg-like teeth. Fossils of these teeth are common, observed Scilla, in both Malta and Sicily. Having a well developed sense of humour, Scilla made a carving of a snake's head and inserted two toadstones in them, like glaring eyes. The specimen still exists today in Scilla's fossil collection.

Another of the fossils Buonamico sent to Scilla was what had long been known on Malta as the impression on rock of a jasmine flower. This was because of the five equidistant 'petals' forming a star-shaped pattern, often on thin, biscuit-like plates. Scilla realized that 'it had been petrified after living out its life as a member of the species of Sea Urchin'. The more he looked at the material that Buonamico had sent him, along with specimens that he himself had collected from Sicily, the more Scilla came to accept Aristotle's view that 'there are many different species of Sea Urchins . . .':

Even among those that are familiar to all, however, there is an enormous variety: some are almost perfect globes on every side; others are somewhat squashed at the poles (so to speak), some slightly dented on one side and bulging out on the other; some have many spines, some have few, some have fat ones, some have thin ones. This applies not only to ordinary Sea Urchins, but also to Sea Potatoes, and other species as well, if they have been given other names by other Writers. By 'Sea Urchins', I mean all those that have spines; I am not bothered about their exact classification. I observe that mother Nature has so designed their internal workings that their shells and external features are divided into five: either five sections, as in the simple ones, or (in all the others) a structure so delicate that it looks like what you call a jasmine flower – at which I smelled the sweet, sweet scent of Truth.

Breaking open a fossil sea urchin, Scilla was astounded by the detail of the tiny structures that he saw:

So artfully were they disposed in that small space that I could only exclaim, 'Oh how provident is Nature, how beautiful is the truth! Nature never has been, and never will be, incapable of skilled operation; Truth is always generous with evidence, so that anyone who does not recognize it is either mentally defective or guilty of impugning an acknowledged truth.'

Scilla argued just as vehemently that fossils long thought to be 'mouths' and found in the limestones around his home in Messina were in fact fossilized crab claws:

In future it will be forgivable to subscribe to an error that has long been common in our part of the world: that of calling big crab-claws, which resemble jawbones, 'mouths', because the one I am showing you [his Plate 19, fig. 1] really does speak, although it has turned to stone. What it says is that while it was being squashed and squeezed by weight and by countless other bodies, it angrily bit into whatever came its way and hung on, all for the sake of persuading you to change your opinion. Has it not bitten into a striated shell? Most certainly

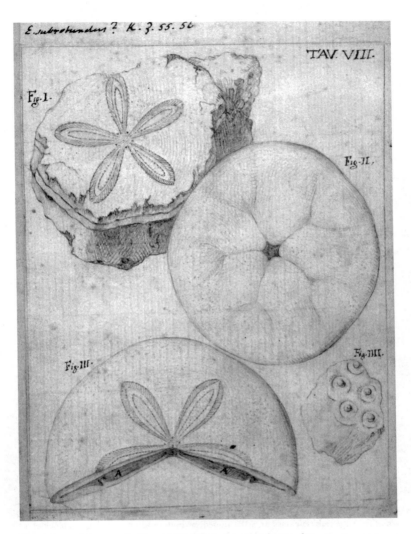

Original pencil drawings for Plate 8 of Scilla's *La vana speculazione disingannata dal senso*, showing clypeasteroid sea urchins (figs 1–3), interpreted on Malta as fossil jasmine flowers.

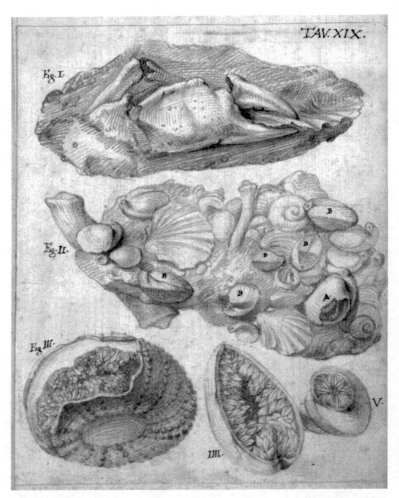

Original pencil drawings for Plate 19 of Scilla's *La vana speculazione disingannata dal senso*. The large crab claw was not, Scilla argued, jawbones and a mouth. Fig. 2, a block of limestone from Messina with brachiopods, scallops and gastropods; Figs 3 to 5, a regular sea urchin, a bivalve and a gastropod, respectively; all show growth of calcite crystals inside the shells, as part of the fossilization process.

it has! And most certainly, I don't think that anybody could suggest that it was born in the hills of Messina, without committing the sin of contesting the known truth.

There were no fossils in the rocks of Malta and those he saw in Sicily that he couldn't assign to living animals. Tongue stones were teeth from different species of fish (though in one case, his Plate 12, dolphin). Serpent's eyes were also teeth, he thought, from wolf-fish. Fossil serpents were in fact calcified tubes of serpulid worms. *Mammelle di San Paolo* were the tubercles on the plates of one kind of sea urchin, to which were attached *Bastoncino di San Paolo*, which were the urchin's spines. Fossilized bivalves, gastropods, corals – all, Scilla showed, once lived in the sea.

Scilla's ideas did not attract much attention, certainly not in England, until a review of his book was published in the *Philosophical Transactions* of the Royal Society for the years 1695–7.[24] The warm review, by Royal Society fellow William Wotton, undoubtedly had a major impact on ideas about fossils in England at the time. Wotton was particularly taken with Scilla's illustrations and how they strengthened his arguments for the organic nature of fossils.[25] Although some naturalists, such as Martin Lister (1639–1712), still clung to the old ideas that fossils grew in the earth, by the turn of the eighteenth century there were few who doubted the organic origin of fossils.

Scilla's book, though, was not the only work that triggered the paradigm shift in palaeontological thinking at this time. Indeed, in 1665, twenty years before Scilla's book was published, Robert Hooke's famous work *Micrographia* appeared. Opening up a new world of the microscopic and minuscule, Hooke took advantage of the use of microscopes to investigate the microscopic detail of thin sections of fossilized wood. He argued cogently for the organic origin of not only the fossilized wood, but fossils in general. Like Scilla, Hooke, applying rational reasoning, could see no other explanation for the origin of fossils. It was 'quite contrary to the infinite prudence of Nature' that they could be anything else.[26] Among his many attributes, Hooke, like Scilla, was a fine artist. He also spent time when he was young wandering the beaches of the southern coast of the Isle of Wight and picking up 'shepherd's crowns', though he called them 'helmet-stones'. Hooke made many beautiful drawings of fossils, but not until after *Micrographia* was published. They appeared in a publication by his friend Richard Waller in 1705, after Hooke's death. It was thought that the originals of Hooke's drawings were lost, until they were recently discovered in the Royal Society's archives in 2012 by Sachiko Kusukawa.[27]

Like Scilla, it was the protracted time spent looking at the fossils in order to produce detailed drawings that enabled Hooke to come to his conclusions as to their origin. The longer they both looked, the surer they were. The artist's eye was unveiling the science. As Hooke pointed out:

> any one that will diligently and impartially examine both the Stones and the Shells, and compare the one with the other, will, I assure him, find greater reason to perswade [*sic*] him of the Truth of my Position, than any I have yet urged, or can well produce in Words; no Perswasions being more prevalent than those which these dumb Witnesses do insinuate.[28]

Hooke detailed how shells and other once-living organisms came to be fossilized:

all these and most other kinds of stony bodies which are formed thus strangely figured, do owe their formation and figuration, not to any kind of *Plastick virtue* inherent in the earth, but to the shells of certain Shell-fishes, which, either by some Deluge, Inundation, Earthquake, or some such other means, came to be thrown to that place, and there to be fill'd with some kind of Mudd or Clay, or *petrifying* Water, or some other substance, which in tract of time has been settled together and hardned in those shelly moulds into those shaped substances we now find them.[29]

Hooke concluded:

from such a History of Observations well rang'd, examin'd and digested, the true original or production of all those kinds of stones might be perfectly and surely known; such as are *Thunderstones, Lapides stellares, Lapides judaici*, and multitudes of other.

In addition to having been appointed as the Royal Society's Curator of Experiments in 1664, Hooke took up the post of Professor of Geometry at Gresham College the following year.[30] And it was here that John Woodward was made Professor of Physicke in 1692. In the following year he became a Fellow of the Royal Society, nominated by Hooke. Both men lived in the college and both had rooms in which they kept their collections: Hooke was responsible for the care of the Royal Society's collection of natural curiosities, 'which included an armadillo, a crocodile, a giant's thighbone and a stone in the shape of "the secret parts of a woman"'.[31] Woodward's collection was more prosaic – his burgeoning geological collection and an assortment of antiquarian objects. Woodward specimens came from far and wide. He actively sought donations, but also bought material. According to entries in the catalogue of his collection he received specimens from Agostino Scilla, presumably in the 1690s before Scilla's death. Unless he knew beforehand, he would have been apprized of the importance of fossil material in Scilla's possession after Wotton's review in *Philosophical Transactions*. Some years after Scilla's death, Woodward managed to acquire his collection, which included most of the material that Scilla had used in his book and upon which his drawings were based. Writing to the Swiss naturalist Johann Jakob Scheuchzer (1672–1733) on 22 June 1717, Woodward told him: 'I purchased all Agostino Scillas Collection of Fossils amongst w'ch there are many Astroita, & other fossil Coralloids: but none calcined.'[32] What he doesn't tell Scheuchzer is that he also obtained the 29 pencil drawings that were used for the book's engravings. Recognizing their importance, he had them bound together. On an inserted title page Woodward wrote:

7 OCTOBER 1727

This Book may properly serve as an Appendix to the Catalogues of the Foreign Fossils; it containing an Account, and the Drawings, of those formerly in the Cabinet of Agostino Scilla; but since purchased and added to my foreign Collection.

These his Fossils are described in those Catalogues; which therefore so frequently refer to this Book that it ought to join and go along with them.

Both Scilla's fossil collection and the drawings of them still form part of Woodward's collection, which he left to the University of

Cambridge in 1728. They now reside in the Sedgwick Museum, the collection in its original mahogany cabinets.

The quest for the meaning of fossils has been a long journey. It has taken over half a million years and involved three species of 'humans'. Fossils have embellished stone tools. They have become tools themselves. Some have decorated and protected the body. Others have acted as medicines, brought good fortune, been buried with the dead, stimulated artistic expression and protected homes. Creators of legends and fragments of myths, they have come from the earth, but were often thought to have been born among the stars. The stories of their origins are myriad. But now, thanks to researchers like Hooke and Scilla, we are intrigued by fossils for very different reasons. They tell us the geological time. They reveal clues to the Earth's ecosystems across billions of years. They show the slow but incessant march of biological evolution, its patterns and processes. And many fossils provide records of past climate changes that have taken place over millions of years. They also document periods of Earth's history when mass extinctions decimated biodiversity. Fossils may have been objects of fascination, inspiration and security for many millennia, but now, having told much of the past history of this planet, the main meaning of fossils to us today may be as the harbingers of things that are to come.

EPILOGUE

Tucked away in the northwest of Western Australia is a region known as the Kimberley. The only sizeable town is Broome. Here, and for some tens of kilometres north along the coastline of the Dampier Peninsula, can be found what those versed in the Western scientific tradition have described as one of the richest tramplings of dinosaur footprints anywhere on Earth: hundreds of individual footprints, some in discernable trackways, representing more than twenty different types.[1] Most distinctive are those made by theropod dinosaurs, ancestors of *T. rex*, with their characteristic three-toed, bird-like footprints. This similarity is probably unsurprising, given that it was from such dinosaurs that birds are thought to have evolved.

The sands upon which these huge predatory animals were striding formed part of a vast deltaic system, where an extensive river drained the ancient Kimberley region into a proto-Indian Ocean. The sands have since cemented together, forming a hard, bright red sandstone, the 130-million-year-old Broome Sandstone. Not only do the rocks preserve evidence of the many animals that lived in this marginal marine setting, but plants also left their mark on the area, quite literally, as impressions in the sandstone. They show a vegetation dominated by conifers, ferns and an extinct group of cycad-like plants with feather-like leaves called bennettitalean seed ferns.[2]

But to the local Aboriginal people, the Bardi, who have lived in this area for nearly 60,000 years, there is quite another way of looking at these fossils. It is a different way of seeing, a different way of trying to bring meaning to these regular patterns in the rocks. Tracks manifest themselves in other, more abstract, ways. Dreaming tracks or song lines are fundamental Aboriginal Creation Time stories. Running across country, song lines define the land's physical and spiritual geography. They are paths taken by mythic beings, singing songs as they go, singing the world into being and creating the spiritual essence of traditional law of the land. In the coastal region of the Dampier Peninsula, the song line across which beings long ago left their mark in the sand is called Bugarrigarra.[3]

One of the most important Bugarrigarra beings is Marala, the Emu Man. He established the codes of behaviour for people in the land to ensure its well-being. As Marala passed along the song cycle, heading north along the coastline, he also passed in and out of the sea. As he did so he left his characteristic three-toed tracks behind. At times he would sit down, leaving impressions of his tail feathers in the sand. The tracks, called *Megalosauropus broomensis* in the Western scientific tradition, and the bennettitalean seed fern *Ptilophyllum cutchense*, are Marala's footprints and his tail feathers respectively in the local Bardi tradition. Sometimes Marala would take on a more human form and leave his human-like imprints in the sand. This is how a set of human footprints, formed about 2,000 years ago in beach rock north of Broome, form part of Marala's story.[4] The fossil leaves also play a significant role in another Bugarrigarra story. They are said to be ceremonial markings belonging to another important mythic being who traversed the Dampier Peninsula.[5]

According to Butcher Joe Nangan, Marala was a great cultural hero. Nangan was both an artist, lawman and custodian of legends.

He tells of how, on his travels along the coast, leaving his footprints as he went, Marala was accosted by a stranger – Warakarna, the Eagle Man. Marala asked him for water, but Warakarna speared him instead. Marala, it is said, left evidence of his passing not only in his footprints and feathers, but in the rock pillars of Gantheaume Point, south of Broome. In one story Marala is said to have used the place as his campsite. But in another, the culture-hero myth is tarnished. The smaller rocks at the point are said to represent crouching Ngaja-Ngaja/Kumanba Sea-women who had been raped by Marala. The single, tall rock pillar is their leader who drove him away to Mangata Spring, on what is now Dampier Downs Station. This is where Marala was speared and killed by the Eagle Man Warakarna.

Marala's country was in the land the Europeans call Dampierland. It was named after the first English explorer and naturalist to set foot in Australia – William Dampier. In 1688 he landed on the coast of what is now the Dampier Peninsula on privateer Charles Swan's ship, the *Cygnet*. In the weeks the ship was careened he undertook preliminary exploration of the country. He returned to Australia in 1699, in command of the *Roebuck*, and landed much further south in Shark Bay. Dampier was the first European to record the fauna and flora of Australia in any detail. He published the accounts of his explorations in Australia in two best-selling books, *A New Voyage Around the World* (1697) and *A Voyage to New Holland* (1703).

Dampier collected 24 plant specimens, representing 23 species, on his second visit to the continent.[6] Carefully following a recently published anonymous pamphlet that had been 'Drawn up at the Request of a Person of Honour and presented to the Royal Society' – *Brief Instructions for Making Observations in all Parts of the World: as also for Collecting, Preserving, and Sending over Natural Things. Being an Attempt to Settle an Universal Correspondence for the*

Advancement of Knowledg [sic] both Natural and Civil (1696) – he preserved them for transport back to England. However, en route at Ascension Island the *Roebuck* sprang leaks and was abandoned. Stranded on the island for five weeks, Dampier and his crew were finally rescued by a passing Royal Navy ship and taken to Barbados. The only item that Dampier rescued from the *Roebuck* was his personal trunk. Fortunately, inside was his herbarium with his 24 plants. From Barbados they transferred to another ship and arrived back in England in 1701.[7] He promptly handed his plants over to the man who had, in fact, written the *Brief Instructions* pamphlet, whose advice on their preservation had ensured the safe transit of the first Australian plants to England.[8] And this was the same man who, eleven years earlier, one cold January morning in 1690, had been wandering through an icy vineyard and chanced upon a small, pebble-like shell – John Woodward.

REFERENCES

ONE: A TIMELESS OBSESSION

1 John Feliks, 'The Impact of Fossils on the Development of Visual Representation', *Rock Art Research*, XV (1998), p. 112.

2 W. Bray, ed., *Memoirs, Illustrative of the Life and Writings of John Evelyn, Esq. F.R.S.*, vol. II (London, 1819), p. 16.

3 J. Woodward, *An Attempt Towards a Natural History of the Fossils of England: In a Catalogue of the English fossils in the Collection of J. Woodward*, vol. I, Pt 2 (London, 1729), p. 1.

4 M. Lister, 'A letter of Mr Martin Lister, written at York August 25, 1671, confirming the observation in No. 74, about Musk sented [*sic*] insects; adding some notes upon D. Swammerdam's book of insects, and on that of M. Steno concerning petrify'd shell', *Philosophical Transactions*, VI (1671), p. 2282.

5 R. Hooke, *Micrographia; or, Some Physiological Descriptions of Minute Bodies Made by Magnifying Glasses, with Observations and Inquiries Thereupon* (London, 1665).

6 A. Scilla, *La vana speculazione disingannata dal senso* (Naples, 1670).

7 J. Woodward, *Fossils of all Kinds, Digested into a Method, Suitable to their Mutual Relation and Affinity* (London, 1728), p. 10.

8 Ibid., p. 11.

9 J. Parkinson, *Organic Remains of a Former World: An Examination of the Mineralized Remains of the Vegetables and Animals of the Antediluvian World Generally Termed Extraneous Fossils* (London, 1804), pp. 2–4.

10 A. Mayor, *The First Fossil Hunters: Paleontology in Greek and Roman Times* (Princeton, NJ, 2000).

11 C. J. Duffin, 'Fossils as Drugs: Pharmaceutical Palaeontology', *Ferrantia* (Luxembourg, 2008).

12 K. J. McNamara, 'Fossil Echinoids from Neolithic and Iron Age Sites in Jordan', in *Echinoids: Munich*, ed. T. Heinzeller and J. Nebelsick (Rotterdam, 2004), pp. 459–66; K. J. McNamara, *The Star-crossed Stone: The Secret Life, Myths and History of a Fascinating Fossil* (Chicago, IL, 2011).

13 K. P. Oakley, 'Folklore of Fossils', *Antiquity*, XXXIX (1965), pp. 117–25.

14 Mayor, *The First Fossil Hunters*.

TWO: IN THE MYTHS OF TIME

1 P. B. Hall, 'Robert Swinhoe (1836–1877), FRS, FZS, FRGS: A Victorian Naturalist in Treaty Port China', *Geographical Journal*, CLIII (1987), pp. 37–47.

2 R. Swinhoe, 'Zoological Notes of a Journey from Canton to Peking and Kalgan', *Proceedings of the Zoological Society of London*, XXIX (1870), pp. 427–51.

3 J. G. Andersson, *Children of the Yellow Earth* (London, 1934), p. 71.

4 Ibid.

5 A. Forke, trans., *Lun Heng Philosophical Essays of Wang Ch'ung* (New York, 1962), p. 357.

6 Andersson, *Children of the Yellow Earth*, p. 74.

7 J. Chinnery, 'China's Heavenly Mandate', in *Mythology: The Illustrated Anthology of World Myth and Storytelling*, ed. C. S. Littleton (San Diego, CA, 2002), p. 404.

8 R. Owen, 'On Fossil Remains Found in China', *Quarterly Journal of the Geological Society of London*, XXVI (1870), pp. 417–36.

9 J. P. McCormick and J. Parascandola, 'Dragon Bones and Drugstores: The Interaction of Pharmacy and Paleontology in the Search for Early Man in China', *Pharmacy in History*, XXIII (1981), p. 56.

10 Ibid.

11 Ibid, p. 57.

12 C. Manias, 'From *Terra incognita* to Garden of Eden: Unveiling the Prehistoric Life of China and Central Asia, 1900–30', in *Treaty Ports in Modern China: Law, Land and Power*, ed. R. Bickers and I. Jackson (London, 2016), p. 185.

13 Ibid., pp. 2016 and 186; Andersson, *Children of the Yellow Earth*, p. 76.

14 M. Schlosser, 'Die fossilen Säugethiere Chinas nebst einer
    Odonto-graphie der recenten Antilopen', *Abhandlungen der
    mathematisch-physikalischen Klasse der königlich Bayerischen
    Akademie der Wissenschaften*, XXII (1906), pp. 5 and 6.

15 Andersson, *Children of the Yellow Earth*, p. 78.

16 Ibid., p. 77.

17 Ibid., pp. 74–80.

18 Ibid., p. 97.

19 Pliny the Elder, *The Historie of the World: Commonly Called,
    The Naturall Historie of C. Plinius Secundus*, trans. Philemon Holland,
    Doctor of Physicke, vol. I (London, 1634), chap. XXXVII, p. 10.
    This translation is preferred to later nineteenth-century and
    twentieth-century translations because it lacks omissions found
    in those editions and is generally a more accurate translation.

20 Agricola quoted in F. D. Adams, *The Birth and Development of the
    Geological Sciences* (New York, 1954), p. 118.

21 R. Plot, *The Natural History of Oxford-shire, Being an Essay toward
    the Natural History of England* (Oxford, 1677), p. 90.

22 H. R. Ellis Davidson, *Myths and Symbols in Pagan Europe: Early
    Scandinavian and Celtic Religions* (Manchester, 1988), pp. 204–5.

23 K. J. McNamara, *The Star-crossed Stone: The Secret Life, Myths and
    History of a Fascinating Fossil* (Chicago, IL, 2011), pp. 145–53.

24 Mark 3:17, King James version: 'And James the son of Zebedee, and
    John the brother of James; and he surnamed them Boanerges, which
    is, The sons of thunder.'

25 McNamara, *The Star-crossed Stone*, p. 48.

26 S. Leslie et al., 'The Fine-scale Genetic Structure of the British
    Population', *Nature*, DIXX (2015), p. 313.

27 J. Kershaw and E. C. Røyrvik, 'The "People of the British Isles" Project
    and Viking Settlement in England', *Antiquity*, XC (2016),
    pp. 1670–80.

28 McNamara, *The Star-crossed Stone*, p. 145.

29 I have to admit that when I was young, and growing up in Sussex, after
    a storm I would rush outside and look for the thunderbolt. What I was
    looking for, though, wasn't a fossil, but what I now know to be nodules
    of iron pyrite that often occur in the Chalk.

30 McNamara, *The Star-crossed Stone*, pp. 135–8.

31 Ibid., p. 127.

THREE: THE STUFF OF LEGENDS

1 J. Needham, *Science and Civilization in China*, vol. III: *Mathematics and the Sciences of the Heavens and the Earth* (Cambridge, 1959), p. 615.

2 K. P. Oakley, 'Animal Fossils as Charms', in *Animals in Folklore*, ed. J. R. Porter and W.M.S. Russell (Cambridge, 1978), p. 214.

3 Ibid.

4 C. C. Emig, '*Nummulus brattenburgensis* and *Crania craniolaris* (Brachiopoda, Craniidae)', *Carnets de Géologie* (2009), p. 1.

5 Ibid.

6 K. J. McNamara and S. P. Radford, 'Professor Tennant's Fossils: A Founding Collection of the Western Australian Museum', *Studies in Western Australian History* (in press).

7 The fossils had been sent to Bernard Woodward by his uncle, Henry Woodward, Keeper of Geology at the Natural History Museum in London. See ibid.

8 A. G. Credland, 'Flint Jack – A Memoir', *Geological Curator*, III (1983), pp. 435–43.

9 W. Camden, *Britannia; or, A Chorographical Description of Great Britain and Ireland, Together with the Adjacent Islands*, trans. W. Gibson (London, 1722), p. 109.

10 Pliny the Elder, *The Historie of the World; Commonly Called, The Naturall Historie of C. Plinius Secundus*, trans. Philemon Holland, Doctor of Physicke, vol. I (London, 1634), Book XXXVII, chap. LX.

11 Gaius Julius Solinus, quoted in C. M. Nelson, 'Ammonites: Ammon's Horns into Cephalopods', *Journal of the Society for the Bibliography of Natural History*, V (1968), p. 2.

12 J. G. Frazer, *The Golden Bough: A Study in Magic and Religion*, 3rd edn (London, 1911), vol. II, p. 26.

13 M. Lister, 'A Description of Certain Stones Figured like Plants, and By Some Observing Men Esteemed to be Plants Petrified', *Philosophical Transactions*, VIII (1673), p. 6186.

14 T. Nicols, *A Lapidary; or, The History of Pretious Stones: With cautions for the Undeceiving of all Those that Deal with Pretious Stones* (Cambridge, 1652).

15 O. Abel, *Vorzeitliche Tierreste im Deutschen Mythus, Brauchtum und Volksglauben* (Jena, 1939).

16 E. Lankester, ed., *Memorials of John Ray, Consisting of his Life by Dr Derham, Biographical and Critical Notices by Sir J. E. Smith, and Cuvier and Dupetit Thouars, With his Itineraries, etc.* (London, 1846), pp. 150–51.

17 N. G. Lane and W. I. Ausich, 'The Legend of St Cuthbert's Beads: A Palaeontological and Geological Perspective', *Folklore*, CXII (2001), p. 66.

18 F. Grose, *The Antiquities of England and Wales*, vol. IV (London, 1783), p. 120.

19 B. Faussett, *Inventorium Sepulchrale: An Account of some Antiquities Dug up at Gilton, Kingston, Sibertswold, Barfriston, Beakesbourne, Chartham, and Crundale, in the County of Kent, from AD 1757 to AD 1773* (London, 1856).

20 The specimens excavated by Faussett are now housed in the Liverpool Museum.

21 Faussett, *Inventorium Sepulchrale*, p. 69.

22 J. Woodward, *An Attempt Towards a Natural History of the Fossils of England: In a Catalogue of the English Fossils in the Collection of J. Woodward*, vol. I (London, 1729), vol. II (London, 1728).

23 H. Hurd, 'Exhibit of Finds from Graves in Anglo-Saxon Cemetery at Broadstairs', *Proceedings of the Society of Antiquaries*, XXIII (1910), pp. 272–6.

24 H. Taylor, 'The Tyning's Barrow Group: Second Report', *Proceedings of the University of Bristol Speleological Society*, IV (1933), p. 92.

25 R. F. Read, 'Second Report on the Excavation of the Mendip Barrows', *Proceedings of the University of Bristol Speleological Society*, II (1924), p. 145, pl. X, no. 6.

26 K. P. Oakley, 'Decorative and Symbolic Uses of Fossils', *Pitt Rivers Museum University of Oxford, Occasional Papers on Technology*, XIII (1985), p. 38.

27 J. W. Jude, ' La Grotte de Rochereil, Station Magdalénienne et Azilienne', *Archives de l'Institut de paléontologie humaine*, XXX (1960), p. 38.

28 N. Goren-Inbar et al., 'Pleistocene Milestones of the Out-of-Africa Corridor at Gesher Benot Ya'aqov, Israel', *Science*, CCLIIIIX (2000), pp. 944–7; and N. Alperson-Afil et al., 'Spatial Organization of Hominin Activities at Gesher Benot Ya'aqov, Israel', *Science*, CCCXXVI (2009), pp. 1677–80.

29 N. Goren-Inbar, Z. Lewy and M. E. Kislev, 'The Taphonomy of a Bead-like Fossil from the Acheulian of Gesher Benot Ya'aqov, Israel', *Rock Art Research*, VIII (1991), pp. 83–7.

30 R. G. Bednarik, 'Middle Pleistocene Beads and Symbolism', *Anthropos*, C (2005), pp. 537–52.

FOUR: FASHIONING THE STONE

1 J. Burnby, 'John Conyers, London's First Archaeologist', *London and Middlesex Archaeological Society*, XXXV (1984).

2 Ibid., p. 64.

3 British Library, Harl MS 5933, ff. 112–13, and ibid., p. 65.

4 K. J. McNamara, *The Star-crossed Stone: The Secret Life, Myths and History of a Fascinating Fossil* (Chicago, IL, 2011), p. 22.

5 J. Feliks, 'The Impact of Fossils on the Development of Visual Representation', *Rock Art Research*, XV (1998), pp. 109–34.

6 K. P. Oakley, 'Decorative and Symbolic Uses of Fossils', *Pitt Rivers Museum University of Oxford, Occasional Papers on Technology*, XIII (1985), pp. 27–8.

7 F. Poplin, 'Aux origines néandertaliennes de l'Art. Matière, forme, symétries. Contribution d'une galène et d'un oursin fossile taillé de Merry-sur-Yonne (France)', *L'Homme de Néandertal*, vol. V: *La Pensée* (Liège, 1988), pp. 109–16.

8 D. L. Hoffmann et al., 'U-Th Dating of Carbonate Crusts Reveals Neandertal Origin of Iberian Cave Art', *Science*, CCCDIX (2018), pp. 912–15.

9 F. A. Karakostis et al., 'Evidence for Precision Grasping in Neandertal Daily Activities', *Science Advances*, IV (2018).

10 D. Néraudeau, 'Les silex fossilifères du nord du littoral Charentais et leur utilisation au Paléolithique', *Bulletin A.M.A.R.A.I.*, no. 17 (2004).

11 McNamara, *Star-crossed Stone*, p. 91.

12 K. J. McNamara, 'Fossil Echinoids from Neolithic and Iron Age Sites in Jordan', in *Echinoids: Munich*, ed. T. Heinzeller and J. Nebelsick (Rotterdam, 2004), pp. 459–66.

13 K. J. McNamara, 'Fossil Echinoids', in *Basta IV.1: The Small Find and Ornament Industries*, ed. H.G.K. Gebel, Bibliotheca neolithica Asiae meridionalis et occidentalis and Yarmouk University, Monograph of the Faculty of Archaeology and Anthropology (in press).

14 D. Reese, K. J. McNamara and C. Sease, 'Fossil and Marine Invertebrates', in *Busayra: Excavations by Crystal M. Bennett, 1971–1980*, ed. P. Bienkowski, British Academy, Monographs in Archaeology (2002), pp. 441–63.

15 F. Demnard and D. Néraudeau, 'L'utilisation des oursines fossilies de la Préhistoire à l'époque gallo-romaine', *Bulletin de la Société préhistorique Française*, XCVIII (2001), pp. 693–715.

16 McNamara, *Star-crossed Stone*, p. 210.

17 S. L. Kuhn et al. 'Ornaments of the Earliest Upper Paleolithic: New Insights from the Levant', *Proceedings of the National Academy of Sciences*, XCVIII (2001), pp. 7641–6.

18 Ibid., p. 7645.

19 P. Valde-Nowak, A. Nadachowski and M. Wolsan, 'Upper Palaeolithic Boomerang Made of a Mammoth Tusk in South Poland', *Nature*, CCCXXIX (1987), pp. 436–8.

20 P. Valde-Nowak, 'Worked *Conus* Shells as Pavlovian Fingerprint: Obłazowa Cave, Southern Poland', *Quaternary International*, CCCDIX–X (2015), pp. 153–6.

21 Valde-Nowak et al., 'Upper Palaeolithic Boomerang', p. 438.

22 A. A. Sinitsyn, 'Figurative and Decorative Art of Kostenki: Chronological and Cultural Differentiation', in *L'Art Pléistocene dans le Monde*, ed. J. Clottes (Tarascon-sur-Ariège, 2012), pp. 1339–59.

23 D. Nuzhnyi, 'The Latest Epigravettian Assemblages of the Middle Dnieper Basin (northern Ukraine)', *Archaeologia Baltica*, VII (2005), pp. 58–93.

24 A. Ficatier, 'Étude Paléoethnologique sur la Grotte Magdalénienne di Trilobite à Arcy-sur-Cure (Yonne)', in *Almanach historique de l'Yonne*, ed. A. Gallet (Auxerre, 1887), pp. 3–25.

25 Sinitsyn, 'Figurative and Decorative Art' (2012).

26 M. Vanhaeren and F. d'Errico, 'Aurignacian Ethno-linguistic Geography of Europe Revealed by Personal Ornaments', *Journal of Archaeological Science*, XXXIII (2006), pp. 1105–128.

27 M. Peresani et al., 'An Ochered Fossil Marine Shell from the Mousterian of Fumane Cave, Italy', *Plos One*, VIII/7 (2013) E68572, https://doi.org/10.1371/journal.pone.0068572.

28 M. Soressi and F. d'Errico, 'Pigments, Gravures, Parures: Les comportements symboliques controversés de Néandertaliens',

in *Les Néandertaliens: Biologie et culture*, ed. B. Vandermeersch and B. Maureille (Paris, 2007), pp. 297–309.

29 D. L. Hoffmann et al., 'Symbolic Use of Marine Shells and Mineral Pigments by Iberian Neandertals 115,000 Years Ago', *Science Advances*, IV (2018), 10.1126/sciadv.aar5255.

30 Hoffmann et al., 'U-Th Dating of Carbonate Crusts', pp. 912–15.

FIVE: DELIGHTING THE MIND

1 G. O. Rollefson, A. H. Simmons and Z. Kafafi, 'Neolithic Cultures at 'Ain Ghazal, Jordan', *Journal of Field Archaeology*, XIX (1992), pp. 443–70.

2 K. J. McNamara, 'Fossil Echinoids from Neolithic and Iron Age Sites in Jordan', in *Echinoids: Munich*, ed. T. Heinzeller and J. Nebelsick (Rotterdam, 2004), pp. 459–66.

3 J. Black, 'Ancient Mesopotamia', in *Mythology: The Illustrated Anthology of World Myth and Storytelling*, ed. C. S. Littleton (San Diego, CA, 2002), pp. 82–133 (p. 5).

4 L. Liu et al., 'Fermented Beverage and Food Storage in 13,000-y-old Stone Mortars at Raqefet Cave, Israel: Investigating Natufian Ritual Feasting', *Journal of Archaeological Sciences: Reports*, XXI (2018), pp. 783–93.

5 A. Arranz-Otaegui et al., 'Archaeobotanical Evidence Reveals the Origins of Bread 14,400 Years Ago in Northeastern Jordan', *PNAS*, CXV/31 (2018), pp. 7925–30.

6 P. C. Edwards, 'Visual Representations in Stone and Bone', in *Wadi Hammeh 27: An Early Natufian Settlement at Pella in Jordan*, ed. P. C. Edwards (Leiden, 2013), pp. 287–320.

7 P. C. Edwards et al., 'The Natural Inspiration for Natufian Art: Cases from Wadi Hammeh 27, Jordan', *Cambridge Archaeological Journal*, XXIX (2019), pp. 607–24.

8 Ibid., fig. 2.

9 Ibid., fig. 5.

10 Ibid., figs 3, 4.

11 Ibid., figs 6, 7.

12 K. P. Oakley, 'Animal Fossils as Charms', in *Animals in Folklore*, ed. J. R. Porter and W.M.S. Russell (Cambridge, 1978), pp. 208–40.

13 C. Ankel, 'Ein fossiler Seeigel vom Euzenberg bie Duderstadt (Süd Hanover)', *Die Kunde. Niedersächsischer Landesverein für Urgeschichte. Sonerdruck*, IX (1958), pp. 130–35.

14 M. Connolly, *Discovering the Neolithic in County Kerry: A Passage Tomb at Ballycarty* (Wicklow, 1999).

15 Ibid.

16 P. N. Wyse and M. Connolly, 'Fossils as Neolithic Funereal Adornments in County Kerry, South-west Ireland', *Geology Today*, XVIII (2002), pp. 139–43.

17 H. O. Hencken, 'A Tumulus at Carrowlisdooaun, County Mayo', *Journal of the Royal Society of Antiquaries of Ireland*, V (1935), pp. 74–83.

18 A. Lynch et al., 'Newgrange Revisited: New Insights from Excavations at the Back of the Mound in 1984–8', *Journal of Irish Archaeology*, XXIII (2014), pp. 13–82.

19 E. Lhwyd, 'Several Observations Relating to the Antiquities and Natural History of Ireland, made by Mr Edw. Lhwyd, in his Travels thro' that Kingdom. In a Letter to Dr. Tancred Robinson, Fellow of the College of Physicians and Royal Society', *Philosophical Transactions*, XXVII (1710), pp. 503–6.

20 J. Feliks, 'The Impact of Fossils on the Development of Visual Representation', *Rock Art Research*, XV (1998), pp. 109–34.

21 R. White, 'The Earliest Images: Ice Age "Art" in Europe', *Expedition*, XXXIV (1992), pp. 37–51, and R. White, 'Technological and Social Dimensions of "Aurignacian-age" Body Ornaments across Europe', in *Before Lascaux: The Complex Record of the Early Upper Paleolithic*, ed. H. Knecht et al. (Boca Raton, FL, 1993), pp. 277–99.

22 K. P. Oakley, 'Folklore of Fossils', *Antiquity*, XXXIX (1965), pp. 117–25.

23 A. Leroi-Gourhan, *Treasures of Prehistoric Art* (New York, 1967), p. 515.

24 Ibid., p. 514.

SIX: SAVING THE SOUL

1 The specimen is housed in the Museo Egizio, Turin. Its registration number is 2761.

2 E. Scamuzzi, 'Fossile Eocenico con Iscrizione Geroglifica rinvenuto in Eliopoli', *Bolletino della Societa Piemontese di Archeologia e di Belle Arte*, n.s. 1 (1947), pp. 11–14.

3 I. M. Schumacher, *Der Gott Sopdu – der Herr der Fremvölker,* (Fribourg, 1988).

4 Susanne Binder, personal communication, 2006.

5 I. Shaw and P. Nicholson, *British Museum Dictionary of Ancient Egypt* (London, 1995), pp. 275–6.

6 Pyramid text 357; 929; 935; 1707. This translation from the Pyramid text, like subsequent ones in this book, is from *The Ancient Egyptian Pyramid Texts*, trans. R. O. Faulkner (Oxford, 1969).

7 D. J. Brewer and E. Teeter, *Egypt and the Egyptians* (Cambridge, 1999).

8 These are the burial chambers of Unas (Dynasty v), Teti (Dynasty vi), Pepy i, Merenre, Pepy ii, Queen Ankhesenmeryre ii, Queen Neith, Queen Iput ii, Queen Wedjebten, King Ibi (Dynasty viii).

9 D. Price, 'Minerals and Fossils', in *The Egyptian Mining Temple at Timna*, ed. B. Rothenberg (London, 1988), pp. 266–7.

10 W. M. Flinders Petrie, *Researches in Sinai* (New York, 1906), p. 69.

11 Ibid., p. 70.

12 P. du Chatellier, *Les Époques Préhistoriques et Gauloises dans la Finistère* (Paris, 1907).

13 G. Chauvet, 'Ovum anguinum', *Revue Archéologique*, i (1900), pp. 281–5.

14 R. J. Schulting, "'. . . Pursuing a Rabbit in Burrington Combe": New Research on the Early Mesolithic Burial Cave of Aveline's Hole', *Proceedings of the University of Bristol Spelaeological Society*, xxiii (2005), pp. 171–265.

15 J. A. Davies, 'Fourth Report on Aveline's Hole', *Proceedings of the University of Bristol Spelaeological Society*, ii (1925), pp. 104–14.

16 D. T. Donovan, 'The Ammonites and Other Fossils from Aveline's Hole (Burrington Combe, Somerset)', *Proceedings of the University of Bristol Spelaeological Society*, xi (1968), pp. 237–42.

17 Ibid.

18 E. Salin, *La Civilisation Mérovingienne*, vol. iv (Paris, 1959), pp. 69 and 70.

19 L. Gardeła and C. Larrington, eds, *Viking Myths and Rituals on the Isle of Man* (Nottingham, 2014), p. 33.

20 D. Krausse et al., 'The "Keltenblock" Project: Discovery and Excavation of a Rich Hallstatt Grave at the Heuneburg, Germany', *Antiquity*, xci (2017), pp. 108–23.

21 Ibid., p. 117.

22 S. West, *The Anglo-Saxon Cemetery at Westgarth Gardens, Bury St Edmunds, Suffolk*, East Anglian Archaeology, Report No. 38 (1988), p. 32, figs 42, 73H.

23 B. Ó Donnchadha, 'The Oldest Church in Ireland's Oldest Town', *Archaeology Ireland* (Spring 2007), pp. 8–10.

24 F. Demnard and D. Néraudeau, 'L'utilisation des oursines fossilies de la Préhistoire à l'époque gallo-romaine', *Bulletin de la Société préhistorique Française*, XCVIII (2001), pp. 693–715.

25 B. Schmidt, 'Die spate Völkerwanderungszeit in Mitteldeutschland', *Veröffentlichungen des Landesmuseums für Vorgeschichte in Halle*, XXV (1970), pl. 3, fig. 2.

26 L.H.D. Buxton, 'Excavations at Frilford', *Antiquaries Journal*, I (1921), pp. 87–97.

27 B. Arnold, '"Soul Stones": Unmodified Quartz and Other Lithic Material in Early Iron Age Burials', in *Archaeological, Cultural and Linguistic Heritage: Festschrift for Erzsébet Jerem in Honour of her 70th Birthday*, ed. P. Anreiter et al. (Budapest, 2012), pp. 47–56.

28 Ibid.

29 T. Malim and J. Hines, 'The Anglo-Saxon Cemetery at Edix Hill (Barrington A), Cambridgeshire: Excavations 1989–1991 and a Summary Catalogue of Material from the 19th Century Interventions', *Council for British Archaeology Research Reports*, CXII (1998), pp. 1–343.

30 E. C. Curwen, *The Archaeology of Sussex* (London, 1954), p. 82.

31 Ibid., pp. 81 and 82.

32 W. G. Smith, *Man, the Primeval Savage* (London, 1894).

33 Ibid., p. 338.

34 This barrow is also known as the Woodchester Beaker Barrow. 'Barrow' is the name given to a burial or ceremonial mound in England. They range in age from the Neolithic (about 6,000 years ago) to the Iron Age (which ended about 2,000 years ago). They are also sometimes known as tumuli.

35 K. P. Oakley, 'Animal Fossils as Charms', in *Animals in Folklore*, ed. J. R. Porter and W.M.S. Russell (Cambridge, 1978), p. 213.

36 P. Raymond, 'L'oursin fossile et les idées religieuses à l'époque préhistorique', *La Revue Préhistorique, Annales de Paléoethnologie*, II (1907), pp. 133–9.

37 S. Heaney, trans.; *Beowulf* (London, 1999).

38 K. Boyadziev, 'Real Arrows or "Darts from Heaven"? Some Ideas on the Interpretation of Belemnites from Neolithic and Chalcolithic Sites in Bulgaria', in *Geoarchaeology and Archaeomineralogy*, ed. R. I. Kostov, B. Gaydarska and M. Gurova (Sofia, 2008), pp. 288–90.

SEVEN: PROTECTING THE BODY

1 'An amulet may be broadly defined as . . . a material object through whose retention there is sought the averting of some result displeasing, or the obtaining of some outcome pleasing, to the possessor of that object, and in a way which seems to be beyond natural laws as proclaimed by persons best qualified to understand them. Primarily it is the retention of the object, for the sake of its presumed apotropaic, medicinal, or magical virtues, which marks it as an amulet.' W. L. Hildburgh, 'Psychology Underlying the Employment of Amulets in Europe', *Folklore*, LXII (1951), p. 231.

2 S. A. Barrett, 'The Blackfoot Iniskim or Buffalo Bundle, Its Origin and Use', *Year Book of the Public Museum of the City of Milwaukee*, 1 (1921), pp. 80–84, fig. 46.

3 T. R. Peck, 'Archaeologically Recovered Ammonites: Evidence for Long-term Continuity of Nitsitapii [*sic*] Ritual', *Plains Anthropologist*, XLVII (2002), pp. 147–64; B. Reeves, 'Iniskim: A Sacred Nitsitapii Religious Tradition', in *Kunaitupii: Coming Together on Native Sacred Sites, Their Sacredness, Conservation, and Interpretation* (Calgary, 1993), pp. 194–259.

4 C. Wissler and D. C. Duvall, 'Mythology of the Blackfoot Indians', *Anthropological Papers of the American Museum of Natural History*, 11 (1909), pp. 1–164.

5 Barrett, 'The Blackfoot Iniskim'.

6 Reeves, 'Iniskim'.

7 R. Scriver, *The Blackfeet: Artists of the Northern Plains* (Kansas City, KS, 1990).

8 A. L. Kroeber, 'Ethnology of the Gros Ventre', *American Museum of Natural History, Anthropological Papers*, 1/4 (1908).

9 Peck, 'Archaeologically Recovered Ammonites'.

10 K. Akerman, 'Two Aboriginal Charms Incorporating Fossil Giant Marsupial Teeth', *Western Australian Naturalist*, XII/6 (1973), pp. 139–41.

11 Kim Akerman, personal communication, 21 January 2019.

12 Ibid.

13 R. Vanderwal and R. Fullagar, 'Engraved *Diprotodon* Tooth from the Spring Creek Locality, Victoria', *Archaeology in Oceania*, XXIV (1989), pp. 13–16.

14 Pliny the Elder, *The Historie of the World: Commonly Called, The Naturall History of C. Plinius Secundus*, trans. Philemon Holland, Doctor of Physicke, vol. I (London, 1634), Book XXXVII, chap. 10.

15 G. Zammit-Maempel, 'Fossil Sharks' Teeth: A Medieval Safeguard Against Poisoning', *Melita Historica*, VI (1975), p. 394.

16 C. Duffin, '*Natternzungen Kredenz*: Tableware for the Renaissance Nobility', *Jewellery History Today* (Spring 2012), p. 4.

17 M. Karamanou et al., 'Toxicology in the Borgias Period: The Mystery of the *Cantarella* Poison', *Toxicology Research and Application*, II (2018), p. 2.

18 M. E. Taylor and R. A. Robison, 'Trilobites in Utah folklore', *Brigham Young University Geology Studies*, XXIII (1976), pp. 1–5.

19 Ibid., p. 2.

20 Ibid., p. 3.

21 H. Toms, 'Wear a Porosphaera?', *Sussex Daily News*, Thursday 26 May 1932, p. 6.

22 H. Toms, 'An Early Bead Necklace found at Higham, Kent', *The Rochester Naturalist* (May 1932), pp. 1–8; C. Duffin, 'Herbert Toms (1874–1940), Witch Stones, and Porosphaera Beads', *Folklore*, CXXII (2011), p. 95.

23 A. L. Meaney, 'Anglo-Saxon Amulets and Curing Stones', *BAR British Series*, no. 96 (1981), p. 115.

24 Ibid., p. 116.

25 Ibid.

26 W. G. Smith, *Man, the Primeval Savage* (London, 1894).

27 S. Rigaud et al., 'Critical Reassessment of Putative Acheulean *Porosphaera globularis* Beads', *Journal of Archaeological Science*, XXXVI (2009), pp. 25–34.

28 R. G. Bednarik, 'Middle Pleistocene Beads and Symbolism', *Anthropos*, C (2005), pp. 537–52.

29 H. Toms, 'Shepherds' Crowns in Archaeology and Folklore', unpublished presentation to the meeting of the Brighton Natural History Society, 6 January 1940.

30 G. E. Evans, *The Pattern Under the Plough: Aspects of the Folk-life of East Anglia* (London, 1966).

31 K. J. McNamara, *The Star-crossed Stone: The Secret Life, Myths and History of a Fascinating Fossil* (Chicago, IL, 2011), p. 131.

32 J. H. Pull, 'Shepherds' Crowns – The Survival of Belief in their Magical Virtues in Sussex', *West Sussex Geological Society Occasional Publication*, no. 3 (2003), pp. 33 and 35.

33 McNamara, *The Star-crossed Stone*, p. 119.

34 Mikael Siversson, personal communication, 2005.

35 C. Blinkenberg, *The Thunderweapon in Religion and Folklore: A Study in Comparative Archaeology* (Cambridge, 1911), p. 81.

36 Ibid., p. 82.

37 Pull, 'Shepherds' Crowns', pp. 33 and 35.

38 Ibid.

39 N. H. Field, 'Fossil Sea-echinoids from a Romano-British Site', *Antiquity*, XXXIX (1965), p. 298.

40 McNamara, *The Star-crossed Stone*, p. 18.

41 G. S. Tyack, *Lore and Legend of the English Church*, ed. William Andrews (London, 1899).

42 A. and B. Smith, personal communication, 2004.

EIGHT: CURING THE BODY

1 George Fabian Lawrence quoted in the *Daily Herald* (1937), quoted in H. Forsyth, *The Cheapside Hoard* (London, 2003).

2 Forsyth, *The Cheapside Hoard*.

3 J. Jonstonus, *An History of the Wonderful Things of Nature: Set Forth in Ten severall Classes . . . And now Rendered into English by a Person of Quality* (London, 1657), p. 116.

4 C. J. Duffin, 'Fossils as Drugs: Pharmaceutical Palaeontology', *Ferrantia*, LIV (2008), p. 44.

5 Forsyth, *The Cheapside Hoard*.

6 Ibid.

7 J. Evans, *Magical Jewels of the Middle Ages and the Renaissance Particularly in England* (Oxford, 1922), p. 19.

8 E. Topsell, *The History of Four-footed Beasts and Serpents* (London, 1658), p. 727.

9 D. Wyckoff, *Albertus Magnus Book of Minerals* (Oxford, 1967), p. 76.

10 C. Leonardus, *The Mirror of Stones: in which the Nature, Generation, Properties, Virtues and Various Species of More Than 200 Different Jewells, are Distinctly Described* (London, 1750), p. 77.

11 S. Batman, *Uppon Bartholome, His Booke de Proprietatibus Rerum* (London, 1582), p. 263.

12 Duffin, 'Fossils as Drugs', p. 43.

13 J. G. Andersson, *Children of the Yellow Earth* (London, 1934).

14 The *hun*-soul is the ethereal soul, as opposed to the *po*-soul, our corporeal soul. It is our creative and poetic soul.

15 Yang Shouzhong, trans., *The Divine Farmer's Materia Medica* (Boulder, CO, 1998).

16 Yang Yifang, *Chinese Herbal Medicines: Comparisons and Characteristics* (London, 2002).

17 G.J.B. Moura and U. P. Albuquerque, 'The First Report on the Medicinal Use of Fossils in Latin America', *Evidence-based Complementary and Alternative Medicine,* Article ID 69171 (2012), p. 2.

18 S. Natarajan et al., 'Nandukkal, A Fossil Crab used in Siddha Medicine and its Therapeutic Usage – A Review', *Malaya Journal of Biosciences,* 11 (2015), pp. 110–14.

19 J. Woodward, *An Attempt Towards a Natural History of the Fossils of England: In a Catalogue of the English Fossils in the Collection of J. Woodward*, vol. 1, Pt 2 (London, 1729), p. 109.

20 [J. Woodward], *Brief Instructions for Making Observations in all Parts of the World: As also for Collecting, Preserving, and Sending over Natural Things. Being an Attempt to settle an Universal Correspondence for the Advancement of Knowledge both Natural and Civil* (London, 1696).

21 Woodward, *An Attempt Towards a Natural History of the Fossils of England*, p. 109.

22 These are 'bots' or the larvae of the equine fly *Gasterophilus*.

23 M. Martin, *A Description of the Western Islands of Scotland* (London, 1703), p. 134.

24 H. Miller, *The Old Red Sandstone* (London, 1841), pp. 10–13.

25 R. Plot, *The Natural History of Oxford-shire, Being an Essay Toward the Natural History of England*, 2nd edn (Oxford, 1705), p. 96.

26 J. Woodward, *Fossils of all Kinds, Digested into a Method, Suitable to their Mutual Relation and Affinity* (London, 1729), p. 17.

27 Duffin, 'Fossils as Drugs', p. 12.

28 P. Tahil, *De Virtutibus Lapidum: The Virtues of Stones Attributed to Damigeron* (Seattle, WA, 1989), p. 4.

29 Dioscorides quoted in Duffin, 'Fossils as Drugs', p. 13.

30 P. Riethe, *Das Buch von den Steinen. Hildegard von Bingen; nach den Quellen übersetzt und erläutert von Peter Riethe* (Salzburg, 1997), p. 110.

31 Duffin, 'Fossils as Drugs', p. 23.

32 Ibid.

33 T. Nicols, *A Lapidary; or, The History of Pretious Stones: With Cautions for the Undeceiving of All Those That Deal with Pretious Stones* (Cambridge, 1652), p. 203.

34 Woodward, *An Attempt Towards a Natural History of the Fossils of England*, p. 8.

35 Technically, all the different types of sea urchin spines are known as 'radioles'.

36 C. O. van Regteren Altena, 'Molluscs and Echinoderms from Palaeolithic Deposits in the Rock Shelter of Ksar'Akil, Lebanon', *Zoologische Mededelingen*, XXXVIII (1962), pp. 87–99.

37 E. Lev, 'Reconstructed *materia medica* of the Medieval and Ottoman al-Sham', *Journal of Ethnopharmacology*, LXXX (2000), pp. 167–79; E. Lev and Z. Amar, 'Ethnopharmacological Survey of Traditional Drugs Sold in the Kingdom of Jordan', *Journal of Ethnopharmacology*, LXXXII (2002), pp. 131–45.

38 O. Fraas, 'Geologisches aus dem Libanon', *Jahrbuch des Vereins für Vaterländische Naturkunde in Württemburg*, XXXIV (1878), pp. 257–81.

39 R. T. Gunther, *The Greek Herbal of Dioscorides Illustrated by a Byzantine AD 512, Englished by John Goodyer AD 1655* (London, 1968), p. 655.

40 Ibid.

41 C. J. Duffin, 'Lapis Judaicus or the Jews' Stone: The Folklore of Fossil Echinoid Spines', *Proceedings of the Geologists' Association*, CXVII (2006), pp. 265–75.

42 W. Bruel, *Praxis Medicinae, or, The Physicians Practice Wherein are Contained Inward Diseases from the Head to the Foote*, 2nd edn (London, 1639), p. 334.

43 Duffin, 'Lapis Judaicus', p. 267; Duffin, 'Fossils as Drugs', p. 31.

44 C. Wirtzung, *The General Practise of Physicke. Conteyning all inward and outward parts of the body, with all the accidents and infirmaties that are incident upon them, even from the crowne of the head to the sole of the foote*, trans. Jacob Mosan (London, 1617), p. 456.

45 Duffin, 'Fossils as Drugs', p. 32.

46 D. Pickering, *The Statutes at Large from the Thirty-ninth Year of Q. Elizabeth, to the Twelfth Year of K. Charles II. Inclusive. To Which is Prefixed, a Table Containing the Titles of all the Statutes During That Period*, vol. VII (Cambridge, 1763).

47 Duffin, 'Fossils as Drugs', p. 33; P. Faridi et al., 'Elemental Analysis, Physicochemical Characterization and Lithontriptic Properties of *Lapis judaicus*', *Pharmacognosy Journal*, V (2013), pp. 94–6.

48 S. Muntner, *The Medical Writings of Moses Maimonides*, vol. II: *Treatise on Poisons and Their Antidotes* (Philadelphia, PA, 1966), p. 14.

49 J. Woodward, *A Catalogue of the Foreign Fossils in the Collection of J. Woodward MD*, part II (London, 1728), p. 19.

50 J. M. Levine, *Dr Woodward's Shield: History, Science, and Satire in Augustan England* (Los Angeles, CA, 1977), pp. 36–40.

51 S. Dale, *Pharmacologia, seu Manuductio ad Materiam Medicam* (Leiden, 1793).

52 Faridi et al., 'Elemental Analysis', pp. 94–6.

53 P. Faridi et al., 'Randomized and Double-blinded Clinical Trial of the Safety and Calcium Stone Dissolving Efficacy of Lapis judaicus', *Journal of Ethnopharmacology*, CLVI (2014), pp. 82–7.

54 T. Browne, *Pseudodoxia epidemica; or, Enquiries into Very Many Received Tenents, and Common'y Presumed Truths* (London, 1646).

NINE: THE DARK SIDE

1 Kim Akerman, personal communication, 21 January 2019.

2 K. Akerman, 'Two Aboriginal Charms Incorporating Fossil Giant Marsupial Teeth', *Western Australian Naturalist*, XII/6 (1973), p. 139.

3 Ibid., p. 141.

4 K. J. McNamara and P. Murray, *Prehistoric Mammals of Western Australia* (Perth, 2010), p. 35.

5 C. Singer, 'Early English Magic and Medicine', *Proceedings of the British Academy*, IX (1919–20), p. 357; A. Hall, 'Calling the Shots: The Old English Remedy and Anglo-Saxon "Elf-shot"', *Neuphilologische Mitteilungen: Bulletin of the Modern Language Society*, CVI (2005), pp. 195–209.

6 A. L. Meaney, 'Anglo-Saxon Amulets and Curing Stones', *BAR British Series*, 96 (1981), p. 109.

7   Ibid.

8   T. Pennant, *A Tour in Scotland in 1769* (London, 1771), p. 99.

9   R. Plot, *The Natural History of Oxfordshire: Being an Essay Towards the Natural History of England*, 2nd edn (Oxford, 1705), p. 94.

10 Meaney, 'Anglo-Saxon Amulets', p. 111.

11 T. Browne, *Pseudodoxia epidemica; or, Enquiries into Very Many Received Tenents, And Common'y Presumed Truths* (London, 1658), p. 104.

12 K. J. McNamara, *The Star-crossed Stone: The Secret Life, Myths, and History of a Fascinating Fossil* (Chicago, IL, 2011).

13 G. E. Evans, *The Pattern Under the Plough: Aspects of the Folk-life of East Anglia* (London, 1966), p. 129.

14 G. Mantell, *The Medals of Creation* (London, 1844), p. 350.

15 Rod Long, personal communication, 2009.

16 Mantell, *The Medals of Creation*, p. 344.

17 H. S. Toms, 'Shepherds' Crowns in Archaeology and Folklore', unpublished presentation to the meeting of the Brighton Natural History Society, 6 January 1940.

18 C. J. Duffin and J. P. Davidson, 'Geology and the Dark Side', *Proceedings of the Geologists' Association*, CXXII (2011), p. 10.

19 J. Woodward, *A Catalogue of the Additional English Native Fossils, in the Collection of J. Woodward MD*, vol. II (1728), p. 51.

20 T. Keightley, *The Fairy Mythology: Illustrative of the Romance and Superstition of Various Countries* (New York, 1968).

21 Evans, *The Pattern Under the Plough*.

22 J. McInnes, 'Celtic Deities and Heroes', in *Mythology: The Illustrated Anthology of World Myth and Storytelling*, ed. C. S. Littleton (San Diego, CA, 2002), pp. 248–73.

23 Duffin and Davidson, 'Geology and the Dark Side', p. 10.

24 P. Mietto, M. Avanzini and G. Rolandi, 'Human Footprints in Pleistocene Volcanic Ash', *Nature*, CCCCXXII (2003), p. 133.

25 A. Mayor and W.A.S. Sarjeant, 'The Folklore of Footprints in Stone: From Classical Antiquity to the Present', *Ichnos*, VIII (2001), pp. 143–63.

26 G. Zammit-Maempel, 'The Folklore of Maltese Fossils', *Papers in Mediterranean Social Studies*, I (1989), p. 12.

27 J. Hála, 'Fossils in the Popular Traditions in Hungary', *Annals of the History of Hungarian Geology*, Special Issue 1 (Rocks, Fossils and History) (1987), p. 206.

28 F. Kendall, *A Descriptive Catalogue of the Minerals, and Fossil Organic Remains of Scarborough, and the Vicinity* (Scarborough, 1816), p. 303.

29 Hála, 'Fossils in the Popular Traditions in Hungary', p. 206.

30 Duffin and Davidson, 'Geology and the Dark Side', pp. 7–15.

31 See M. Rudwick, *The Meaning of Fossils: Essays in the History of Paleontology* (New York, 1972).

32 F. D. Adams, *The Birth and Development of the Geological Sciences* (New York, 1954), p. 179.

33 Ibid., pp. 106 and 107.

34 Pliny the Elder, *The Historie of the World: Commonly Called, The Naturall Historie of C. Plinius Secundus*, trans. P. Holland, vol. I (London, 1634), ch xiii.

35 D. Siculus, *The Library of History of Diodorus Siculus*, Book V, Section 31, para. 3, vol. III of the Loeb Classical library Edition (1939).

TEN: A JOKE OF TIME

1 A. Whittle, *Europe in the Neolithic: The Creation of New Worlds* (Cambridge, 1996), p. 317.

2 T. Zammit, *Prehistoric Malta: The Tarxien Temples* (Oxford, 1930).

3 S. Stoddart et al., 'Cult in an Island Society: Prehistoric Malta in the Tarxien Period', *Cambridge Archaeological Journal*, III (1993), pp. 3–19.

4 Zammit, *Prehistoric Malta*.

5 J. D. Evans, *The Prehistoric Antiquities of the Maltese Islands: A Survey* (London, 1971), p. 115.

6 Ibid., Pl. 52, fig. 15.

7 Ibid., Pl. 57, figs 1–3.

8 F. Legge, trans., *Philosophumena or the Refutation of all Heresies, Formerly Attributed to Origen, but now to Hippolytus, Bishop and Martyr, who Flourished about 220 AD* (London, 1921), p. 50.

9 F. D. Adams, *The Birth and Development of the Geological Sciences* (New York, 1954), p. 13.

10 M. M. Al-Rawi, 'The Contribution of Ibn Sina (Avicenna) to the Development of Earth Sciences', *Foundation for Science Technology and Civilisation*, no. 4039 (2002), p. 5.

11 G. Zammit-Maempel, 'The Folklore of Maltese Fossils', *Papers in Mediterranean Studies*, I (1989), pp. 1–29.

12 Ibid.

13 Ibid.

14 Ibid., p. 19.

15 Ibid.

16 Ibid., p. 21, Pl. 3, figs 1–3.

17 G. Zammit-Maempel, 'Two Contra-veleno Cups made from Terra Sigillata Melitensis', *The St Luke's Hospital Gazette, Malta*, x/2 (1975), p. 85.

18 British Museum, Hans Sloane Collection, no. 541.

19 Ibid., p. 394; G. Zammit-Maempel, 'Fossil Sharks' Teeth: A Medieval Safeguard against Poisoning', *Melita Historica*, vi (1975), pp. 391–410.

20 Zammit-Maempel, 'The Folklore of Maltese Fossils', p. 24.

21 B. Accordi, 'Agostino Scilla, Painter from Messina (1629–1700), and his Experimental Studies on the True Nature of Fossils', *Geologica Romana*, xvii (1978), p. 129.

22 Scilla's 1670 original was written in Italian, although it was subsequently reprinted many times in Latin. Despite being a book of such importance to the history of palaeontology, it has only in recent times been translated into English, by Rodney Palmer, Rosemary Williams and Ilaria Bernocchi, and edited by Dan Pemberton. All quotes from Scilla's *La vana speculazione disingannata dal senso* are taken from this translation. You can download your very own copy of this, replete with his drawings, from the website of the Sedgwick Museum, University of Cambridge.

23 A. Cutler, *The Seashell on the Mountaintop: A Story of Science, Sainthood, and the Humble Genius Who Discovered a New History of the Earth* (Cambridge, 2003), p. 58.

24 [William Wotton], '*La vana speculazione disingannata dal senso: Lettera Risponsiva Circa i Corpi Marini, che Petrificati si trovano in varii luoghi terrestri. Di Agostino Scilla Pittore Academico della Fucina*, in Napoli, 1670. 4to. With short Notes, by a Fellow of the Royal Society', *Philosophical Transactions*, xix (1695–7), pp. 181–201.

25 P. Findlen, 'The Specimen and the Image: John Woodward, Agostino Scilla, and the Depiction of Fossils', *Huntington Library Quarterly*, lxxviii (2015), pp. 217–61.

26 R. Hooke, *Micrographia; or, Some Physiological Descriptions of Minute Bodies Made by Magnifying Glasses, with Observations and Inquiries Thereupon* (London, 1665), p. 112.

27 S. Kusukawa, 'Drawings of Fossils by Robert Hooke and Richard Waller', *Notes and Records of the Royal Society*, LXVII (2013), https://doi.org/10.1098/rsnr.2013.0013.

28 R. Waller, *The Posthumous Works of Robert Hooke, M.D., S.R.S., Geom. Prof. Gresh. Ec. Containing his Cutlerian Lectures, and other Discourses read at the meetings of the illustrious Royal Society*; facsimile reprint (New York, 1969), p. 284.

29 Hooke, *Micrographia*, p. 111.

30 S. Inwood, *The Man Who Knew Too Much: The Strange and Inventive Life of Robert Hooke, 1635–1703* (London, 2002), p. 32.

31 Ibid., p. 86.

32 Correspondence, John Woodward to Johann Scheuchzer, 22 June 1717, Ms H 294, S. 67 Zentralbibliothek Zürich.

EPILOGUE

1 S. W. Salisbury et al., 'The Dinosaurian Ichnofauna of the Lower Cretaceous (Valanginian–Barremian) Broome Sandstone of the Walmadany Area (James Price Point), Dampier Peninsula, Western Australia', *Journal of Vertebrate Paleontology*, XXXVI, Suppl. 1 (2016), pp. 1–152.

2 S. McLoughlin, 'Early Cretaceous Macrofloras of Western Australia', *Records of the Western Australian Museum*, XVIII (1996), pp. 19–65.

3 Salisbury et al., 'Dinosaurian Ichnofauna', p. 2.

4 D. M. Welch, 'Fossilised Human Footprints on the Coast of North Western Australia', *The Artefact*, XXII (1999), pp. 3–19.

5 Kim Akerman, personal communication, 6 April 2019.

6 A. S. George, *William Dampier in New Holland: Australia's First Natural Historian* (Melbourne, 1999).

7 Ibid., p. 17.

8 Woodward passed the plants to botanists John Ray and Leonard Plukenet for description. Some years after receiving them back he passed them to the botanist William Sherard who, in his will, left them to the University of Oxford. The plants are still in excellent condition today in the herbarium of the University of Oxford Botanic Garden.

BIBLIOGRAPHY

Adams, Frank, *The Birth and Development of the Geological Sciences*
  (New York, 1954)
Andersson, Johan, *Children of the Yellow Earth* (London, 1934)
Bienkowski, Piotr, ed., *Busayra: Excavations by Crystal M. Bennett,
  1971–1980* (Oxford, 2002)
Connolly, Michael, *Discovering the Neolithic in County Kerry: A Passage
  Tomb at Ballycarty* (Wicklow, 1999)
Duffin, Christopher, *Fossils as Drugs: Pharmaceutical Palaeontology*
  (Luxembourg, 2008)
Edwards, Phillip, ed., *Wadi Hammeh 27: An Early Natufian Settlement at
  Pella in Jordan* (Leiden, 2013)
Ellis Davidson, Hilda, *Myths and Symbols in Pagan Europe: Early
  Scandinavian and Celtic Religions* (Manchester, 1988)
George, Alex, *William Dampier in New Holland: Australia's First Natural
  Historian* (Melbourne, 1999)
Inwood, Stephen, *The Man Who Knew Too Much: The Strange and
  Inventive Life of Robert Hooke, 1635–1703* (London, 2002)
Leroi-Gourhan, André, *Treasures of Prehistoric Art* (New York, 1967)
McNamara, Kenneth, *The Star-crossed Stone: The Secret Life, Myths and
  History of a Fascinating Fossil* (Chicago, IL, 2011)
Mayor, Adrienne, *The First Fossil Hunters: Paleontology in Greek and
  Roman Times* (Princeton, NJ, 2000)
Meaney, Audrey, *Anglo-Saxon Amulets and Curing Stones* (Oxford, 1981)
Murphy, Anthony, *Newgrange: Monument to Immortality* (Dublin, 2012)
Needham, Joseph, *Science and Civilization in China*, vol. III: *Mathematics
  and the Sciences of the Heavens and the Earth* (Cambridge, 1959)

Palmer, Rodney, Rosemary Williams and Ilaria Bernocchi, trans.,
  Vain Speculation Undeceived by Sense (Cambridge, 2016)
Rudwick, Martin, *The Meaning of Fossils: Essays in the History of
  Paleontology* (New York, 1972)
Scilla, Agostino, *La vana speculazione disingannata dal senso* (Naples, 1670)
Scriver, Robert, *The Blackfeet: Artists of the Northern Plains* (Kansas City,
  KS, 1990)
Smith, Worthington, *Man, the Primeval Savage* (London, 1894)
Whittle, Alasdair, *Europe in the Neolithic: The Creation of New Worlds*
  (Cambridge, 1996)
Woodward, John, *An Attempt Towards a Natural History of the Fossils
  of England: In a Catalogue of the English fossils in the Collection
  of J. Woodward, M. D.* (London, 1729)
Zammit, Themistocles, *Prehistoric Malta: The Tarxien Temples*
  (Oxford, 1930)

ACKNOWLEDGEMENTS

The information upon which this book is based has been gathered over more decades than I care to remember. Throughout that time, I have enjoyed the support and encouragement of my wife, Sue Radford. I offer her my heartfelt thanks and gratitude for much discussion about how and why people have collected fossils, and for accompanying me on so many visits to museum collections, and archaeological and historical sites, as well as for putting up with me during those times when I disappeared off into the Palaeolithic. I am also most thankful to my son, Jamie McNamara, for reading the text and providing much encouragement, as well as sage and sound advice.

For making specimens in their care accessible to me I wish to thank Moya Smith and Ross Chadwick of the Western Australian Museum; Helen O'Carroll of the Kerry County Museum; Ian Beavis of the Tunbridge Wells Museum; Gary Brown of the Liverpool Museum and Dan Pemberton of the Sedgwick Museum. For assistance with information over the years I wish to thank James Dyer, Ellen Dissanayake, John Cooper, Christian Neumann, Sten Vikner, Michael Connolly, Andrei Sinitsyn, Dirk Krause, Dawn Scher Thomae, Richard Cushing, Dawn Cansfield, Patrick Wyse Jackson and Lars Kremers. For assistance with photographs I wish to thank Imogen Gunn, Gary Rollefson, Phillip Edwards, Ian Beavis, Sarah Hammond, Tony Roche, Yael Barschak, Stephen Atkinson and Enrichetta Leospo.

I am most grateful to David Reese, who many years ago introduced me to fossil sea urchins in archaeological sites in Jordan and encouraged me to study them. I am very appreciative of the help that Kim Akerman has given me on matters associated with Australian Aboriginal interest in fossils. Chris Duffin has helped greatly with the provision of literature on the folklore of fossils over the years. I also particularly wish to thank Roland Meuris who, with the help of John Jagt, sent me many photographs of the fossil-bearing artefacts he has found in Belgium.

Many thanks to Michael Leaman of Reaktion for so enthusiastically supporting this book, Amy Salter for her astute text editing and Harry Gilonis for helping me with the illustrations with such skill, good grace and humour.

In the hope that few, if any, errors are to be found in the book (for which I naturally accept full responsibility), I feel that the last word should go to Agostino Scilla and his opening statement in *La vana speculazione disingannata dal senso*:

> Kind reader, I know that I must address some words to you, now that I see my letter published; but I will not follow the style of some, who gladly take the opportunity to disclaim their own errors, laying them on the Printer. I have never known how or why it has become the custom, even for very socially inept people, to insult a gentleman: instead of thanking him at the end of the work that he has provided, they dismiss him as a careless and ignorant sleepyhead; even though all men are so prone to making mistakes that it is impossible to imagine anything easier for, or less unique to, a writer. I will therefore conclude this part by saying that if you are an erudite man, familiar with good spelling, you will certainly be able to forgive me and the Printer, correcting the errors perhaps of both of us; and if you are otherwise, it will all seem well and good to you, and I do not wish to give you the additional obligation of excusing me.

PHOTO
ACKNOWLEDGEMENTS

The author and publishers wish to express their thanks to the following sources of illustrative material and/or permission to reproduce it. Some locations are given below in the interests of brevity.

Author's collection: pp. 29, 42; courtesy the author: pp. 54, 221; photos by the author: pp. 42, 107, 115, 128, 148, 162, 174; photos courtesy Brighton Museum: pp. 143, 144; British Museum, London: p. 179; photos courtesy of Michael Connolly: pp. 113, 114; photo Phillip Edwards: p. 109; from Adrien-Jacques-François Ficatier, 'Communication de M. Philippe Salmon, L'Age de la Pierre', in *Bulletin de la société d'anthropologie et de biologie de Lyon*, VI (1891): p. 96; from Conrad Gesner, *De Rerum fossilium, lapidum et gemmarum maximè, figuris & similitudinibus liber*... (Zürich, 1565): p. 191; from [Robert Hooke], *The Posthumous Works of Robert Hooke, M.D., S.R.S., Geom. Prof. Gresh. Ec. Containing his Cutlerian Lectures, and other Discourses read at the meetings of the illustrious Royal Society* (London, 1705): p. 12; Institute of Archaeology and Anthropology, Yarmouk University, Jordan (photos K. Brimmell): pp. 89, 107; photos courtesy John Jagt: pp. 21, 86; The Jordan Museum, Amman (on loan to the Musée du Louvre, Paris): p. 105; Kerry County Museum, Tralee, Co. Kerry: pp. 115, 116; courtesy Dirk Krause: p. 139; Department of Archaeology, La Trobe University, Melbourne, Australia: p. 109; Landesamt für Denkmalpflege im Regierungspräsidium Stuttgart: p. 139; Liverpool Museum: p. 78; photo courtesy Museo Egizio, Torino, Italy, used by permission of Ministero per I Beni e le Attività Culturali-Soprintendenza per I Beni Archeologici del Piemonte e del Museo Antichità Egizie: p. 127; Museum of Archaeology and Anthropology, University of Cambridge: p. 82; photos © National Monuments Service, Department of Culture, Heritage and

INDEX

Page numbers in *italics* refer to illustrations